AN ANTHOLOGY

Writing the Circle

Native Women Of Western Canada

Compiled and Edited by
Jeanne Perreault and Sylvia Vance

Introduction by Gloria Bird
Preface by Emma LaRocque

D1041367

University of Oklahoma Press : Norman and London

Library of Congress Cataloging-in-Publication Data

Writing the circle : native women of western Canada, an anthology /
  compiled and edited by Jeanne Perreault and Sylvia Vance ;
  introduction by Gloria Bird ; preface by Emma LaRocque.
       p.   cm.
    ISBN 0-8061-2437-7 (pbk.)
    1. Indians of North America—Canada, Western—Women—Literary
collections.   2. Eskimos—Canada, Western—Women—Literary collections.   3. Canadian literature—Indian authors.   4. Canadian literature—Eskimo authors.   5. Canadian literature—Women authors.
6. Canadian literature—20th century.   I. Perreault, Jeanne Martha.
II. Vance, Sylvia.
PR9194.5.I5W74   1993
810.9'9287—dc20   91-50857
                                                                    CIP

The paper in this book meets the guidelines for permanence and durability of
the Committee on Production Guidelines for Book Longevity of the Council
on Library Resources, Inc. ∞

1   2   3   4   5   6   7   8   9   10

We dedicate this book
to the contributors,
to their children,
and to ours.

Contents

Introduction

or

The First Circle — Native Women's Voice

By Gloria Bird

The title of this collection invokes the major paradigm of Native thought: life, time, seasons, cosmology, birth, womb, and earth are intrinsically located in the symbology of the circle. Within this circle we are returned to beginnings to consider how far we have come as Native women. For those of us who are also writers, the Native literary tradition resulting in a publication such as *Writing the Circle* suggests the state of the circle: in flux, encompassing and reflexive, a reciprocal meeting of beginnings and possible futures. What is recalled are the influences on our individual way of knowing the cultural landscape of being Indian and woman, the women who are an integral part of our lives: mothers, grandmothers, sisters, aunts, and friends. While reading *Writing the Circle* for the first time I began to feel I knew these women, that what they had to say and, in particular, the way they conveyed their stories to me reminded me of a cousin or old childhood friend, someone I once knew or someone I used to be. In essence, I was being reminded of where I have come from, and how much I myself have survived.

The recognition of similarities in the experiences of Native women has culminated in much thought on the dichotomous relationship between written and oral forms of communication. That the majority of the writing collected here resembles the oral tradition cannot be mistaken.

There is a marked discrepancy between the oral and the written, which is highlighted by the juxtaposition of what we normally consider literature and the way we communicate to one another through speech. Education conditions us to read with a critical eye that has much to do with the value Western culture attributes to the written over oral forms of communication. As I read through this body of work for the first time, I found myself wanting to stifle that response, and floundered in my reading. I felt the need to *give name* to what I was reading/remembering, and decided that in some sense I was reading journal writing. Whether or not this is an accurate assumption on my part is a secondary consideration, and probably it says more about formal education than it is a true reflection of the following writing by Canadian Native women. On some deeper level, *naming* serves an important function as a way of participating in the discourse. It has, as a consequence, freed me from the critical activity that accompanied my first reading; the channels for communication were opened.

The whole of what I have witnessed in my own life and learned in the educational system is distilled into my being. Like many of the women speaking here, I was raised Catholic and for a time attended a mission school on the reservation. Two incidents from my time there stay with me. On the occasion of my great-grandmother's passing, my grandmother, for whatever reasons, did not come for me to take me to my great-grand-mother's wake or funeral, but instead afterwards sent me a letter advising me to "pray to the Blessed Virgin." I felt as a child that my grief was being denied, and I was angry at my grandmother, who offered as substitute for my loss the Blessed Virgin, one who as far as I could tell was neither real nor Indian. At the time I was able to process neither my grief nor my anger. This has only come with age.

The other incident occurred when I was nine. I wanted to buy two pencils from the sisters' store, and the nun who was there that day to sell us candies and supplies from the store refused to sell me more than one pencil. I remember the look she directed at me, evil in intent and full of loathing, as she informed me that I was greedy. The same nun was the teacher of the first and second grades. I carried the guilt of greed with me for years afterwards. Again, only time healed the wounds, and as I look back now, I can see how that particular nun might have been angry with me for destroying her preconceived notions of Indians as both poor and ignorant. It would never have occurred to me as a child that nuns could be prejudiced against Indians and that her action was based upon racist, prejudiced beliefs. Again, only age has provided me an insight into the motives of this particular damaging woman, who happened to be a nun.

Which is all to say, as I perceive these experiences as having a negative impact upon my life, that they have formed me with the same degree of intensity as have the births of my children, for instance, which I regard as miracles. I recognize the process by which as a child I took these negative experiences and turned them into a false image of myself, owning them. Not only was I greedy, but I was disrespectful in being angry at my grandmother. I have come to an age in which I have only recently recognized that even negative experiences can be useful, that they can be turned around and that they need not remain damaging. I no longer have to own a nun's hate of me as an internalized hate of myself, and I do not have to be angry at my grandmother for neglecting to acknowledge my childhood right to feel grief. And I can identify my anger at Christianity in general, which took my grandmother from me and from herself.

As I look back to the parallels between my life and the lives of other Native women writers, I notice that issues of silence (or shame, as Joy Harjo tells me) afflict us in the subterranean levels of our being. Negative self-images have been internalized, pitting culture and identity against a romanticized version of who and what we are as people. Everything is turned inward. These issues are relevant to all of our lives.

As Indian women we are taught through stereotypes in literature and pop culture to believe that "traditionally" it is our duty to be long-suffering, to not complain. Possibly it is most damaging that we are not allowed to express our anger. It is good, for a different perspective, to note that during my grandmother's time there were no support services, much less a social consciousness, available to women to deal with issues of rape, abortion, incest, and the general violence perpetrated against women. In many ways, the recognition of the similarities in our experiences is a humbling reminder of the legacy of pain that we inherit. It is also a testament to the strength and power of women to continue. And while it is certainly true that the realities of our lives are more complicated than simply transcending pain, and that pain is not the only measure of our existence, we cannot deny its impact on that experience. It is a place of beginning, as writing for catharsis is; and it is a place of ending the cycles of abuse, or any of the damaging cycles that are quickly becoming primary concerns in Indian communities.

When we make the decision not to teach our children our Native language, as my own mother chose, that is another form of silencing. My own recognition of the loss of my Native language is felt as a poignant self-consciousness. It is only recently that I have come to the realization that silence gets us nowhere. I don't believe that writing comes easy for any of us who have broken through the manifestations of silencing. It is difficult and exposing, yet is necessary to our well-being and the well-being of our children. With it also comes healing, as is evident in the following stories.

The reality of women's voice in published literature depends on some literary criteria that posit another contemporary concern. To date, the firsthand experience of Native women has been expressed in two categories: anthropological life histories and the sophisticated writing of Native women. The criteria for publication, often a painful process in itself, neglect much of what has been written simply because it does not fit the standards as they are applied in order to make that judgment. This suggests to me, as a consequence, the silencing of Native women within the literary community, and represents another form of controlling the dialogue.

Recently, in the preparation of another Native women's anthology, I confronted the control of the dialogue inherent in the act of rejection, recognizing that rejection *is* a form of censorship. This became a moral dilemma for me, and initiated a questioning of the standards by which we judge a piece of work. Do I have the right to make the judgment that one human being's voice, or way of *saying*, is less valuable than another's? Yet, we live in a world where words are commodified and where the works of well-known writers, as well as those of writers who are merely able to follow the standard conventions of writing, are indeed more valuable as products than are those of others.

I truly admire the efforts of Jeanne Perreault and Sylvia Vance, who had the courage and freedom to disregard those imposed "standards of literary excellence" in compiling *Writing the Circle*. In validating the voice of Native women, this anthology breaks through the boundaries that prevent Native women from speaking, without subjecting them to either censorship or editorialization. More important, the anthology legitimizes the importance of this voice to our communal story and existence.

We are at an opportune moment in the formation of a new awareness and direction for the portrayal of Native women in Native literature, and for shaping the course of the dialogue from here. The growing influence of the society we live in is exemplified by the voices of the women published here, as some of them struggle to own the language of anthropology, linguistics, and other disciplines. This places Native women as participants in the discourse about Indian people, within a power structure that tends to marginalize us.

One of the many strengths of *Writing the Circle* is that it has challenged me to confront my own biases, to define learned habits of reading texts, and to differentiate between the values of the oral and written traditions. It also discloses the cathartic nature of writing through pain in order to transcend it. I find this a very healthy aspect. I don't come away with a feeling of resignation, but with a necessary healing that comes with sharing our stories in a community that nurtures us. I can remember that it wasn't that long ago that I lived alone in a remote area of the reservation and wrote in isolation, feeling as though my life were lived in a vacuum. What I find particularly moving about *Writing the Circle* is that through it we are once again connected by our stories that merge into one. That story is the one we share where the dialogue continues between Native women. It has transcended individual isolation, estrangement, and is alive and wonderful.

Foreword
By Jeanne Perreault and Sylvia Vance

Unlike most anthologies, which are compiled to serve a preconceived set of expectations, *Native Women of Western Canada: Writing the Circle — An Anthology* was initiated for only one purpose — to give a place for Native women to speak. We realize that this is a radical departure from the usual sense of what an anthology does, in that our agenda was not specifically literary nor narrowly political. Conventional standards of literary excellence in no way prepare a reader for the complexity of responses the writing contained here will evoke. Readers will discover the limitations of their own reading practices as they encounter the emotional and intellectual demands of this collection.

Writing the Circle is a collection of voices. They are voices that have not been widely heard until now and that have been missing from all Canadians' understanding of our society and literature. These voices will challenge expectations of what Aboriginal women are or should be saying. They demonstrate a wide range of values, attitudes, experiences, and political perspectives. At the same time, no reader could fail to recognize a deeply held commitment to an Aboriginal heritage.

This book appears at a moment of profound change within Aboriginal communities and in relationships between Native and non-Native Canadians. Among the most significant of these changes is the increasing number of Aboriginal writers making their literary presence felt. This is a change that has been desperately needed for a long time. The conception of this collection of western Canadian Native women's writings was prompted by our inability to find many voices of Native writers in bookstores and libraries (by western Canada, we mean Manitoba, Saskatchewan, Alberta, Northwest Territories, and Yukon).

In 1986, we began to hunt in bookstores for the Canadian Native poets, novelists, short-story writers, and essayists who would teach us in the same way the USA writers Leslie Marmon Silko, Wendy Rose, Joy Harjo, Chrystos, and Paula Gunn Allen were teaching American readers — to read in a new way, to see the world in new ways. Of course, we knew Maria Campbell's powerful memoir *Halfbreed* (1979) and later found the deeply moving novel *In Search of April*

Raintree, which Beatrice Culleton published in 1983. These and the intense selections by Jeannette Armstrong and Beth Cuthand in *in the feminine* (1983) were the only readily (and not all that readily) available works by Native women. We knew that we needed to hear the words of Aboriginal women in order to understand this country, its history, and its present. As well, hearing them would be an important part of the social changes that Canada clearly needs to undergo. We also knew that systemic racism and sexism in our society makes every stage of writing and publishing less accessible to Native women than it is to others. We promised ourselves then that we would attempt to make public the words of western Canadian Native women.

Following those early conversations, we found ourselves in professional positions that allowed us to make our early wish for a collection of Native women's writings a reality. Although we are not Native, we felt then, as we do now, that anything we could do to work to lift the blanket of silence would be of value. Since that time, several collections of Native writings have appeared (and even more by individual authors — among many are Armstrong's *Slash*, Baker's *Being on the Moon*, Cuthand's *Voices in the Waterfall*, Maracle's *I Am Woman*), including Thomas King's edition of *Canadian Fiction Magazine: Native Issue* 60 (1987) and his anthology *All My Relations* (1990) and Heather Hodgson's *Seventh Generation* (1989), a collection of poetry. We fully trust and expect that *Writing the Circle* will be only one of many anthologies that will appear this decade.

One of the truths this collection tells is that there is no more a monolithic "Native" world any more than there is a uniform "white" world. In fact, Thomas King suggests that the automatic assumption that "the matter of race imparts to the Native writer a tribal understanding of the universe" is "romantic, mystical, and in many instances, a self-serving notion" (King, *Native Issue*, 4-5). King, here, is working against a limited view of racial identity, while understanding that community, history, tradition, culture, and heritage carry lines of selfhood that cannot be erased, that must not be lost. We made no attempt to define "Nativeness." We know that we are in no position to establish definitions or determine categories. Each contributor, therefore, is self-defined as Native, and the pride and self-affirmation of that identity speaks for itself.

Writing the Circle is part of a tradition that began to find its way into print almost four hundred years ago. This integration of an ancient and ongoing tradition of oral history and literature with the

printed word has been troubled, struggling against the overt destruction of ancient communities and violent abuses at the hands of
Europeans. Despite the damage done to Indian and Métis peoples, the
will to be heard has remained strong, and their refusal to be silenced
finds an image in the words of Alanis Obomsawin: "I know I'm a
bridge between two worlds" (Penny Petrone, ed., *First People, First
Voices*, Toronto: The University of Toronto Press, p. 201).

Each of the writers who appears in this anthology is also a
bridge, making a connection between herself and every reader, woman
or man, Native or not. These individual bridges link us all in a common
humanity at the points where experiences of love, pain, fear, and hope
cut across differences. These individual connections are primary, but
others are equally as important. Links among all women are forged in
the bridges of pain inscribed here — the horror of rape, the anguish of
a child's death — and bridges of tenderness, too, in the sweet moments
of childhood and the loving memories of a grandparent. But specific
and precise evocations of Aboriginal experience are also powerfully
articulated in humour and in the righteous anger that resists the
injustices and brutality of a white culture. The insularity of the white
world, the *de facto* apartheid that reigns here in western Canada, is
being challenged by these writers. Sometimes, unspeakable sorrow
cries out in the face of a damaged way of life. However, most powerful
of all is the voice of spiritual energy speaking through the words of
many writers.

Because our primary goal was to be able to hear the words of
people who conventionally, as women and as Aboriginal people, were
silenced, we wanted to hear whatever they wished to say. No boundaries were made as to what forms writers could choose, nor were there
any suggestions or restrictions about content. We certainly had no cri-
terion in mind about the "Indianness" of the writing. We had heard
the laughter of an Aboriginal woman whose story had been rejected by
a publisher because it was "not Indian enough"! We were grateful for
the responses of Native readers who helped us look at aspects of the
writings that we otherwise would not have appreciated. Our aim has
been to listen and to learn, not to restrict and define.

Most of the writers here sent a variety of pieces. This allowed
us to choose work on the basis of the anthology as a whole as well as
according to individual pieces. Some writers whose work appears here
have been wrestling with their craft for a lifetime. Others sent us their
first attempts to express their thoughts and feelings. Whatever the

writer's individual history, we could feel the strength of mind and heart in each piece. We followed conventional editorial policy, making grammar, spelling, and punctuation consistent throughout the manuscript and working with individual authors to rework and rewrite a piece at the author's request. But, any substantial editorial changes we wanted to make were only made with the approval of the individual writers and, sometimes, that was not given. One observed that if you change the words you change the feelings; another wanted her story left alone, since it already had been "improved" by a helpful schoolteacher. The author had rewritten the piece from scratch, reclaiming the flavour of her own words that had been lost in the revision. Yet another, who initially had given us editorial carte blanche, insisted that a section we had removed be put back in, since it explained to Native people why she was making a certain argument. Because of the issue of appropriation or misuse of literary production, we wanted to make sure that the words of each writer would appear just as she wished them to.

The results of this editorial decision are apparent. Each piece of writing speaks clearly and forcefully from the experiences and modes of expression that its author has had at hand. These vary as the personal and cultural background of the writers vary, and the words and deeds, the thoughts and feeling recorded here engage the reader in a complex reality. The cruel racism of the past and present can no longer be understood merely as an abstraction by the white reader. Whites, too, must feel the pain of that reality and must look into the reflections of ourselves these words make for us. If we don't like what we see in the mirror of these works, we have been offered the gift of change by the truths told here.

The work of compiling and editing this book has been very exciting, because of the people we have met and the friends we have made and because of the intrinsic value of this collection. But, we are conscious that the historical moment of its inception (1986) has been supplanted by a better time: one in which non-Native people involved in such projects will work alongside Aboriginal anthologists in the production of literary collections. We are deeply honoured by the trust that has been placed in us by the contributors to this anthology. We share the view of one contributor, who wrote, "I believe we can all grow from this, Native and non-Native sisters, alike." The words that appear here will, we believe, stand together with past and future collections as Native women continue writing the circle.

Preface

or
Here Are Our Voices—Who Will Hear?
By Emma LaRocque

To be a Native writer of some consciousness is to be in a lonely place. Happily, our isolation is about to come apart at the seams. This collection, which represents some fifty voices and has already engendered much discussion, is one of a growing number of anthologies reflecting nothing short of a revolution in Native literature.

To discuss Native literature is to tangle with a myriad of issues: voicelessness, accessibility, stereotypes, appropriation, ghettoization, linguistic, cultural, sexual, and colonial roots of experience, and, therefore, of self-expression — all issues that bang at the door of conventional notions about Canada and about literature.

It was not too long ago that Native peoples were referred to as voiceless, even wordless, sometimes with the association of these with illiteracy. But were Indian and Métis voiceless? And what did it mean to be classified as illiterate? To be sure, many Natives were illiterate up to the 1970s, even into the 1990s, due to the unconscionable failure of the Canadian education system to impart to Native youth basic reading and writing skills. And illiteracy does render people voiceless in the life of a country that revolves around the printed word. But what other nuances may be found in these terms? Did it mean Native peoples spoke no words? And since illiteracy is often associated with lack of literature, even lack of intelligence, did it imply that Native peoples were bereft of literature or of knowledge?

In contrast to the inane stereotype of the Indian as soundless, we know from the vast storehouse of our oral traditions that Aboriginal peoples were peoples of words. Many words. Amazing words. Cultivated words. They were neither wordless nor illiterate in the context of their linguistic and cultural roots. The issue is not that Native peoples were ever wordless but that, in Canada, their words were literally and politically negated.

It is now well known that Indian and Métis children in residential or public schools were not allowed to speak their Native languages. What is perhaps less well known are all the ways our words have been usurped, belittled, distorted, and blockaded in Canadian culture. Whether we spoke or wrote in Cree or in English, we had very little access to mainline communication systems.

Literature is political in that its linguistic and ideological transmission is defined and determined by those in power. This is why Shakespeare rather than Wisakehcha is classified as "classical" in our school curriculums. And, of course, the written word is advanced as superior to the spoken word. Oral traditions have been dismissed as savage or primitive folklore. Such dismissal has been based on the self-serving colonial cultural myth that Europeans (and descendants thereof) were/are more developed ("civilized") than Aboriginal peoples ("savage"). So arrogant is this myth and so arrogantly held has this myth been that, except for Christian or scholarly purposes, the colonizers have not bothered to learn Aboriginal languages. To this day, inept and ideologically informed translations of legends or myths are infantilizing Aboriginal literatures.

Power politics in literature is also evident in the decisions of publishers and in audience reception. For example, around the time we were being described as "voiceless," hundreds of us were actually articulating our colonized conditions throughout Canada. Much of this articulation came in the form of speech, but it also came in the form of writing, for there were already a number of very fine Native writers by the later 1960s to the mid-1970s. But rarely were these writers approached or included in the existing literatures of those times. Publishers, including editors and journalists, turned to white authors to speak on our behalf. Just two examples: in *Native Peoples in Canadian Literature* (William and Christine Mowat, eds., Toronto: Macmillan of Canada, 1975), the majority of authors are white, including Hugh Dempsey, Rudy Wiebe, Emily Carr, Al Purdy, and George Ryga; in *Many Voices: An Anthology of Contemporary Indian Poetry* (David Day and Marilyn Bowering, eds., Vancouver: J.J. Douglas Ltd., 1977), there are four poets, one of which is Cam Hubert, whose identities are put in such a way that it is difficult to tell whether they are "Indian poets" or not.

The interplay between audience reception and publishing cannot be minimized. As one of those earlier Native writers, I experienced and studied what may be called the Native-voice/white-audience dynamic. The interactions were often poignant. On another level, we were again rendered voiceless no matter how articulate we were. Apparently unable to understand or accept the truth of our experiences and perceptions, many white audiences, journalists, and critics resorted to racist techniques of psychologically labelling and blaming us. We were psychologized as "bitter," which was equated with emotional incapacitation, and once thus dismissed we did not have to be taken seriously.

We were branded as "biased," as if whites were not! Sometimes, we were even unabashedly charged with lying. The innocence and goodness of white Canada was stridently defended: How could all this oppression happen? How could police, priests, and teachers be so awful?

Our anger, legitimate as it was and is, was exaggerated as "militant" and used as an excuse not to hear us. There was little comprehension of an articulate anger reflecting an awakening and a call to liberation, not a psychological problem to be defused in a therapist's room.

Influenced by uncomprehending critics and audiences, publishers controlled the type of material that was published. It is no surprise that whatever Native protest literature was produced from authors like Harold Cardinal, Howard Adams, George Manual, Duke Redbird, Wilfred Pelletier, or Waubageshig was short-lived. In direct contrast to the hailing given "Black protest literature" as a new genre by white American intellectuals, Canadian critics accused us of "blustering and bludgeoning society." Basically, we were directed just to tell our "stories" (and the more tragic the better) not, in a manner reminiscent of archival descriptions reflecting earlier colonial attitudes, to be so "arrogant" or so daring as to analyze or to call on Canadian society for its injustices.

From about the mid-1970s, there was a noticeable turn to soft-sell Native literature. Personal narratives, autobiographies, children's stories, legends, interviews with elders, cultural tidbits, and "I remember" sorts of materials were encouraged. Here, I must hasten to say that it isn't the Native efforts I am criticizing; given all the suppression, misinformation, and stereotypes that exist, we can never speak enough or do enough correction or debunking. It is the white Canadian response to and use of this literature I am addressing.

Even soft-sell literature has been misunderstood and abused. I recall reading an incoherent review of Beatrice Culleton's moving allegory *Spirit of the White Bison* with the general accusation that "minorities" were "strangling in their own roots" (*Winnipeg Free Press*, 10 August 1986)! Maria Campbell's *Halfbreed* and Culleton's

In Search of April Raintree have been reduced, at times, to grist for social workers rather than being treated as the powerful mirrors to Canadian society that they are.

Actually, much of Native writing, whether blunt or subtle, is protest literature in that it speaks to the processes of our colonization: dispossession, objectification, marginalization, and that constant struggle for cultural survival expressed in the movement for structural and psychological self-determination. Ruby Slipperjack's gentle and wonderfully written novel *Honour the Sun* and even Chief Dan George's Hiawathian prose reflect protest.

Native writers have been creating new genres in Canadian English literature, but this fact has been largely missed by readers and critics. For example, the more overt protest books of the 1970s often combined their sharp analyses of society with wit, humour, poetry, history, anthropology, and/or personal reflections. Authors turned to facts of biography to humanize the much dehumanized "Indian." Instead of being read as new genres, they were attacked as biased and parochial. Few bookstores, libraries, or professors knew what to do with Native writing that crossed or integrated well-defined genres, styles, or schools. Native writing soon got thrown into one pot variously called "Native Literature" or "Native Studies."

I have viewed such hashing of our writing with considerable ambivalence. On one hand, Native literature has become a new genre, and Native studies has certainly become a well-respected field of study in the university. On the other hand, categorizing literature on the basis of ethnicity, gender, or politics raises the spectre of ghettoization. While one must be supportive of both Native literature and Native studies, one must be concerned about ghettoization because of its effects on Native writers and writing.

The lumping of our writing under the category "Native" means that our discussion of issues and ideas that are universally applicable may not reach the general public. For example, an analysis of the Canadian school system by a Native author is rarely placed under "education" or "sociology" or "social issues." The poetry and poetic prose in much of the writing of the 1970s is rarely, if ever, placed under poetry or literature proper. And what about Native writers who do not write about Native themes? What about Native women writers who do not write specifically or only about women, and so get excluded from "women's writing" shelves?

Perhaps the ugliest effect of ghettoization is that it raises doubts in the deeps of a writer. Is our writing published because we are good writers or because we are Native? Of course, we may never know, judging from the contradictory responses from editors and publishers. I will never forget a new Winnipeg magazine of poetry returning my poems with a rejection slip that read, "Not Indian enough"! And several years ago, a major literary journal chose a poem (out of perhaps twenty) because, I believe, it has one Cree word at the end. Indeed, one of the editors even suggested that my poems were not authentic because they played too much with words. I do wish I could recall her exact words, since they were quite stunning in their implications — especially since I worry that my poems do not have enough "word play."

Occasionally, I collect my poems, along with my courage, and take them to a reputable poet with the request that he or she critique my works strictly on their poetic merits, not on the basis of my ethnicity or gender. I take some consolation from the fact that there are many white people who get published not necessarily because they are good writers but more because they have access to the publishing world. And that Native writers choose to explore Native themes does not mean they are incompetent. After all, most white writers deal with white issues or characters, but no one thinks of this as either parochial or ghettoized.

Still, the ramifications of ghettoization are unsettling. Generally, the Canadian intellectual establishment has disregarded Native writing. Such disregard reveals a profound Canadian contradiction: even as Native voices are silenced, the writings and movements of other oppressed peoples around the world are saluted. Yet, a study of Albert Memmi's portrait of the colonizer and the colonized in Tunisia reveals a striking similarity to the faces of the colonizer and the colonized of Canada (*The Colonizer and the Colonized*, 1957, 1967). Indeed, the very resistance of the Native's use of the colonizer's language is consistent with this portrait.

So is the belittlement and stereotyping of Native cultures. Canadian society has not understood that earlier Native writing styles have reflected a holistic way of seeing and placing space and time that produced a sense of integration with the variant aspects of life. This has been confused with the misguided notions of Indian culture (still prevalent today), notions that portray Indians as having taken no direct control over their environment, their children, their urges, their resources, their art, their thoughts, or their knowledge. A presentation that blurs Indians with their landscape only serves to de-culturalize them. In fact, Indians were multifaceted and cultivated peoples who acknowledged and practised a host of distinctions, yet maintained a functional connectedness between parts. And despite the disintegrative forces on Native cultures, many of us grew up with a holistic rather than an atomistic or discrete *Weltanschauung*.

There are numerous Native peoples yet who live or carry this world view. And every Native author of my generation or older has tried, in philosophy and in praxis (in the blending of genres), to teach our audiences our way of seeing and naming our worlds. It appears we have not been received. Superficial, even flaky, conceptions and objectifications of Indian culture have muted the deeper, life-sustaining currents of cultural continuity.

It must also be understood that Native writers have a dialectical relationship to the English (or French) language. Not only do we have to learn English, we must then deal with its ideology. To a Native woman, English is like an ideological onion whose stinging layers of racism and sexism must be peeled away before it can be fully enjoyed.

A word must be said about words. Native readers and writers do not look at English words the same way as non-Natives may, for we have certain associations with a host of them. It is difficult to accept the following terms as neutral: savage, primitive, pagan, medicine man, shaman, warrior, squaw, redskin, hostile, civilization, developed, progress, the national interest, bitter, angry, happy hunting grounds, brave, buck, redman, chief, tribe, or even Indian. These are just a few of the string of epithets that have been pejoratively used to *specifically* indicate the ranking of Indian peoples as inferior to Europeans, thus to perpetuate their dehumanization. This is why I often use a lot of quotation marks even though standard editorial practice discourages it. Then, there is the challenge of wanting to use soul language, which for me is Cree, but having to explain it with a running bracketed glossary is distracting. This is made even more difficult by the fact that there is no standard way to spell Cree words in English. Kokom, which can be spelled in at least five different ways, is just such an example. We may also disagree with what is aesthetically pleasing. We may prefer Basil Johnston or Louise Erdrich over Stephen Leacock. We may bring our oratorical backgrounds to our writing and not see it as a weakness. What is at work is the power struggle between the oral and the written, between the Native in us and the English. And even though we know the English language well, we may sometimes pay little attention to its logic — perhaps we will always feel a bit rebellious about it all. For, it must be said, that perhaps the height of cheekiness in a colonizer is to steal your language, withhold his from you as long as he can, then turn around and demand that you speak or write better than he does. And when you do, he accuses you of "uppityness" or inauthenticity.

The Native intellectual struggle to maintain our cultural integrity at these profound levels is perhaps most severely tested within the confines of scholarship and scholarly writing. Some of us de-colonizing Native scholars are challenging existing conventions in research methodology, notions of objectivity, and writing styles. So far, there has been little comprehension on the part of our colleagues. The academic world may be the hardest nut to crack. Long-standing conventions hold that objectivity must necessarily entail the separation of the "word" from the "self." As a scholar, I am expected to remain aloof from my words; I am expected to not speak in my own voice. But I am a Native woman writer/scholar engaged in this exciting evolution/revolution of Native thought and action. My primary socialization is rooted in the oral literatures of the Plains Cree Métis, which does not separate the word from the self and certainly knows the difference between atowkehwin (stories of legendary bent or sacred origin) and achimowin (factual and objective accounts). Further, there is ample evidence in the study of justification literature for the argument that objectivity can be a self-serving tool of those accustomed to managing history. This is not to mention my feminist understanding of the use of the English language. So, as an integrated person, I choose to use my own voice whether I am writing history or whether I am writing poetry. I may not always speak in my own voice, but when I do I experience no disconnection between my "self" and my footnotes.

With respect to scholarship and Native literature, many professors still turn to Rudy Wiebe, George Ryga, Robert Kroetsch, or Kinsella when discussing Native themes. Yet, there are numerous Native authors available. To list just a few more (at the risk of offending many, and in addition to the ones referred to already): George Kenny (*Indians Don't Cry*, 1977), Sarain Stump (*And There Is My People Sleeping*, 1971), Marty Dunn (*Red On White: The Biography of Duke Redbird*, 1971), Basil Johnston (*Moosemeat and Wild Rice*, 1980), Jeanette Armstrong (*Slash*, 1985), Lee Maracle (*I Am Woman*, 1988), Maria Campbell/Linda Griffiths (*The Book of Jessica*, 1989), Beth Cuthand (*Voices In the Waterfall*, 1989), Jane Willis (*Geneish: An Indian Girlhood*, 1973), Tomson Highway (*The Rez Sisters*, 1987),

Arthur Shilling (*The Ojibway Dream: Faces of my People*, 1986), Rita Joe (*Song of Eskasoni: More Poems of Rita Joe*, 1988). This is not to mention a number of older compilations of Native essays and poetry. And now there is such a spate of new Native writers (in a wild variety of anthologies and special features) that I cannot keep up with them. There are new poets, short story writers, novelists, and playwrights. There are also new autobiographies, protest literature, children's literature, and more recollections of legends, myths, and earlier times. Even as I write this preface, I have received three different calls for submissions to Native women's anthologies. So, it cannot be said that we have been wordless from lack of skill or effort. Yet, we have been silenced in numerous and ingenious ways. In effect, we have been censored.

For the last two decades, we have been faced with the weary task of having to educate our audiences before we could even begin dialoguing with them! Our energies have been derailed from purely creative pursuits. Many speakers and writers have been cornered into the hapless role of apologists, incessant (and very patient) explainers, and overnight experts on all things Native. And in response to the negation and falsification of our histories and cultures, some have been pushed to cultural romanticism, even perhaps cultural self-righteousness. But, incidentally, nobody on earth has ever romanticized their culture to such mythic proportions (cowboys moving west and killing Indians being equated with moral and human progress) as white North Americans.

A sentence in Marlene Nourbese Philip's delightful article, "The Disappearing Debate: Or how the discussion of racism has been taken over by the censorship issue" (*This Magazine*, July-August 1989), gripped me: "No work is in any full practical sense produced unless it is also received." If Native writers have felt like they have been speaking into a vacuum, it is because we have. Neither the white nor the Native audience has received us. If white audiences have largely misunderstood us, Native audiences have been virtually non-existent. Linguistic, cultural, geographic, and social distances fostered by colonial forces have prevented the development of a broadly based Native intellectual community. And those few of us who have been around for a while do not speak with each other as much as we speak to audiences. This has been due, in part, to unavoidable political and economic circumstances.

The lonely echoes of our own words have been amplified by a

strange but perhaps predictable colonial phenomenon: white intellectual judgement and shunning of Native intellectuals. The dearth of Native intellectual voices and artists in the media and in Canadian creative pursuits makes one wonder if the media is aware of our existence. Or are they avoiding us? Or is our invisibility an indication of the extent to which we are ghettoized?

The most distressing thing I have observed is the assumed estrangement between Native intellectuals from "the real people." How it is that white rather than Native intellectuals can better speak for the "real Natives" remains a puzzle. But the following is a typical, if bizarre, scenario: when white journalists "discover" an "articulate" or "bright" Native, they proceed to judge her as an intellectual, then bypass her in their liberal search for the grassroots.

In 1985, Métis writers, including myself, were unearthed. One incident remains for my memoirs: a CBC radio journalist from Regina called for cultural sorts of information. After regaling him (about bears, blueberries, fiddles, ghosts, and things) for about an hour, it somehow dawned on him he was speaking to a professor. He abruptly ended his interview with this request: "Could you tell me where I could find a *real* Métis storyteller?"

During the first Constitutional Conference on Self-Government, Barbara Frum interviewed a white sociologist who off-handedly accused " the Native intellectual elite" of "leading their people down the garden path." (He was from Regina too.) Perhaps because there is no Native intellectual elite, Barbara couldn't find one to interview. Seriously, I know there have not been a vast number of us intellectuals and/or writers around and I know perhaps we do not hustle for the spotlight as much as we should, but we are around. And there are more of us every day.

More seriously, we are not alienated from our roots. Society has made sure of that. And unlike many white intellectuals, we were not born into our stations in life. This is another reason why our selves are not (yet) separated from our words. To be exceptionalized is but another rung on the ghettoization ladder.

It is against this backdrop of keeping us voiceless that a movement against the appropriation of Aboriginal literatures has been born. There is absolutely no question but that radical intellectual surgery is required in the existing literatures on Aboriginal peoples. There are not enough superlatives in English to say how deeply Aboriginal peoples' worlds have been falsified in white North American literary traditions and popular culture. I, for one, have long been calling for the dismantling of racist thought and language in scholarly and popular works. Again, recently, I addressed my fellow scholars in an essay on the ethics of publishing those historical documents that qualify as hate literature against Indian and Métis peoples ("On The Ethics of Publishing Historical Documents," in Brown and Brightman, 1988). Some missionary and fur-trade journals, even some standard Canadian history books, would qualify as hate literature, even under the most stringent court requirements. But who will go to court against this hate literature? Who will face charges for falsifying Aboriginal histories? For that essay, I have received some thoughtful reviews. But several reviewers have dismissed my legitimate and scholastically sound concerns with the accusation that I am into "censorship."

Ironically, these silly charges came at a time (early 1990) when I was contemplating my continued involvement with this anthology, which was catapulted into the appropriation controversy because several Native women have felt that white editorship of Native women's literature constitutes appropriation. There is an obvious need for clarification and debate on the definition, direction, representation, and strategy of this issue. For now, I will simply submit that the editors of this anthology have not appropriated this literature; instead, they have facilitated its possibilities and transmission. They outline their work and approach in their prefatory comments. If I thought appropriation was involved, I would have removed my materials. For the record, however, I would not have tried to stop the publishing process.

But I do call on *all* writers of consciousness to address the continuing dehumanization of Indians as grunting and bloodthirsty savages in the cowboy and Indian movies and comic books, both of which are amply available on late night shows, VCRs, or comic book stands. All must challenge the exploitation of Indian motifs in the media and marketplace. How, I have wondered so many times, is it possible in our era of supposed awareness about "minority rights" that there are still teams called Washington Redskins, Cleveland Indians, Atlanta Braves (hasn't anyone seen their jerseys?), or Edmonton Eskimos? Then there are the archival materials protected as historical documents no matter what racist and inflammatory language they carry. And what could we ever do with the fathomless well of novels that qualify as hate literature but are also protected as classics in our libraries and schools? Then, there are those individual authors who presume to speak from the Native point of view, though this to me is a grey area, depending on how it is done. For instance, I value Cam Hubert's short story "Dreamspeaker" while, on the other hand, David Williams's *The Burning Wood*, Betty Wilson's *Andre Tom Macgregor*, and Mort Forer's *The Humback*, among many others, would have been better left unwritten. Even so, I have my students read these books for critical purposes. All of this and more needs urgent attention. But what kind and degree of attention? And where might we begin? And since racism informs so much of mainstream literature, surely the onus cannot be on Native writers to address it all. Natives cannot be the only ones responsible for confronting racism and hate literature of this magnitude. Colonized peoples often end up cleaning up the debris colonizers have left — can we refuse to do it this time? That we are raising our voices provocatively (see, for example, Lenore Keeshig-Tobias's important article "Stop Stealing Native Stories" in *The Globe and Mail*, 26 January 1990) should not be used as an excuse to further ignore us or to wash one's hands from the responsibility of fighting racism with respect to Native peoples in literature (and everywhere else, for that matter).

Appropriation is one of many issues that should be addressed by white or Native anthologists of Native literature. The irony is that, after reading this manuscript for purposes of writing the preface, I wanted more editorial changes, particularly with several pieces because they may, however unconsciously, perpetuate stereotypes. After all, much of my life has been spent "defeathering" stereotypes. But my concern (and it is legitimate) is one among many other considerations here. Even though I can rhetorically ask, "What good is the democratization of voice if it is one more avenue for the transmission of stereotypes?", I am painfully aware of the long history of suppressing Native voices, especially women's voices, and I am as anxious as anyone to help facilitate their/our expression. What a bizarre situation to be in: to know so well the nooks and crannies of colonization that this "knowing" threatens to stand in the way of other voices. Happily, this dilemma was resolved for me because, in the main, this anthology carries many good and worthy words.

And I do care about the quality of writing within the Native community. I do believe in such a thing as literary excellence (albeit dialectical as discussed above) in the tradition of the Cree who were known as Nehiyawak, The Exact Speaking People (although in some dialects it could refer to People of Four Directions). It is in keeping with the spirit of our original cultures to produce excellence in the contemporary context. Accordingly, I do call for an "exact" articulation of our humanity and our oppressed conditions in the advancement of our liberation.

Native peoples, however, are still making a transition from oral to written literatures, from aboriginal to foreign languages. This is both a gift and a challenge. It is a gift to know more than one language, more than one culture. It is a challenge to be able to fly with "the gift," given the colonial state of affairs in our country. But this is 1990. To speak, read, and write in English is the birthright of contemporary Native peoples. It may be said that linguistic "appropriation" can go both ways. My first language is Plains Cree. My parents were forced to allow me to go to school where I was forced to learn English. In due time, I have "appropriated" this language without abandoning my Cree. I have sought to master this language so that it would no longer master me.

Colonization works itself out in unpredictable ways. The fact is that English is the new Native language, literally and politically. English is the common language of Aboriginal peoples. It is English that is serving to raise the political consciousness in our community; it is English that is serving to de-colonize and to unite Aboriginal peoples. Personally, I see much poetic justice in this process.

To be sure, we must attend to the task of "recreating the enemy's language," as Native American poet Joy Harjo put it (at a Native Women Speaker Series in 1989 at the University of Manitoba). This does take some skill, but our survival, as always, depends on skill. Native writers, like all writers everywhere, must have access to and must avail themselves of good and conscious editing and editors. To that end, then, we can make a distinction between editing as craft and editing as ideology. We must make room for the advancement of skill.

Native writers face a monumental but purposeful task: that of giving voice to a people's journey that spans centuries, a journey that at once says so much about white Canada. Alanis Obomsawin, Abenaki filmmaker, singer, and poet from Quebec, in explaining the purpose of her films, said:

> The basic purpose is for our people to have a voice. To be heard is the important thing, no matter what it is we're talking about. . . . And that we have a lot to offer our society. But

we also have to look at the bad stuff, and what has happened
to us, and why.... We cannot do this without going through
the past, and watching ourselves and analyzing ourselves,
because we're carrying a pain that is 400 years old. We don't
carry just our everyday pain. We're carrying the pain of our
fathers, our mothers, our grandfathers, our grandmothers —
it's part of this land." (Maurie Alioff and Susan Schouten
Levine, "Interview: The Long Walk of Alanis Obomsawin,"
Cinema Canada, June 1987: 13).

Much of that 400-year-old pain has been expressed in the war
of words against us. And to that, we are pressed to explain, to debunk,
and to dismantle. To the war of ways against us, we are moved to
retrieve, redefine, and reconcile our scattered pieces. To the voices of
despair among us and in us, we are challenged to dream new visions
to bring hope for the future.

We are the keepers of time. We must know the places of invasion
in our histories and in ourselves so that we may illumine the paths of
those who cannot see or who do not know. Because our pain is a "part
of this land," we are also the Uncomfortable Mirrors to Canadian
society. And few can look at the glaring reflections our mirrors
provide. "My knee is so badly wounded no one will look at it/The pus
of the past oozes from every pore/... Anger is my crutch/I hold myself
upright with it" writes Native American poet Chrystos (*Not Vanishing,*
1988).

Finally, we cannot be cast as voices of the past, or even of the
present. As writers, we are seekers of truth. We are called to transcend
our own prejudices and politics, even our centuries-old pain, so that
we can do what writers must do — tell the truth about the human
condition. In this task, we cannot spare our own human make-up,
which, however, must be done with an awareness of the social
dimensions influencing it.

This anthology gives voice to Native women, and these women,
in unexpected ways, tell the truth about this land, about the oppressor,
and about the oppressed in us all. Ideologists will find this wonderfully
democratic collection puzzling. It is clear that Native women are not
in any uniform stage of political consciousness (but whose "consciousness"?), either about the oppression of Natives or of women. Nor are
they at a uniform level of ability. Both are to be expected, because the
tidal waves of colonization have hit Native communities at different

times in different ways over a span of five centuries. This is not to mention that Aboriginal peoples are also *different* from each other, quite apart from European influences. Represented here are women of different languages, religions, cultures, generations, educational levels, and personal circumstances.

There is a range of movement in theme and style that reflects the transitional nature of contemporary Native consciousness and writing: from oral to written, from ambiguity to clarity, from hesitation to self-assertion, from internalization of stereotypes to an articulation of our colonial experience, and from romanticization to quiet criticism of "our people" and "our culture" (a hint of what is to come). Some themes unique to a people dispossessed stand out: a haunting and hounding sense of loss that drives one to reminisce. "I remember," many of us write, "I remember."

The poignancy of "taking on" the historical millstone of keeping our ancestors' memories alive comes through in our unsettling dreams and visions. "It's with terror, sometimes/That I hear them calling me" wrote Sarain Stump (*And There Is My People Sleeping*, 1971). Then there is the plodding through the maze of identity crises that come from the political burdens and contradictions of our times. Questions of religion, traditionalism, modernism, racially mixed ancestries or offspring, mixed marriages, or feminism all pull at our loyalties.

There is the loneliness that comes from so many places: forced separation from one's children or parents, emotional and intellectual isolation, the experiencing of daily indecencies inherent in a racist society, the grieving that follows death.

Nor is there any escape from having to live in the eye of the storm — a storm one cannot tangibly touch or immediately give voice to, but still it is there. Always there. Like Pakak, the "thousand year companion" who "pierces the heart" with his "socket eyes" (see Halfe). And *forever* trying to remove the speck of self-doubt from one's eyes, and the boulder of arrogance from the whites of others' eyes.

So we share our humanity — over and over again. We share our dreams, our fears, our loves, our hates, our mourning for the dying of the Grandmother, our culture, the Mother, our land, the Children, our future.

Themes specific to Native women are, of course, here: birthing, children, nurturing, sense of vulnerability, fear of violence, wife battering, and sexual assault. And there is some allusion to the developing tensions between male-defined traditions at variance with the women's spirituality, suffering, and perceptions. There is eloquence in the humour, wit, and gentle chiding employed on self and others on issues such as loss of innocence, sexism, hypocrisy, personal foibles, sexuality, and even betrayal.

Finally, a word must be said about the theme of the spectrum of betrayal that permeates these writings. There is betrayal that a child feels about being sent to a hospital, a residential school, or fostering. There is the priestly betrayal of a child in the confessional (see Higgins), of a teenager in "the black sedan" (see Barton). There is the beastly betrayal in the policeman's frenzied raping of a six-year-old child, left alone in the woods during the traitorous treaty days, a story that must be set in a Hiawathian garden to accent the profound loss of innocence (see Gladue). There is "the man in the shadows" who must be "masked" yet (see Chisaakay). There is betrayal by men who jump into children's beds in their own home (see Alice Lee).

The metaphorical layers of betrayal are just as damning, and infinitely more difficult to say: Where were the grandmothers, the mothers, the fathers, the brothers, the "warriors"? Why did they not protect? Too, there is the disloyalty of kin and community in looking the other way, even blaming. And what more can one say about the betrayal of "coldstone Canada" for creating the conditions, then abandoning the oppressed to the oppressed, and to snake priests and yellow-striped sons of . . . Her Majesty?

To these devastations of war-time proportions, and to all the other indignities available in our society, women here write with such subtlety and restraint, it brought a hammer to my guts and stinging water to my eyes. And with some amazement, I notice a remarkable lack of despair. Or rage.

No one can read these words and say they cannot understand — there is no mystification here. No longer can our words be discarded "as irrelevant as Native poetry" (*The Globe and Mail*, 16 November 1985). Nor should Native women's writing form a new body of ghettoized literature. Both white and Native communities are implicated; both are invited to hear.

Aiy Aiy my sisters for writing with such honesty and courage. Aiy Aiy Jeanne and Sylvia for "sweating" this through. Our loneliness has been lifted.

Aiy Aiy I offer you this poem:

Brown Sister

O my beautiful brown sister
your eyes are deep pools of pain
your face is prematurely lined
your Soul of Sorrow
is the Sorrow of Every Woman
Every Native
My beautiful brown sister
I know you
I know you
you heal me
you sweep sweetgrass over
the scars of my Exile

Emma LaRocque
Winnipeg July 1990

Acknowledgements

Thanks are due the Alberta Foundation for the Literary Arts, Multiculturalism Canada, and the University of Calgary for providing grants that absorbed some of the expenses of producing this collection and that allowed us to provide honoraria for the contributors. The University of Calgary's Department of English is owed particular thanks for its unstinting material support and its enthusiastic endorsement of this project. We thank Myrna Ruth Sentes, who cheerfully and accurately typed the manuscript for us.

We are pleased to acknowledge the early encouragement of Marilyn Dumont and the ongoing help and advice given us by Thomas King, Emma LaRocque, and Eva Radford. The title, *Writing the Circle*, comes from Robin Melting Tallow, a contributor and much valued friend. We also wish to thank those individuals who urged their friends, students, and relatives to submit material for this anthology, and we thank our own special people who lived this long and rich experience with us. Finally, we thank Bill Law for his unflagging support — emotional, physical, and financial.

Della Anaquod-Williams

I am thirty-four years old, the mother of Charlie, Candace, and Carin. I am primarily of Sioux and Cree descent and am a member of the Muscowpetun Band in Saskatchewan.

I am currently attending the Saskatchewan Indian Federated College in Regina. I plan to have a bachelor of arts, with a major in Indian Studies, and a bachelor of administration by the spring of 1991. Thereafter, I have plans to attend law school.

I feel that my education is an investment for the future, as well as an avenue to break the cycle of poverty so prevalent in Native society.

Editors' note — The following is a portion of the letter we received accompanying the poem "Bill":

I wrote this poem in memory of my late Uncle Bill. Unfortunately, my uncle Bill, who was once a proud Indian, died of alcohol and diabetes. More sadly, during his funeral service, a Christian preacher, more or less, condemned the living instead of delivering a eulogy. This, of course, started arguments among the living about who was to blame for hiring the preacher. However, our elders took over the services and Uncle Bill was put to rest with dignity.

In memory of Bill Oliver, White Bear Reserve, I submit this poem, and, if you can use it, then justice will be served.

Bill

We had great grief
    when he left us.

We had great grief
    on how he left us.

We had great grief
    when the preacher gave
    hell-fire and brimstone.

We had greater grief
    when in their grief
    it tore them apart.

We had great grief
    for that moment
    with song, prayer, and sweetgrass.

We had greater grief
    but we did it our way
    we buried him the Indian way.

My Reason

In pursuit of a post-secondary dream,
I have studied by the desk lamp's gleam.
Many theories, I have learned,
While the washing machine churned.
I have read my classroom notes,
Through the scribbles of a small one's quotes.
I have memorized numerous math formulas,
While I prepared the baby's midnight formula.
I have typed many long term papers,
With the help of my two-finger typers.

I have learned the secret to focus in
Amidst the noise created by my children.
Until, of course, I'm needed elsewhere,
By the cries of "Mom" echoing in the air.
With hugs and kisses and supper dishes,
My children are why I fulfill my wishes.

Death Chant

Crying to the spirits above,
Echoing into the cold, still night,
Piercing winter's darkness,
Knowing what is done,
Falling on to his knees,
Realizing no greater loss,
Mourning the young warrior's death,
Unending sorrow,
Emptying the heart,
Filling the air.

Sharon C. Anderson

I was born in Winnipeg in 1953. I am Scottish on my father's side and Cree and Saulteaux on my mother's side. I am a single parent with two children, Tiffany (ten) and Danny (nine). I lost my baby Bella on 14 April 1990, when she was sixteen months. She died of a rare blood syndrome. Bella was named after my late kohkom (grandmother) Bella Stonechild, who was one of the strongest influences on my life. When my baby died, I thought that Easter, a time of resurrection, was a beautiful time for her to join her great-grandmother, who was a staunch Christian. I am a member of the Baha'i faith. My future includes plans of teaching art and English in elementary school. I want to pursue both art and writing as part of my own creative work, as well.

Mothers and Daughters:
A Narrative Analysis of Linda Hogan's "New Shoes"

"New Shoes," by Linda Hogan, is the story of the dilemma a pair of new shoes creates for a mother in her relationship with her daughter. Hogan's use of a third-person omniscient point of view allows the reader to see what all the characters are doing, hear what they are saying, thinking, and feeling, with the main character, Sullie, receiving the majority of attention in the story. This point of view also allows the narrator to pass judgement on the character of Sullie. The narrator has already decided what kind of character Sullie has, proceeds to develop that character, and shapes the reader's feelings toward the character. Sullie's character is seen as more positive compared with the other characters in the story. The contrasts between the distant past, the past, and present are presented along with Sullie's private thoughts and dreams as she faces the realities of her life.

Narrator comments and judgements give the reader a positive feeling for Sullie and a more negative one for the other characters she encounters in the story. As Sullie rides home on the bus, the two women in front of her talk incessantly and simultaneously and neither hears what the other has said. Sullie does not say much or speak often, so her words do not reveal her deep emotions and feelings, but the intrusions into her private thoughts by the omniscient point of view make the reader aware of the true depth of her emotional turmoil. Sullie stays home from work and spends the entire day thinking of her daughter, their relationship, their private lives, their past, and their future. She is deeply troubled by the new shoes and what their origin might mean in terms of Donna's private life and future. When she finally sees Donna, her young daughter, after school, she only says, "No." In another incident when Sullie remains silent, Donna's teacher pays a visit to their home. Sullie believes the teacher is examining everything critically when she will not make eye contact with Sullie but, instead, seems to look everywhere except at Sullie. She has brought nothing but bad news of Donna's failures at school. Sullie reacts by bringing out Donna's exceptional artwork, only to realize the teacher is not able to see or appreciate Donna's talent. Sullie feels ashamed for having shown the pictures, as if maybe she is the one who is mistaken about Donna's abilities, because the teacher gives no reaction.

Also, when Mrs. Meers, the motel manageress, brings a message from Sullie's employers, Sullie says, "I'm not going in." Mrs. Meers assumes that Sullie is pretending to be sick in order to avoid work, and she is incensed at the thought of such laziness. She does not listen to Sullie's answer to her message from Sullie's employers and says that she would not lie for Sullie. When Sullie emphasizes that she is neither sick nor lying, the manageress wants to know why her tenant has put her job at risk, but Sullie distracts her. As the manageress takes her leave, she speaks all manner of insult against Sullie and Donna under her breath after she has seen the new shoes on the table. The negative traits that the manageress has decided as to Sullie's character are in direct opposition to the positive traits that the reader has seen to be the actual truth.

The contrasts between Sullie's memories of her long-ago childhood, the more recent past after her leaving home, and the present time of loneliness and poverty give us further knowledge and understanding of Sullie's character. Her remembrances of childhood evoke feelings of longing and sadness for the character herself and for the reader. The cigarette smoke of a fellow passenger on the bus causes discomfort to others but provides a comforting reminder of the lake at home for Sullie, with mist rising in the dawn and the smell of the tobacco sweet to her, perhaps reminding her of ceremonial offerings.

Later, as she examines her quilt, she remembers the events, the places, and the people in her life. She is sentimental about the distant past, but time and alcohol have made more recent memories into painful things. Many people she had loved have died, and those left are ravaged by alcohol, so things are no longer the same for her.

She chooses to go with Donna's father rather than stay home and endure the changes in her life, but she only finds another kind of despair and loneliness in the city. It is a place where her little girl would not be able to enjoy even the simple pleasures that nature can provide the poorest person. Donna is growing up in the white world, where Indians are low on the social order, a world where Indian women were used by men and abandoned and where the richness and spirituality of Indian culture counted for very little. Sullie has the courage and determination to be trying to change things for herself and her daughter.

We are drawn closer to Sullie by the narrator intruding on the character's thoughts and feelings. We know the intimate and painful details of Sullie's life, things that only someone very close to her would know. We know she took great joy in the simple beauty of her surroundings. The most beautiful thing for her in her motel room was the crystal doorknob, which she decided to hang her apron on since it would conceal its loveliness. Extravagance for Sullie is buying the new orange dish drainer that was the same colour as wildflowers from home. We know about her shame and self-consciousness concerning her appearance, with her thin clothes and worn-out shoes, and we are aware of her beauty of spirit, her honesty, her goodness, and her great love for her daughter. The discovery of the new shoes hidden under the couch serves as a focal point for the emotions Sullie has been feeling for many years. The unknown origin of the new shoes serves to heighten her misgivings about Donna's private life. She feels that her daughter is growing away from her, and she does not want this to happen. She has dreams and hopes for her daughter, and she does not want to drive her further away by making the new shoes a source of contention between them. Sullie accepts the realities of their present life and realizes the possibilities the future actually holds for Donna. She has seen her daughter play-acting in front of the mirror with her mother's clothes and lipstick, and Sullie fears that Donna may already have been taking a woman's role in the world outside the home.

By using the third-person omniscient point of view, Hogan has drawn the reader into Sullie's life and relationship with her daughter by revealing Sullie's personality. The narrator has revealed the contributing incidents that lead the reader to understand the basis of Sullie's decision about what she finally does about the new shoes. The reader shares in her moral dilemma and, with the knowledge of her character, can accept her final decision.

Hogan, Linda. "New Shoes." In *That's What She Said: Contemporary Poetry and Fiction by Native American Women*, edited by Rayna Green. Bloomington: Indiana University Press, 1984.

Willow Barton

My people (on mother's side) are first listed on government papers in 1879 as being from the Yellow Sky Band. This is now the Red Pheasant Band.

My father's people were Norwegian. He was one-eighth Sioux. His family came to Canada in the early 1900s. All of the men worked for the railway, beginning with my great-grandfather, Diamond Jim.

Much of my childhood was spent in a non-Native residential school. Consequently, I was isolated from Native culture. I suppose my mother believed it would be best for me and my sister Bernadette. I also have a brother, Cory. Both of our parents passed away at an early age.

In my later years (I am thirty-eight), I began to wonder about Native social issues. Questions arose as to what circumstances contribute to a Native person's success in life. Thus the poem "Where Have the Warriors Gone?" was written.

I am married. Bob and I have two wonderful children, Darryl and Candace. In the near future, I plan to attend university, majoring in either art or writing.

Where Have the Warriors Gone?

i am i was a child
cold in the rain
stone grey cold

from the mouth of anguish i am born
out of the flashing star of death
my mourning cry takes form

the first rays of the summer sun
warm my face and naked body
held up from the earth to the sky and wind

to my grandmother i am the morning star
i am the candle that brings light
to brighten her sightless night

love of life through the indian way
i am taught the secrets of earth and wind
and the song of the willow tree

it is a life of innocence of crystalline snow
a time of snaring truths
but now the white man comes

with strange white words of silver tone
he speaks of a stepping stone
where whites and us could live as one

education will give us the magic key
to open the white-man's book of knowledge
unlocking understanding and dignity

grandmother laughs and throws him out
what world is this? says she
a world of stardust that could never be

next came a man with long black robes
to save our souls salvation was the way
and i was thirteen that year in may

the rain is beating angry on his roof
splattering mud on his black sedan
today he took something he didn't own

grandmother, he didn't take a woman
today he took away the child
the sky is crying and i am cold

what god are you to let this happen?
i turn my back and soul on you
for you are a white god and stone

now i hear and see the children play
but it is no use for i cannot stay
how can i tell them of salvation?

stealing away under the moon-drenched night
i am a running rabbit, a sparrow in flight
frightened by a shadow i cannot comprehend

forgive me, grandmother, for i leave
with a secret burning in my soul
how can i tell you of your new-found god?

to a place of wonder and glass
i come, a sea of faces swims before me
i am a hawk with no place to land

my eyes are full of electric lights
my mouth is dust and the hunger burns
my soul longs for the open space

i lay myself on a patch of land
the white man calls a park
my eyes searching for a friendly face

another indian who speaks a strange cree
laughed when i asked if the jobs were free
little girl, he said, go home with dignity

there are no buttercups or wild blue violets
i am walking concrete look at me
a grand madam no grass beneath my feet

walking in pink patent leather shoes
grandmother, i am barefoot no more
but why is it i feel so cold?

i am i was a child
oh it is true men like us young
i am fourteen, i feel so old

body and soul belonging to no one
but for a fee they can rent me
they cannot give me laughter

not the grey men young or old
who own rough hands that rip
then turn and leave a dollar tip

call me child of the morn
i was so named in spite of life
but i am a child of night

there is a game the white-faced children play
step on a crack, break your grandmother's back
i cannot go home nor step back

i remember the line and reason
grandmother, there are no satin cushions
that cradle my heart like your bosom

body and soul belongs to no one
i need you, you are the one link
between my heart and soul

i dream of my childhood friends
now my eyes deceive me, it cannot be
the little girl i laughed with is on the street

reflections of what i am are shining
in her smiling eyes but she doesn't see
i cry out though i want to run and hide

she doesn't say while you are away
your one and only grandmother died
instead, three owls sat upon her roof

but your grandmother didn't stay
she lived long, eighty-three summers
and winters, following the old ways

some say it wasn't fair to raise you
that way for a life that cannot be
better to hit civilization, she smiled at me

standing all alone i wondered
if anyone went to grandmother with tea
and bannock, cowards, did they whisper secretly?

did they wonder of the money i sent
to buy her medicine and tea?
did they ask or whisper openly?

all i can hear is the song of the willow tree
all i can remember are the red tracks
in the snow when we went hunting

i am i was a child
inside my levi jeans a stirring
i am i think a woman

which one was it that sired
this flicker of love that begins?
although i belong to no man but his seed

my belly is growing round and taut
still they want a warm brown girl
to chase away grey hairs, doubts of virility

grandmother, can i speak with you again?
i'm sure you can finally forgive and forget
now that you can look down and see

life on the reservation was nowhere
a shrinking circle getting smaller
choking up old ideals and dreams

there are no warriors riding strong and brave
they cannot see the enemy's face
nor swing a hatchet against white-man's ways

reaching into the flames
searching for rhyme or reason
i am burning slowly into ashes

look! look at me! you men in large cars
with calculating eyes, can you really see?
i was a fawn with trusting eyes

sometimes my legs are trembling still
wondering if i should pause or run
or brace my heart against assault

now autumn walks in golden moccasins
i have a baby and call him Donovan
a white name, it means dark warrior

what better name for a child half-white?
i do not think that he will mind
that his name was given from a book

i hold his tiny perfect hand
in it he holds my soul
i sing a lullaby of joy

he is safe here in my arms
but there are bills to pay and i
am father, mother, provider, protector

room 22 down the hall and to the right
here lives an old indian woman, aunt
we are bonded now by necessity

she holds my child and smiles
a shy smile and slowly quietly
i walk away from my heart

cold fingers loosen my hair sighing
the wind is caressing my cheek
when a car stops, i get in willingly

my steps bring me closer yet
a welcoming light beneath her door
my sleeping child waits, my warrior

the battered red rocking chair is empty
somewhere a radio is blaring loud
a neon light is flashing yellow

where is my child? i fling her around
her wrist is dry bone, a winter twig
it will snap beneath my hand

my battle cry where is my child?
i hold her braid shamelessly
her answer stabs me softly

the people from the welfare came
they heard the news
two children are living here alone

i am i was a child
cold in the rain
i am a child of pain

there are no warriors riding strong and brave
we cannot see the enemies' faces
cannot swing a hatchet against white-man's ways

in the bottle is the amber grace
that washes away my boy-child's face
i am just another drunken indian

walking in tattered grey running shoes
grandmother, i am barefoot no more
but why do i feel so cold?

the seedy bars and bar-room brawls
have turned my forehead and mouth
into a line of well-earned scars

it is spring again
i am i was a child
i am fifteen

grandmother, you wouldn't know my face
you, who called me morning star
held me up to the sun, sky, and wind

i woke today in a dark dirty alley
paying tribute to me are two rubbies
who laugh and call me skin and bone

my hands are sea-gulls, tiny beggars
asking for some tidbit of knowledge
from a god i thought i had forgot

why is it that we, wooden children, unborn
are waiting for the carver's knife
to shape and whittle us into form?

my life has become a question, a puzzle
incomplete fragments of me lie here, there
please, who has the piece in their pocket?

progress is the white-child's game, may i?
take two giant steps forward and then
take ten small steps backward when

will the savior be acoming?
on sleep-winged feet in snow-white coating
to carry me off to clouds of oblivion

a gentle thief the old doctor sneaks
within the pocket of my soul to steal
sleeping secrets where they lie hidden

under the covers of my childhood
undisturbed cowering from his naked eye
is the child, cold in the rain

mister fixer of broken souls and dreams
you cannot give me back a dream
you cannot glue a soul with words

the white man has many words
if they are not sitting on his tongue
then he manufactures them in his mind

he frames his ideas in scarlet letters
and in wise phrases, home is where the heart is
but my people would say, my heart is the home

my heart was my home a fire glowing
in the hearth which my soul built stone by stone
home, where my love was served in ivory chalice

no, my home didn't have four walls
it wasn't large or grand
enough for a child to hold in his hand

grandmother will you tell me the truth
can there really be a reason why
trust grows like a wild flower after fire?

i thought all knowledge was bound, held
by the pages in the white-man's books
i was angered that he was the chosen one

in this place of madness i hear the drums
of the white-man's heart same as mine
i see his eyes fill with sadness, as mine

grandmother, you would call me crazy
tell me that i should spit in their eyes
that i shouldn't linger in this place of fire

like dry buffalo skulls, bare of meat
filigreed with silver light, row in row
the patients sleep on white meadow

cross-legged i sit by the window
calls through the bars my heart
like a lone coyote against the moon

across the sky a thousand warriors dance
with undulating sapphire steps, shivering
when a thousand luminous heads bend low

from the valley of peace, i call you
as my ancestors called before me
dear grandmother, i have need of a dream

the white man, the old one, i call nestow
my brother with smiling heart and eyes
came with his woman here today

the arms of the old ones are empty
they have no child to help or hold
they have no child to pass on their dreams

but i am half child, half woman
i cannot be a white nor indian
i do not know that i can love again

dear grandmother what would you do?
would you laugh or would you cry?
the only friends i have, the white man

i see a vision in my mind of an old porcupine
remember how he came to us in darkness
we wondered why he didn't fear or hate us

how we marvelled that he didn't associate us
with the traps other brown hands had set
instead carried a dead reminder on three good legs

and i with a question that any child would
turned my face to your years of wisdom
asked why he didn't shower us with quills

didn't you say because he hungered, needed
he had to learn to trust another face
not of his colour, not of his creed, or kind

didn't you say forgiving is the lame old leg
we sometimes have to carry around reminding
that we cannot hate all for one sin done

beneath our skin, sinew for sinew, bone for bone
white or brown, yellow or black, skin for skin
we are all the same, we love, we die, we sin

i have a long way to travel on life's road
i cannot carry hate upon my back and yet
i cannot forget that i am cree

my child will look upon my face
it will not be with shame or hate
i will dance my dreams upon an eagle's wing
and fly high, higher, higher

Bertha Blondin

Bertha Blondin runs Naoka Enterprises Limited and is a consultant in all aspects of a cultural wholistic approach to community development. She worked for the Dene Nation from 1987 to 1989, as manager of the health and social development program. Her work has resulted in a number of publications about traditional medicine in the North and a cultural wholistic approach to family violence, education, and community development.

She writes, "This article is dedicated, with thanks, to my father, who taught me and gave me an education on many cultural aspects of life, to Dene elders, who have also shared their knowledge of medicine, and, most of all, to children and youth, who have the opportunity to learn traditional medicine."

Native Traditional Medicine:
Its Place in Northern Health Care

Traditional medicine and healing is to be considered as an essential service to the Dene (recommendation from the Dene Health Conference).

Past

The Dene were and still are gifted with medicine power, counselling, teaching, hunting, and laws that function as self-determination powers.

The Dene have always talked about prevention of sickness and intervention for health and strength through the cultural wholistic approach to health. We talk about mind, body, and spirit and how we have to integrate all of these factors together.

For centuries, Dene had control over the power of life. Our great-great-grandfathers lived on the land, with special powers of four directions, water, animals, land, and weather reporting. Some of the

Dene were born with these medicine powers. Others had visions
through their dreams, and the ones who didn't have these powers had
to work very hard day and night to earn their power. Sometimes, it
took them years.

We respect and have pride in our medicine powers and in always
being watched by the Creator and spirits and by our people to keep and
look after the medicine man and woman with respect. The people
hunted, fished, and gathered wood, and women provided clothing.
We didn't need money in those days to offer for healing or medicine,
but we offered food, clothing, tools, and crafts. These laws are related
balances of all the components in nature and were the daily science of
the Dene people.

Women are taught about womanhood, about their *time*, and to
respect the medicine man's powers. She is taught not to ask for help
during her *time*, because her powers can destroy the power of the
medicine man.

Fasting was one of the healing methods of clearing and cleansing your mind, your body, and your spirit. Fasting could last up to one
day to seven days or more. Food was carried by their side — roots, dry
meat or poundmeat (pemmican), berries, and water — until the fast
was over. But, prayers and offerings could be done anytime of the day
on the land. Water and fire were offered to ask for forgiveness,
understanding, trust, respect and love, and to have a strong positive
value of life.

Many Dene travelled hundreds of miles by foot to the mountains or sacred place to give offerings and ask the Creator to help them
in healing waters to take the sickness away and put the sickness in a safe
place where no one could get harmed by it, which is still in effect today
to cure any type of sickness.

For thousands of years, Dene understood both the theory and
practice of healing plants. In the culture and lifestyle was an expertise
to identify, gather, and use the healing plants in our environment.
Through generations, this traditional knowledge and wisdom of
plants' usefulness grew and expanded.

All the medicine is picked by the medicine man, who has the
power to pick the right medicine in all of the four seasons. The
medicine cannot be handled by anyone else but the medicine man.
Before the medicine man can offer you medicine for healing, he has to
know your illness by talking and by feeling the infected area with his
hand.

Our Dene lived a life of natural dependence on the forest for many generations, depending on the season of the year. Before the Dene began to use the white-man's food, they lived on a simple diet. Choice was limited and cooking simple. Yet, they lived in perfect health and strength. They had mental strength and active healthy well-balanced growth to live a long life with all parts of the body connected that puts to shame the strength and power of civilized man. Dene and Inuit people survived on unprocessed food close to nature, which was the elemental key to preventing all forms of physical and mental degenerations.

Many foods commonly eaten were gathered directly from the land. These included onions, currants, rosehips, strawberries, blackberries, blueberries, raspberries, tea, and roots.

Four Seasons Traditional Medicine

Spring Medicine
Berries picked in the spring are berries that didn't fall in autumn. They are used to keep our blood circulating in our mind, body, and spirit and to awaken us from the long winter.

Summer Medicine
Blossoms of herbs, muskeg, grass, and roots are picked and used when needed.

Fall Medicine
Autumn food. Cranberries are considered blood and liver boosters.

Winter Medicine
Bearberry roots, spruce gum, and spruce bud are frostbite and cold medicine. Most of these herbs are boiled in water to give to patients to drink. Some of the medicine is chewed or used rough and applied to your illness.

There are over two hundred medicines used by the medicine man, from herbs, berries, roots, and, most important, the animals and fish. Bone and animal bladder are used to medicate wounds, as well as to draw blood from bruises.

Present

In the late 1800s, settlers came and imposed foreign education, religion, health, and social programs that took away our powers, resulting in loss of pride and respect. They brought among us diseases that were very difficult to heal because we were not aware of new diseases.

The question of past and present relationships between Dene and modern medicine, however, are perhaps best commented upon by a non-medical person, who lacks the "blinders" that too often develop from training in a specialized field. Many people will question the value of examining aspects of Dene medicine, for modern science would seem to have displaced traditional practices.

Such, however, is not the case. Some traditional practices persist in many communities, and health-care professionals can use their strength or attempt the concept of Dene medicine. Today's traditional medicine is self-defeating if it is approached with negative attitudes.

Dene people have no difficulty dealing with issues of traditional and modern approaches to health care. They use both, and such an attitude is pragmatic and sensible. From a nurse's or doctor's viewpoint, it may seem crude and even dangerous to apply spruce gum to a badly cut foot. Modern medicine has expanded treatment and access to that treatment. However, it is not possible if an injured person is in a trapper's cabin a hundred miles from a nursing station. In this circumstance, traditional medicine is a sensible alternative.

Over the generations, traditional medicine and Dene practices have been ridiculed by many health-care professionals, with the result that its practice has gone underground and, in certain communities, much of the knowledge has been lost.

Although modern drugs from plants are used in Dene medicine, we have a "special power" aspect that caused most professionals to reject all Dene medicine. Some of the "power" aspect still remains.

For a long time, doctors refused to believe that anything could be learned from the "uncivilized" Dene. Only in this century have some learned doctors and biologists given serious attention to Dene medicine. But, unfortunately, their changes in attitude have not filtered down to the common Dene nor to the many practitioners in medical services.

The competition with modern medicine caused much traditional matter and power to disappear, and what was retained were only those medicines that proved to be of equal value to those of European origin. Today, some modern drugs are taken from the same natural substances that form the basis of traditional herbal medicines.

Medicine men are still very secretive because of persecution by non-Natives in the past to make profits from our medicine.

Communities today depend highly upon professional assistance from the nursing stations. It seems that many people even come to get a band-aid or an aspirin. The reason for this is that they have been told for so long that their traditional medicine was useless that many came to believe it. Many now think that even if you are capable of treating yourself or a neighbour, you must see the nurse. Rarely do these overly dependent patients treat themselves even when they know what to do.

Today's Healing Approach

Mind: Mental health is taken care of by the psychiatrist.
Body: Physical health is taken care of by the doctor.
Spirit: Spiritual health is taken care of by the clergyman.

In Dene practice, one person helps to look after all three aspects of healing. In some areas of Canada, medicine men are allowed to practice in hospitals and nursing stations. In one of the provinces of Canada, 38.5 per cent of the medical profession is now actively referring patients to medicine men and 52 per cent are directing patients to elders to receive relief from medical problems related to mental health. Moreover, the Federal Health and Welfare Department has agreed to pay the air fare and travel expenses of Natives who visit a medicine man in a remote community. Most of the referrals are patients who have had failures with modern medicine.

Imagine how many experiences the Dene had to go through all these years, with stress, frustration, language barriers, poor food, and illnesses that they don't understand or that no one takes the time to explain to them. Doctors come to the community for one to three days to see hundreds of patients. Each one of these patients is seen for approximately five to fifteen minutes, or doctors rush the patients through to meet that time. It is the same with any other medical treatment.

For many years, Dene have suffered through no understanding of or by lack of communication about modern medicine. But, again, we have created another confusion and frustration with the transfer of health services that will take years to develop and implement in the communities.

Some of the frustration we face in the present comes from patients having to travel away from home to get healed or treatment, where they have no family or friends. They can't speak English to ask, Who is my doctor? Is my sickness serious? One elder rode the elevator for a full morning because no one explained it to him or assisted him to his room, and he could not speak English. Another elder went home from the hospital with no parka in the middle of winter. On the way there, security at the airport got him to take off his parka but never returned it to the elder. It caused a lot of anger within the community because no one has respect for the elder.

For years, we didn't have escort services for patients. We struggled to find suitable persons in the community, but most of the escorts were involved with alcohol instead of looking after the patient.

Shy young people are going through the same situation as the elders, because they have to leave home for medical treatment. They can speak English, but they still have that fear. Hospital orientation should be given to patients about what is available for them.

Elders and other patients become addicted to pills. Common pills are 222s, 292s, valium, and others. These pills come from nursing stations, hospitals, and family or friends travelling to the closest drug store.

Some of our relatives are gone from our life to the spirit world, because they were poorly diagnosed by medical professionals that were wrong and, by the time they found out, it was too late.

Most of all is the difficulty of the language barrier between health care professionals and the patients, while using interpretation to try and translate medical terms. Translation is very difficult, because most of the medical terms are not developed in our language, and, again, we have to struggle because no one wants to change the system.

For years, we have been treated as third-class people who can be experimented on with drugs. If the pills work, then they are used in the south.

If we work toward developing the cultural wholistic approach, it will take off a lot of the workload from the health professionals, because we will be able to cure our people with the help of the professionals and the medicine man.

Future

It seems clear that medicine is most effective for patients who have favourable attitudes toward medicine and doctors. Two factors are implied: suggestion and social support. Medical professionals, whether traditional or modern, work with faith. A weakness may be that modern medicine ignores the necessary social support. To rectify this, a detailed knowledge of the local cultural systems would seem to be *essential.*

Because of the responsibility for health being transferred from federal to territorial government, we Dene hope in the future to focus on our traditional medicine and to develop a strong working relationship with the medical professionals in the community, the region, and the nation.

First, the only way to improve our health and social problems is to work toward the cultural wholistic approach *again.*

Wholistic health deals with prevention and making a person as healthy as he or she can be and with working at building the positive aspects of the individual and the strength of the individual toward self-determination to *control* his or her value of life.

Secondly, we have to work together to build stronger individual self-esteem, self-confidence, self-awareness within communities, regions, and the nation in order to rebuild the traditional healing and medicine ways. If we have the vision of control of our nation, we have to change our attitudes toward self-determination, self-esteem, and self-government. If we are weak physically, mentally, emotionally, and spiritually, then everything falls apart — the individual, family, and community — but we can rebuild ourselves through healing power from the land, water, animals, and environment.

To strengthen our cultural wholistic approach toward traditional medicine, we have to work together with the medicine men and elders:

1. To give medical professionals more understanding of our culture and how to use the referring system to our medicine men.

2. To culturally orientate medical professionals before or after being stationed in the community.

3. To teach interested groups of women and medical professionals why it is so important for us to start rebuilding midwifery so that our children will be delivered in our own homes and in our own communities.

4. To educate the student about traditional medicine, the values of life, and the importance of the cultural wholistic approach to healing self, family, community, and nation.

5. To develop a system with the doctors and nurses in large hospitals to work along with the medicine men by referring their patients to medicine men.

6. To educate our children, students, and youth on how very important it is to have them in medical professions and also to have traditional medicine and learn to be medicine men with a medical profession combined as one.

7. Since mental health is affected by many changes today, which are multiplying every day, to educate the community on the meaning of treatment, prevention, and intervention.

8. To revise the whole of social programs to meet the needs of the people to improve their live, working toward a positive way of life.

With this information I have shared with you, which is very precious and important to the Dene, we will one day grow to strengthen ourselves to rebuild our mind, body, and spirit and build our power of medicine to help others with pride.

Molly Chisaakay

Molly Chisaakay is a single parent with two daughters, Carla (sixteen) and Jocelyn (eleven). She is originally treaty status from Assumption, Alberta. She has lived on reserves and in High Level, Calgary, and Edmonton, for the last twelve years, experiencing challenges in these transitions and making choices through many obstacles. She attended high-school in Grande Prairie, took hair-styling at NAIT in Edmonton, and studied at Grant MacEwan College in Edmonton and at Mount Royal College in Calgary.

She worked for the Calgary Separate School Board, in the cross-cultural program, and helped develop a speaker's manual for the Calgary Separate School Board. She has also worked for the *Kainai News*, Dene Indian Affairs, the Dene Society for Social Development Program, and for various alcohol and drug treatment centres.

Molly Chisaakay says that she believes in self-determination for Native people and emphasizes the need for Native communities to integrate traditional values with healthy values from the majority culture. She believes that all people have a purpose and to realize their potential is to recognize the inherent value and worth of all individuals to themselves and to others.

She writes: "I want to thank my invaluable friends, Mary Stacey, Dave Belleau, and Rosemary Brown, for encouraging me and believing in me."

The Elder's Drum

The smoke rises from the sacrificial fire,
the circle is getting bigger, and many share hope,
the elder begins to drum and circles with song,
my love for the people in the circle exuberates,
the many other times I have shared these rituals,
noticing the whiteness, and the age of my grandfather's hair,
he seems frail and yet the song comes with such clarity,

and my spirit rejoices, in the song of my people,
that we all have the dignity to be,
to determine the spirit, to be like the man who sings,
and yet be proud of the heritage,
our grandfathers leave us the path,
the song, the sacred song.

Existing Beyond Fear

Reach for me as I lay numb, thoughtless, heartless, faceless,
the cries, silence, dry tears, I am a Tomb.
The rage of the menace strikes again, driven to beat me,
fists flying, purple, blue, black,
the swollen ugly face stares back through the looking glass,
angry growls, cold chilled stares, forever a reminder,
the looming towering striking fists,
stored in my memory,
the vengence of rage, the alien stares back at me,
someone might hear, no one must know, a sacred vow,
the cutting words burn holes,
the face has become immune to pain,
I involuntarily serve as a punching bag,
his vow to punish, the hatred, the bitterness hovered constant,
every nerve awakened, on edge,
stomping footsteps send me hurriedly to tend chores,
the attempts to erase the journey a harrowing one,
bald spots on my scalp, I laugh about, hairs uprooted and
I'd been scalped, mirrors shattered.
Fear is not good enough, listless minutes taunt the silence,
the echo of footsteps fading breaks the sobs,
the aging soul is free to fly.

Waiting

She never asked what it is that makes systems inconsistent,
or who is to blame, where does justice begin or end?
Who does make decisions for the Lubicon Lake Band?
She just listened and voiced opinions, poverty is normal,
especially on those northern Indian reserves, she voiced.
Poverty permeates every area of the system, when there is no
economic, social, political infusion, or is it intrusion?
The poverty reigns, and the waiting is what they all talk about.
It becomes a long wait.
An unending existence, housing is still bad, no water, no sewage.
Politicians visit other poor countries but refuse to visit the
Indian reserves, and many bands are affected with this waiting.
We are waiting they say,
for the papers of change they say, so many more deaths, violent deaths,
nothing to do they say, no jobs.
Now there are a few who are still talking of the so-called waiting,
or know of the waiting.
Talk of the elders and the coming of this change that is to come.
So many bands of Indians are affected
with this waiting.

Habay

The blue skies reach far to the horizon,
clouds move lazily overhead, and the camp-fire crackles,
the soft breeze touches the tall grass,
the loon calls far away, the mosquitoes hum, and swarm around
my child, she listens with wide eyes as the loon calls once more,
blinking she points to the fox which darts into the tall grass,
the lazy river moves slowly, and she throws rocks,
squealing with laughter,
the horse-flies buzz about, huge ones too,
the small log cabins still stand from years past,
the floor-boards, the moss on the walls,
I raced down these trails, barefoot,
the dust flew as horses picked up speed, down this road,
and the creaking of the wagons,
brief, memories.

Mother

She is a fair lady,
gentle, soft,
with years of hardship resting on the hands,
that gently touched a babe, that washed bruises,
that sliced wild meat, that held rosaries,
the voice soft and yet tainted with years of poverty,
as she tells the tales, in the late eve,
as the children listen, with huge eyes,
the ugly broken doors of the cupboards draw the
attention, as little hands break a piece of bannock,
and you smile, the warmth, present, always
your door has no locks, just a rope,
the richness is not in the doors of the home,
but in your eyes, and in your heart,
mother.

I Remember

I remember when days were unending, the long spring mornings,
and grandmother cooking, baking huge chunks of bannock,
the barge we made floating off to distant lands,
mother chatting, laughing, energetic,
father hunting, proud, and tall,
everyone gathering to feast on the fat goose,
the moccasins beaded, so much pride taken in showing them off,
at the fireside tea dances,
the tea that was drunk instead of the liquor,
the hearty laughter, real laughter,
the round faces of children,
the many family members that gathered, to visit,
doors without locks,
the potato sack races,
I remember
the stories told of adventures, instead of gossip in hushed tones,
the faces, pictures in clouds,
the pretty rows of peas,
Uncle Jon's treehouse,
the wild roses, the old mare, with seven children on for the ride,
the saskatoon berry patch,
the camp-fires, the rosy cheeks of children,
the long horse buggy rides,

the freedom to roam,
watching the young foxes at play, the fishing trips,
I remember . . .

Shadows

The masked man lurks in shadows, waiting, be careful,
monitor the acute sensory clocks, ticking,
in the shadows he lurks, blinking, big hands, big eyes,
black nights,
he lurks, in the shadows of the night, the rolling clouds
come thundering, heavy, rolling, heavy weight,
deep in my soul I dropped, into nothingness,
endless waiting, a thousand times it came, stabbing pain,
rain pours, silently trickling,
the shadow comes, a ritual begins, a thousand screams,
a lightning bolt piercing my head,
my body, as the spirit lifts, to drift,
the heaviness of the weight, all consuming,
in the heat of the darkness, the ugly grunts, and groans,
of a trapped animal leaves me, scurries to safety,
all dead inside cowering in dread, unkempt and dirty,
the untidy filth, scrubbing, rinsing the milky stinky pools of mud,
so small, so pure, yet the torrents keep me looking on,
while others laugh, real tears never came,
the heaviness of the rage, forever a companion,
frozen, until you came, I saw the layers of many masks,
many plays, the many colours I wore in pretence,
the puppet I became,
dancing to every tune, games, and façades, yet time stood still,
the shadows lurking,
many faces he wore,
all elusive, I dodged his plans,
his presence,
suffocating,
the rolling clouds choked me,
again, I suppressed myself, to disappear,
to a million pieces,
when you asked, with warmth,
you knew,
I saw me.
A tiny speck it was, so far far away,
to emerge, from the thick fog.

Pat Deiter-McArthur
(Day Woman)

Pat Deiter-McArthur is a Cree Indian and a member of the fifth generation. She has a bachelor of education degree and has written two books, *Dances of the Northern Plain* and *Games of the Plains Cree*. She runs a consulting firm, giving Indian employment and Indian awareness seminars, and is now on contract to the Federation of Saskatchewan Indian Nations to set up an Indian employment agency.

The Vision Quest

I am an Indian and a member of the Fifth Generation.

I have choice, strength, and freedom.

I have an obligation to my Treaty-Signers,
    and others who knew no freedom,
    and to my future — to be the
    best I can be.

What I dream, I am. The fulfillment of
    my dream is my Vision Quest

Saskatchewan's Indian People —
Five Generations

It has been about five generations since Saskatchewan Indian people have had significant contact with European settlers. The First Generation strongly influenced by Europeans were the treaty-signers. The key characteristic of this generation was their ability to have some input into their future. They retained their tribal cultures but realized that they had to negotiate with the Europans for the betterment of future generations. They did not give up their language or religion or the political structures of nationhood. They were perceived by government as an "alien" nation to be dealt with by treaty.

The Second Generation (1867-1910) of Indian people were the objects of legal oppression by the government. This generation lived under the absolute rule of an Indian agent, a government employee. Through the Indian Act, this generation was denied their religion, political rights, and freedom to travel off their reserves. A pass and permit system was strictly adhered to on the prairies; every Indian person required a pass to leave the reserve and a permit to sell any agricultural produce. All children were required to attend residential schools run by the churches. The goals of their schools were, first, to make Christians out of their students and to rid them of their pagan lifestyles and, second, to provide a vocational education.

Tuberculosis was a major killer of Indian people during this time and contributed to decimating their population in Saskatchewan to a low of five thousand in 1910. This generation was treated as wards and aliens of Canada.

The laws which served to oppress the second generation were in place until the early 1950s. The Third Generation (1910-1945) was greatly affected by these laws and schooling. This generation can be described as the lost generation. These people were psychologically oppressed. They rejected their Indianness but found that because of the laws for treaty Indians they could not enjoy the privileges accorded to whites. This third generation was our grandfathers' generation. Many Indians at this time could speak their language but would not because of shame of their Indianness. They were still required by law to send their children to residential schools, to send their sick to Indian hospitals, and to abide by the Indian agent. They rarely had a sense of control over their own lives. This generation was considered wards of the government and denied citizenship.

Our fathers' time, the Fourth Generation since treaty-signing, can best be described as the generation of an Indian rebirth. This generation (1945-1980) is characterized by a movement of growing awareness — awareness that being Indian was okay and that Indian people from all tribes are united through their aboriginality, historical development, and special status.

This generation saw the rise of Indian and Native organizations across Canada, the return of traditional ceremonies, and an acknowledgement of the need to retain traditional languages and cultural ways.

Indian people of this generation were given the right to vote in 1960. The pass and permit system was abandoned in the late 1930s. In 1956, Indian children could attend either residential schools or the local public schools. However, the effects of this generation being raised within an institution and their parents being raised in the same way had a severe impact on these individuals. The residential school not only taught them to suppress their language but also to suppress their feelings and sense of individualism. The continued attack on Indian languages by residential schools left this generation with an ability to only understand their language, but many were not sufficiently fluent to call their Native language their first language.

During the sixties, there was a rise in Indian urbanization, a trend that continues today. This generation also contributed to an Indian baby boom that is estimated to be eight to ten years behind the non-Indian baby boomers. The federal and provincial vote allowed Indian people to legally consume alcohol. Alcoholism, suicides, and violent deaths were on the rise for this generation.

This was a period of experimentation by both the Indian communities and the government. Unfortunately, neither side was ready for each other. The intended government goal of assimilation was besieged with problems of racism, poverty, maladjustment, and cultural shock.

Today's Indian people are part of the Fifth Generation. The fifth generation is faced with choices: assimilation, integration, or separation. Indian people are now able to intermarry or assimilate with non-Indian without the loss of their Indian status. Indian leaders across Canada are seeking a separate and constitutionally recognized Indian government. Indian government is to provide its own services within Indian reserves. Integration allows Indian people to retain a sense of their cultural background while working and living within the larger society.

The fifth generation people are the first children since treaty-signing to be raised by their parents. Many of this fifth generation are not able to understand a native language. Their first and only language is English. This generation is generally comfortable about their Indianness without strong prejudicial feelings to others. However, this generation is challenged to retain the meaning of Indian identity for their children.

Tracey Dodging Horse

I am twenty-four years old and the mother of three. I was raised on the Sarcee Reserve and now live in Calgary. I plan to write more and am making a collection of my poems.

The Gifted One

Entangled white strands of knowledge
Braided in a manner of pride
He had mastered the patience of being
As displayed in his warmest smiles

His wrinkled skin and frail frame
Did not allow for disrespect
And though silence was his most trusted friend
He was followed by seekers, none the less

Magical, harmonious chants
Fulfilled each listening ear
He sang with his open mind and heart
Touching all who were near

Guidance was sought from swaying souls
Lost amongst the growing cold
He took within him the aching pain
Then released it as a cloud would rain

Somewhere, there is an entity
Brightly streaming of unwielding power
With all his faith he had worshipped
Remaining humble to the last hour

Georgina Ducharme

I wrote "A Dream" after a vivid dream I had one night. I felt so strongly about the dream that I had to express myself through writing. I write from life experiences and messages from within and from events occurring around me. As a single mother of a lovely son, who is nine, and a teacher, I find that I don't spend enough time writing.

A Dream

In a dream
So misty and vague
Struggling and clawing
Climbing and crawling
Up a mountain
Ahead walks the eldest son
At last!
The summit
In my arms
A faceless child
I am falling and sliding
Down into an abyss
Full of nothingness
Emptiness
Behind are loved ones
Encouraging and supporting
I stand
Straight and tall
On the mountain top
Unburdened
Behold the beauty!

Jenine Dumont

I am presently forty-four years old, have a bachelor of science in nursing, and am working full-time. I live with my husband and three children in Edmonton, Alberta.

I Didn't Know I was Different

I was born in 1944 to Gabriel Dumont and Victoria Lafromboise at Duck Lake, Saskatchewan. My father was a grandnephew of the famous or infamous Gabriel Dumont of the Northwest Rebellion. To the Métis, Gabriel Dumont was always considered famous, but as a child I interpreted from history that the accepted adjective was infamous.

I was born in Duck Lake but did not live there. My mother returned to her home town to have two children after moving to the Birch River area in Manitoba. My first home was a ranch in the Old Fort district on the Woody River. My father managed the ranch that was owned by a wealthy Duck Lake resident. We probably lived there until I was two years old. I was the first girl after three boys, so I was given a lot of attention by family and friends alike. I was six years younger than the youngest boy and exactly twelve years younger than the oldest whose birthday was two days before mine in December. My oldest brother and I had a special relationship.

We moved to the town of Birch River after leaving the ranch and rented an old house which first looked like an old store-front finished in grey stucco, sprinkled with coloured glass. I remember enjoying the two years we lived there. My brother and I played with neighbouring children without incident. My father worked at various jobs, one I remember was bull cook for the provincial government road gang who were building roads eight miles north of Birch River in the Pasadena district. This led to a job as manager of the community pasture in the area, owned by the Department of Lands Branch and Wildlife. In the summer of 1949, the family moved out to the pasture and lived in two railroad shacks. The larger building was used for a kitchen, living-room, and sleeping area for my parents and my sister and me. The boys slept out in the smaller shack. In the fall, we moved back into town and rented a small but comfortable house behind the Royal Cafe. My oldest brother had to quit school to help out financially; this was a sore point with him all of his life. I remember that he bought a brown snowsuit for my sister, who was somewhat of a tomboy; it really made her look like a tough little boy. On 9 April 1950, Easter Sunday, my youngest sister was born. When mom brought her home, I said, "She looks like an Indian." I didn't know I was part Indian, and it was two years before I knew.

The next summer, we went back to the pasture and lived in the two railroad shacks again. We spent the winter there, too. The next year, the government built a two-bedroom house with a big yard landscaped by elm and spruce trees and a caragana hedge in the front. We thought it was heaven. The government officials thought they could use the smaller bedroom for an office; I don't know where they thought we would all sleep. They ended up using the larger railroad shack for an office down by the corrals, where it was more appropriately situated.

I began grade one when I was six and a half years old because of my December birthday. I loved school and knew a lot before I started. My youngest brother, who was in grade six, and I were the only family members attending the school. The school was a one-room school with grades one to nine. The two or three pupils in grade nine took correspondence courses and were supervised by the teacher. My first year passed without incident.

For my second year of school, we had the same teacher, and everyone was pleased because she was superb. My brother was in grade seven, and they happened to be studying social studies one day when Duck Lake and the Rebellion was discussed. The teacher, who knew our family, asked my brother if that was where our father was from. His reply was, "Yes, they're all a bunch of Indians there."

Nothing more was said, but a few days later or perhaps the next day the kids started teasing us, calling us Indians and half-breeds! This went on for some time. I couldn't understand why the teacher did not stop them, although the teasing occurred at lunch time and recess. One lunch hour, all the kids stayed inside the school while my brother and I were outside alone. Then one day, because we were Catholic, my brother and I were let out of school half an hour early when the Anglican missionaries came to the school to give a service. We walked and ran the two miles home as fast as we could to get home before the other kids. Our parents were surprised to see us home in thirty minutes. I had a sore throat that night, was in bed with a chest cold the next day, and missed school for two weeks. We must have told our parents about the teasing then. When I went back to school, the teasing had stopped. I assume my parents had intervened. My brother skipped school a lot that year and eventually dropped out. He was fourteen years old.

That was when I realized I was part Indian. I believe that was also the first time my father talked to me about being proud of my heritage. Over the years, he would often say, "Hold your head up high and be proud; it doesn't matter what they say."

I was particularly close to my father and believed him, so I did as I was told.

I walked that way so much that in high school people thought I was a snob; I really was shy and afraid of being hurt. I had some difficulty being proud of my Indian ancestry, as there were constant reminders that Indians were inferior. My own mother referred to Indians as "les sauvages" (the savages), as if they were inferior. I remember thinking, "Why are you saying that, we're part Indian too?"

I got a lot of mixed messages. We had a group of Métis friends with whom we spent holidays. All the women were the same, trying to be white and rather intolerant of Indians or the mixed bloods who had more Indian ancestry than we did. I remember my father as being very tolerant and being friendly to Indians. I never heard any of the other men make any racial statements.

Other memories stay with me. Once, when we lived in Birch River, I went to the butcher shop for my mother. The owner was always very nice to us. He used to give us wieners when we came into the store. This particular day I went in while a salesman was there, and the butcher gave me a wiener as usual. As I took it and turned to leave, the salesman, addressing the butcher, said with a laugh, "One of your little Native friends?"

I remember seeing that the butcher was somewhat embarrassed. Little things like that would keep reminding me that I was not white.

I spent a lot of years trying to be white. We used to always say that we were French. Shortly after I met my husband, I asked him if he was prejudiced. I think he must have replied negatively. It never seemed important to tell him I was part Indian. I think he figured it out himself. He's of Icelandic ancestry, and they seem to be a rather non-judgemental people.

After we were married, we lived in northern Manitoba for a year in a town that had a large Native population. I remember denying my ancestry once while I was there. That bothered me for a long time. It took me until I was thirty years old to really come to terms with being part Indian. I had two children of my own by then, and you can be sure I told them they were part Indian. When my daughter was in grade two she told a friend about her Indian ancestry and this girl started to tease her and call her Indian. I went to the child's mother who stopped the teasing. I certainly didn't want history repeating itself.

When I was thirty-five and my last child was a precocious two year old, we stopped in a small northern Alberta town to buy something at a drugstore. My son was touching things, etc. When I went to the counter to pay for my purchase, the clerk looked through me with disdain and I got this terribly chilled feeling. It's a feeling that I cannot describe. It comes when you know that someone dislikes you because of your race. I thought I had come to terms with my Native blood. Maybe I have, but other people have not.

I think the prejudice I was exposed to as a child affects the way I interact with people as I am not an open person and do not make friends easily. When I compare myself to my sisters, who did not suffer the same prejudices I did, I find them to be much more open and congenial. I would like to think there is less prejudice in the world, but is there? I have a ten-year-old son writing a story about an Indian Chief who killed a white-man's wife and then this white man relentlessly hunts down the Indian. The story is supposed to take place one hundred years ago. I guess the stereotypes are still there. Where else would this ten year old get his ideas?

Marilyn Dumont

I am thirty-five years old and have taken my writing seriously for about
five years, having kept a journal for about eight. I taught myself to
write by reading everything I could, including Canadian and interna-
tional poets. I write for my own sanity, not for art's sake.

Spring breathing

the night-birds assure me
    you're ready,
    that even though
    you're silent
    you're ready,
    that even though
    you're still
    you've changed
    and that even though
    you're reticent
    you're
        resolute
            like the grandfathers.
    and I go on moving
    and disguise
    my doubt.
    for shamefully
    I know
    I have lost
the meaning of your signs
    and the trust
    in your breathing.

One Day in May

A photographer exposed you
making a late night phone call
from a closing greyhound station

Seven years ago you were accused
of stealing dark glasses;
you always were lean and hungry
a tall thin Indian going nowhere.
It was then you thought
you could beat your way through hell,
instead you escaped
on a braided bedsheet
and never stopped letting go.

First published in *Contemporary Verse 2*, 10 (4):27.

we are desperate

we are desperate
voices
        echoing
against
        each
threatening pause.

prairie within us
stretches between us.

we are separate
        words

hyphenated by these lines
that breach this distance
called
        place.

I am a place; I am told I have a sense of.

I have never felt
this sense of place more
now
        alone
                cold

north of you.

Spineless

the most welcome image I have of you
is gone.
the most unwelcome image I have of me
is still here
big, loud, and bitching,
bigger still are my myths,
the ones I threaten your small frightened
                                frame
of mind
with
finally shrunken to life
size
now.

all you've heard are lies.

and hear me
bigger than life
too damn wise and smiling
bitch of the north
colder than Jasper & 101st
in a minus forty wind
waiting for a bus
nose dripping
short a quarter
and too mute to ask for change.

recovery

it may be too deep
        for you to enter
            now
      you can enter slowly
          you know
you enter by breathing in deep
          and when you breathe out
              you're inside
a tree branching out
       your palms running up
          the inside of trunks
into limbs that reach
       for spring air and hope,
          spreading fingers that point
into leaves
    blades of grass,
         now fingers running through
black
   moist
      edible
        earth
that you inhale
     and enter birth

The Gift

Who knows what it's like to leave, to give up a piece of land? If you do it might haunt you forever, follow you till you come back.

My father and I climbed the steep hill in a hot noon sun to see the old homestead at Goodridge. I worried about his health as we climbed. I wondered if he knew how dangerous this climb would be for his heart. My mother knew. I wasn't sure I wanted to be the one there if he collapsed. I wondered if this was why she stayed behind in the truck and coaxed me to follow him. I envied her ability to delegate this to me. She was shrewd.

Like a cub, I followed on the heels of my father. The hot dry earth shifted like sand underfoot and made climbing punishment. The bush was thick and dusty, but we pushed through, leaving the sound of branches and twigs snapping behind us. Finally, we reached the top, our lungs madly sucking in hot air that pushed more sweat to our faces.

Trying to imagine what the house and barn looked like, I watched my father's eyes as he pointed to where the house stood, where the barn started, and where he, his brothers, and his dad pitched horse shit over the bank by the barn into the coulee. Then he pointed out the garden with its rows of potatoes, beans, and onions.

I followed his eyes out over an endless field of timothy, clover, and foxtail. It was as flat as any real farmer's field. Moving his arm over it, he said, "That a-l-l used to be bush."

Toward the valley, I could see the winding Beaver for miles. The green cover of poplar, spruce, and fir spread out between the low-lying fields in all directions. Down the middle ran the Beaver.

I would have chosen this spot like my grandpa Pete. Thinking I might be likened to him unsettled me. He was a horseman: cocky and stern. He wore the dark and dusty clothes of the depression years, a shaped black felt hat, a handkerchief gathered round his neck with a bolo, a thick brown leather belt, and a pocket watch. In photographs, he'd stand leaning with one hand on his hip and stare stone-faced into the camera. Maybe the one difference between him and me was that I couldn't conceive of giving up this land. He did.

Life for the Métis was to improve in 1938 with the Métis Betterment Act and the development of the Métis Settlements. My grandpa was one of the Métis who accepted the offer of land and "relief" at Kikino, sixty miles to the west of Goodridge.

My parents were married in the spring of 1938, and my father was given the homestead as a marriage gift. "Dad left me the homestead, one holstein cow, and a calf."

I thought I recognized pride in my father's voice at the mention of this gift. And, at first, I think my young parents felt promise in this gesture. But farmers even in 1938 needed money to buy farm machinery. So what pride there was in my father's voice turned bitter with, "But we starved out of here. You couldn't make a go of it. Without water, a piece of land is no good for nothing."

Grandpa Pete had dug a well, but it yielded enough water for his family's use only and not enough for stock or farming.

My father was never one to give in. Years later, when we lived in Sundre and my father was a logger, he froze his lungs one winter working in the bush. So I knew that when my father said, "But we starved out of here," he hadn't given up easily.

My father tucked some blades of grass and twigs into his wallet. As he did, things stopped. The Old Ones breathed on us. The flies and grasshoppers were quiet. The light changed. My father's face tightened. I turned away, breathing silently and pretending not to notice. It was better that way. My father brushed his hand across his face. It could have been sweat.

He started down. My thoughts raced. I wanted to take something too. Something to say I'd been here. My eyes searched in the grass. A light flickered. I picked up a brown piece of glass. The heavy broken bottom of a jug. I didn't know what I'd do with it. It didn't matter; I gripped it against me.

There used to be a road up the side we climbed down. My grandpa plowed a road up to the top with a team of horses. The trail was overgrown now with tall grass and saplings.

My parents left Goodridge two years after my grandpa. My father gave up "the quarter" to the Land Improvement District, sold the holstein cow and calf for fifteen dollars a piece, and joined his relatives in Kikino.

Goodridge followed me long after I left it, not because I had any real hope of reclaiming it but because my small past had been tangibly placed by it in the history of Métis people. And knowing this history placed the history of my father's bitter and shameful struggle into the history of failure of the government to recognize that the Métis were hunters and trappers and guides and traders but not farmers. The Métis were never farmers.

Vicki English-Currie

Vicki English-Currie is a Blackfoot Indian doing graduate studies at Carleton University in Ottawa. She is in Canadian studies and is doing a thesis on Native women's issue. She writes: "Without the friendship and support from Dr. Yvonne Hebert, I would have found it very difficult to choose graduate studies. I thank her for showing confidence in my work and the encouragement to cut ties in Calgary and attend university in Ottawa. She also encouraged me to write and submit this article for publication. I must also thank my mother Philomena English, who has blessed and allowed me to use her family as an example to make a point."

The Need for Re-evaluation in Native Education

From 1949 to about 1960, my immediate family unit consisted of my parents, brother, three sisters, and grandfather. We lived on and off the reserve for about seven of those years. Happy and content, we children learned the way of life taught to us by our grandfather and parents. For me, it was a free and positive learning experience.

The hierarchical independent group approach typical of many Indian families was the lifestyle we lived. My grandfather was consulted on most things that happened in the family. If there was sickness, a problem, or a move to another residence or work place, we were all involved. Even if the children did not speak their minds, we were allowed to listen and be aware of family decisions and problems. There was no need to ask questions and become anxious; in time, we would experience and understand the decisions made by the adults. Growing up, we learned that it was more important to observe and listen rather than waste time asking questions that would not be answered immediately. The answers would come with time.

Those children who asked too many questions were seen as being problem children. They were dealt with by public ridicule, which served to check the actions of inappropriate behaviour. Discipline was prominent but was done indirectly. One technique involved shaming the child, often performed through story-telling about the child. Everyone knew who was being disciplined and for what reason, since it was generally performed at a family or community gathering.

At the gatherings, there was no separation of the children and the adults. It was an extended family; even community members could become involved. All of the talk was comprehensible so the children were included in the conversation, although the adults did most of the talking and the children mostly listened.

Often, at play, the children would discuss earlier conversations amongst themselves. Girls would ask questions of their mothers when they were alone. The mother would answer with a story relating to the questions asked. That would end the question period. If more questions were asked by the child, the mother would notice she had a problem child. Because it was a matriarchal family, it was a mother's duty to talk to our maternal grandfather, who would then talk with the child. I remember spending many days walking with my grandfather in the woods or down the road. Many of the stories he told me were turned into a life-lasting informal education of values.

As we were Blackfoot, many stories were about Napi, a legendary being who is responsible for many unexplained happenings in our lives. He is also responsible for punishing those who do wrong. For example, if someone steals, that person will never become rich, because every time he or she steals something Napi will take something of the thief's own belongings. Never, at any time, did my grandfather or mother directly tell me not to steal. By the story-telling, I should be able to make up my mind if I wanted to become a poor thief or become an honest person.

Decision-making was imposed very early in life on Native children. We were made responsible for ourselves and for our siblings. One had to decide when to eat, sleep, wash, or take a bath, for oneself and for younger siblings. I remember preparing to give my one-year-old brother a bath in the creek running behind our house. For most of the morning, I heated water and poured it into the creek so that the water would not be too cold for him. No one told me to stop. Everyone just laughed and went about their business. No one questioned the action of children or directly criticized the action. One was expected to come to a realization of the goodness or folly of her or his actions by oneself.

Time was not an important factor in our lives, so we could eat whenever we were hungry. There was always a pot of soup on the stove and bread in the cupboard. On a daily basis, children were not held to waiting for set times for meals. The only time we had to wait was at a feast where an elder prayed over the food. At this time, the prayer could last for five minutes or five hours, depending on the choice of the elder. In the evening, the whole family prayed together, and, then, whenever we were tired we could go to bed. There was no such thing as a curfew. Much of the evening was spent listening to legends told by my grandfather. I rose whenever I woke. Life at home was a whole, not separated into work time, sleep time, or eat time.

Physical contact was not a part of our culture. Gift-giving was the traditional way to show love or affection. For example, Native mothers did not hug their children or tell them they loved them. However, Native children knew their mothers loved them because of their mothers' actions of cooking and sewing clothing for them. The girls could and sometimes would put on the new clothing and parade in front of everyone while they cheered and clapped their hands. This helped to build Native children's self-esteem and acceptance as individual and as family members. They lived in close proximity but had a well-developed sense of personal privacy. There was no positive body contact, but, in the same respect, there was no negative body contact. I do not ever remember my parents slapping or hitting me for any reason, not even for discipline.

My parents did not tell me to lower my eyes when they were speaking to me. We learned this behaviour from observing older people and from the community. It was a gesture of respect for authority. One could disagree with what was being said by occasionally looking at the speaker. This would tell that person that there was disagreement or something more to the whole situation. Then, it was the adult's turn to listen and observe the child. Grandfather served as the bridge many a time. It was okay for grandfather to ask about the problem. This was when the child had a chance to story-tell.

All activities were performed according to each person's ability, and his/her self-determination to help oneself become independent. Work was shared by the whole family or with other relatives. It was a time of laughter, talking, and sharing. Many times, jokes and stories were told. I recall picking berries together and later drying them or picking firewood and carrying it home. We always waited for the slower ones, teasing and joking with them. It was a community effort in that we all left together and we all finished together. All work or activity would always end in eating, even if it was only bread and tea.

Even though we worked as a group, every individual had their own chores and each person was rewarded for his or her effort and ability to perform on their own accord. The reward, stimulations, and encouragement were not expressed in words; rather, it was body language of a smile of approval. We all knew who was performing and who was not. If an individual was not performing to capacity, she or he would be punished. If all was not done well or not done at all, few words were said. Silence and negative eye contact were used as punishment. For example, teenagers who had a friend of whom the family did not approve were ostracized. No one spoke to them until they stopped seeing that friend, a bad influence. The Native teenagers try to avoid mentioning the friend's name around the adults, mostly because mothers' eyes would blatantly express their disapproval of the friend when the name was mentioned.

By this time most of these teenagers were in the Indian residential school. Caught between two cultures, they were not sure how to deal with ostracism. They might rather have had the family members yell at them, being conditioned to that type of behaviour in school. When this happened to me, it was time-consuming and difficult for me to understand at this point, but I never forgot the negative reinforcement I received and a few months later I became aware of the reasons for their disapproval.

The Indian people's non-directive approach is a way of guiding offspring. It determined a basis for a future lifestyle. We matured rapidly and we became adept at determining our own actions and making our own decisions, while being sensitive to the expectations of the collective and of our elders.

This short sketch of an earlier lifestyle does not necessarily mean we had no family problems or negative experiences as children. Because we were Indians, there was the painful fact that we were forced to live in a confined area, on the Indian reserve, unless one had a permit to leave. Also, we were forced to obey the govenment, through its instrument, the Indian agent, or our parents could go to jail.

As mentioned earlier, it was through stories, observation, and reflection that we learned and were encouraged to change our negative behaviour. This early education built our self-esteem, confidence, and acceptance of who we were. We learned to accept others and respect adults. On the other hand, we were not being prepared for a life of totally opposite values, rules, and regulations. No one ever spoke of it until it was time to leave. Then there was only the physical preparation such as hair-cutting, new clothes, and the goodbyes.

This strength, which was being implanted in the process of primary socialization, was much needed later. Without this strength, the Indian child could never have survived the future in residential school — away from parents, community, and natural environment. The oppression experienced on the reserve was mild compared to the era of the residential school and its missionaries. For myself, in the setting of the residential school, life became very confusing; the kind of work interpretation I lived with while growing up was in sharp contrast to what was learned later in residential school. The conditioning of our early life resulted in a lot of hurt and pain in a different setting.

Before entering residential school, my accumulated hurts, both physical and mental, were not so drastic, but they were there as a normal child would have. Once in residential school, I learned to close out and build defences, which affected my performance after leaving this setting. Suddenly, a way of life had been snatched from me. In 1954, I entered the confinement of the Roman Catholic Indian Residential School at Brocket, Alberta. Suddenly, there was a loss of individual privacy and personal decision-making.

According to the rules of the Indian Agent and the religious missionaries, they had the authority to remove all Indian children, at age seven, from their family, to put them into a residential school to receive a formal education until the age of sixteen. At this age, one was considered ready for marriage or a farming and domestic lifestyle.

The government took no responsibility for the formal education of the Indian children sent to residential schools. The missionaries had total responsibility to house, clothe, rear, and educate these Indian children. The missionaries signed contacts and were employed by the government. The missionaries had total control over the lives of these Indian children and, indirectly, over their parents.

My experiences in a Roman Catholic residential school were parallel to those of other Native people in similar schools. This overnight transformation in my life was a total shock and an interruption of a well-learned childhood lifestyle. This was an enormous setback and the beginning of a lifetime cultural tragedy. All the formal education that I had learned in these first few years of my life in residential school was soon overshadowed by the stress, anger, fear, and hostility that was accumulating. One of the most damaging aspects

was the change from a non-directive way of living to a directive
approach. This new lifestyle was not understood. As described earlier,
questions were not asked directly because that was the way we had
learned in our culture.

As my parents before me had attended a residential school with
the nuns, we had a strong syncretic mixture of Indian and Catholic
religion that was practised regularly. We did not speak an Indian
language, so religious concepts were accepted and familiar in English.

I remember so well the first day of school in September of 1954.
I was so excited and eager to get to the school, because it meant
reading, writing, games, children, and those Grey nuns who I thought
were gods. I had wanted to become a nun so I would never sin and
go to hell forever. My mother brought me to the door and left. A nun
took me to a room and pushed me inside with my bag and closed the
door. This was one of the very first times I experienced violence. There
was a lot more physical violence later at school, but this was one
instance I was never able to forget.

When I saw all those Indian children, I tried to run away, but
the door was locked. Just the panic of not knowing any of these kids
or never having seen them before made me want to go back home.
They just stared at me and it made me more afraid than I had ever been
before. I was almost paralyzed by fear, and no one seemed to notice.

This was the beginning of an education of oppression and the
end to family life. We did not realize at that time that oppression and
a limited education was an effective way of controlling the Indian
people. In this way, the government could keep the Indian people
divided and restrained. No matter how the parent felt or objected, the
child was taken from age seven to sixteen. They were kept undereducated, in poverty, and dependent on the false charity of the Indian
agent and the mission schools.

There was no way our parents could question this educational
system. They did not know their rights under the law. In actuality, they
had very few rights. They were told outright by the missionaries that
they should be grateful for what they got. What was taught very well
in residential school was how to feel guilty and to be grateful to the
religious orders for "all they were doing" for us and our people.

There may have been non-Indian residential schools in Canada,
but none of them came close to what the government contracted with
the religious orders for Indian people. The reason for these schools
was not for the betterment of the Indian child or to give that child an

opportunity to excel in a formal educational setting. It was a way for the government to control the Indian people, using a religious order where the church was the instrument of the state. The way I see it, the missionaries were interested in converting people and the government was interested in keeping the Indian people quiet and out of the way. The two really did not care how it was done, as long as they achieved the goals they had set out to achieve.

The type of teachers who were employed in the residential schools were hardly qualified to teach, particularly proper English. For example, my grade two and three teacher was French and spoke very little English. She taught us to write the way she spoke. Her accent was so strong that many times we could not understand her at all. Many of the Indian children picked up this accent and made it part of their language. It is ironic that I do not speak a second language but have a pronunciation that the French-speaking nun left with me. As an example, I have to be very careful to remember to pronounce the "th" in a word.

The education so important in the first grades was so badly reduced by religious studies and by half-days in the kitchen for the girls or in the field for the boys that many of the children had an inadequate basis upon which to attend successfully a provincial school system. Classroom work was modified to a cut-and-paste type of instruction. For art, we cut pictures out and constructed a scenery. In religion, we cut out people who served God and made a booklet. The curriculum was modified to what the teacher felt was important to teach Indian children.

All of the people in the pictures in our textbooks were white and middle-class; nurses, doctors, dentists, lawyers, and nuns were depicted, creating the impression that those were the only worthwhile persons in life. Native traditional leaders were never used. As a result, the students' self-esteem, self-determination, self-worth, pride, and confidence slowly dwindled away to a desire to be white, because being brown was not made to seem right somehow. All authority was white. Indian culture taught us to have and to show respect for anyone in an authoritarian position. Indian people were not allowed by law to leave the reserve to attend higher educational institutions unless one joined a religious ministry. What possible point was there to use all these professional white, middle-class role models with the children during those primary years of schooling if they were to be denied by law ever achieving any of the roles of their models?

We were told outright that not only all Indian religion was heathen and should not be practised but also that Indian culture and language were savagery. This further oppressed Native people and created a false belief that our culture, language, and religion were degrading and insignificant.

In spite of the oppressive residential schools, Indian people resisted and maintained their culture. They became aware and began searching for a new identity that would lend a positive image to Indian people. In the sixties, many minority groups began looking for their distinctive places in society. Assimilation was rejected. Hippies formed communes and expressed ideas of personal freedom and individualism. "Human rights" and "multiculturalism" surfaced as new words and ideas to use as weapons.

Society was not sure how to categorize the Indian people. A very limited aspect of Indian culture was seen in ceremonial dances and in Indian artwork yet was considered representative of our whole culture. Furthermore, contemporary psychological theories such as Tony Buzan's were used to label us once again — as right-brain people. According to Buzan, we, as right-brain people, are good at things such as singing, art, and creativity.

> In most people the left side of the brain deals with logic, language, reasoning, numbers, linearity, and analysis, etc., the so-called academic activities. While the left side of the brain is engaged in these activities, the right side is the "alpha wave" or resting state. The right side of the brain deals with rhythm, music, images, and imagination, colour, parallel processing, day dreaming, face recognition, pattern, or map recognition (1974:14).

This is the way Indian people were perceived. People had seen only the surface of our culture and had formed conclusions about what they thought we were. We were considered to be cognitively deficient, because of this limited perception, the poverty we were obliged to live in, and our low social status.

Psychological testing was used to legitimize the treatment we had received. It is not surprising to find we have been perceived this way. We had learned so well in our formative, primary years of schooling only how to cut and paste different forms, shapes, and sizes. The core subjects such as math (beyond basic elements of addition and subtraction), reading, and phonics were not available as a major focus of our formal education. How could we have developed those academic skills? Given the opportunities and an appropriate education, Native people would not only be right-brain, we would also be left-brain, or as academic as any other cross-section of society. In reality, many Indian persons are capable of higher order cognitive-analytic thinking, as are, for example, many wise elders, sage mothers, and cunning chiefs. Educational policies, however, were based on similar limited perceptions of the value and abilities of Native peoples.

The operating framework for the Indian residential schools that I experienced was contained in a policy statement given to the school by Indian Affairs in the 1950s. In 1952, the Indian Act was revised and many changes were made. One of the changes made concerned the organization of federal responsibility for Native education (Barman et al., 1986). Academic authorization was now the responsibility of the Federal Indian school inspector, as a representative of the Indian Affairs Department. The curriculum was geared toward changing the children. We would no longer continue our old ways or be confined to the reserve. The children would serve as catalysts of integration and assimilation of the Indian people. This, in turn, drew a wedge between ourselves and our parents. If we did not all die out, we would have to become domestically inclined. As farmers, we would become entrenched into the Canadian mosaic at the lower rungs of society (King, 1967).

The children were sent to provincial schools with their substandard education. Many felt degraded by this experience. Many eventually dropped out. These children came from a school system that was not concerned with academic achievement. However, Indian Affairs, non-Indian teachers, and the provincial system expected Indian children to compete.

I was one of those who was put through this system, experiencing a transfer from residential schools to the provincial school system at grade nine. What a catastrophe! Scanty cumulative records were kept in residential schools; these pointed in the direction of a very low level of educational curriculum and instruction: "Testing policies — and, in some cases, even basic record-keeping was ignored. A permanent record card is made for each child. It is devised to provide final course grades and certain test results over the years" (King, 1967:49).

Not only the academic portion but the total residential school system has caused the Indian child/person to become a straggler in

Canadian society, lacking higher education and professional status: "University enrollment has shown great proportional and numerical improvement over the last 15 years, but participation is one-half the national level. This is probably a reflection of the number of Indians who do not complete the secondary level" (Indian and Northern Affairs, 1980:52).

This system of secondary education has also caused repressed anger and a lack of maturation in adulthood. For the first eight years of education, all self-determination was removed from one's life. Now, the fear to be free is an additional problem — a problem many may not be aware of or even want to admit. Accepting or not accepting the responsibility for making major decisions to plan a life constructively, outside the confines of Indian residential school, is a crippling factor in the lives of many Indian people: "The fear of freedom which afflicts the oppressed, a fear which may equally well lead them to desire the role of an oppressor or bind them to the role of the oppressed" (Freire, 1968:35). Indian persons have a limited idea of how to set priorities, to make major life decisions effectively, and to carry them out. All this stems from the early education of Indian people, the dichotomy between the primary and secondary socialization, and the oppressive nature of the latter.

In 1961-62, the Department of Indian Affairs closed down some of the Indian residential schools across Alberta and bussed the children to the nearest integrated provincial school. This was all done without band council, parent, or student input or consent. This was another violation of Native traditions and the Native way of coming to decisions. Again, it was a time of fear, excitement, and unforeseen disaster. Being young and inexperienced people meant that we were unaware of the haphazard integration into a provincial school. What pride we brought with us as Indian students was soon cut down, as a result of being two or three grades behind our peers, so we were further degraded and dehumanized. Our first reaction was to withdraw into our individual selves. We began to feel as though we deserved all the name-calling and ostracism, because we were not as smart and as good as the white students. We were lost academically and socially. With respect to our dress, we appeared as strange and foreign as the children from the nearby Hutterite colonies, compared to the other students. Our exposure to what was acceptable dress for a classroom had been taught to us by the Grey nuns.

The Alberta drop-out rate for Indian children in the 1961-62 school year went from zero per cent in the residential school to 29 per cent in one integrated Alberta school with an enrolment of 341, losing 141 students. In a twelve-year period, there was a 94 per cent drop-out rate, in comparison to the 12 per cent national drop-out rate (Hawthorne, 1970:78-79). Registered were 8,441 high-school students, and yet 8,282 did not complete grade twelve. The Hawthorne Report identifies cultural differences as the dominant factor in the drop-out rate of Indian children in integrated schools. Furthermore, since 1969-70 when the White Paper was introduced and slowly implemented under the aegis of Indian Affairs, we had no choice but to join the integrated educational system and make the best of it. At the time, the Minister of Indian Affairs, J. Chrétien, sought an end to federal responsibility for the education of Native people and transferred funds to the provincial government for the education of Indian students. In a letter dated 20 February 1970, Chrétien states that, "monies would be made available to the province for the point of termination for Federal responsibility for Indian education" (Hawthorne, 1970:2).

The provincial school system continued the directive approach to the socialization of children, including Indian children. For some of these children, being in a directive setting where all decisions were made for them had a lasting conditioning effect on their lives. The parents didn't change; they continued to use a non-directive approach in dealing with the young people. The young people were totally confused. A large generation gap developed that could not mend without professional outside help. All of these feelings of misunderstanding between parent and child contributed to family breakdown. Today, this situation has not improved significantly and a degenerative familial cycle has set in.

A Re-evaluation of Self

Many of the adults of that era walk around with anger and resentment. These feelings inhibit their ability to venture forward in education, careers, or marriage. They are carrying bitterness toward the white man; many have become alcoholic or have committed suicide. As a result of the lack of self-esteem and self-determination taken from them in residential schools, they are demonstrating self-destructive, self-deprecating behaviour.

For example, let us take a quick glance at the students of my era, who attended the same residential school. I am one of the remaining few who is still struggling to obtain a higher education in an academic setting. I am aware that it is because I had to come to a crisis in my life, forcing me to make a decision to re-evaluate my life, resolve the past, and get on with a clear mind to take advantage of life's alternatives. I could have allowed myself to become an alcoholic, like the other four friends who have already died in car accidents, or from suicide, or from cirrhosis of the liver, a consequence of alcoholism.

Many Indian people who are experiencing inner conflict are under the impression that we are born with this anguish and it is part of an Indian lifestyle. We seem to accept this self-concept, with all its negativity. We must realize that we can choose to step back and withdraw from the confusion of our dilemma in order to take a better look at our roots — a cultural, non-directive lifesytle — and re-examine these from a vantage point prior to the change in our childhood development — the residential school. Underneath all of this hurt and anger, there are the real people that Indian parents reared us to be.

Upon entering the strange and new environment of the residential school, we were subjected to a conditioning for a lifestyle contradictory to our parental teachings at home. This contradiction is what Indian people are trying to deal with today. Many accept living within their former negative conditioning or are unaware that they can take charge of their own lives and seek help to change them.

Today, in Alberta, we are not much further ahead in educating Indian people than we were in 1962 at the beginning of mass integration. We cannot continue at our presently diminished success rate. We must look at another possibility, that is, the development of holistic programs for all age groups, which will not only include religion, culture, language, and core subjects but another component that is badly needed — an area that will deal with the ethnohistory of Indian people.

Professional Indian people are currently struggling to develop education programs that can prepare Indian people to take a significant place in society. Focussing on the present, they are trying to achieve positive results in educational programs. However, I feel they are missing a major issue in ignoring the negative impact of the Indian residential schools on Indian people's lives.

Indian people still have a great deal of leftover anger. Group work could benefit people who have been mistreated in earlier life situations by giving them the support of people who have had common experiences and a basis to re-evaluate. I feel if people begin to re-evaluate their behaviour, they can start to make positive changes in their lifestyle. In this way, they can become aware of their actions and then begin to do something about them.

From working as a social worker and as an educator for Indian Affairs and for numerous reserves in Alberta, I have come to realize what the institutional racism of the residential school has done to the motivation and self-determination of many Indian people. Recently, I spoke with an Indian woman who went through the residential school system of the late 1940s and early 1950s. She said, "All my life, I have blamed the past situation for my present instability of life and feelings of being cheated and short-changed in how I feel about myself and this terrible feeling of never being good or smart enough. Also, when I am happy, I feel that I do not deserve to be happy and have the fear that I am doing something wrong and at any minute the happiness will end." She went on to say, "I was never able to talk about my feelings and this affected my job, friends, and everyone I met. Now, I have done something about it. I have taken it upon myself to attend seminars, learn to talk about the past, and read a lot of human growth type of books. Most of all, I have turned back to a supernatural being for divine help."

I see how Indian people and children have been subjected to numerous major changes in their lifetime. These changes have disrupted our traditional lifestyle and have caused enormous confusion and chaos.

In addition to all the chaos we have experienced, we have received an inferior formal education. This should have been a prosperous time of growth in our lives, but, instead, the schooling experience caused dissension, prolonged guilt, and accumulated anger. The government residential schools, western religion, and poverty have systematically robbed Indian people of our identity, self-esteem, and self-worth. The formal education offered could have complemented the informal education of the child's culture; instead, it degraded the child's cultural life and prohibited the development of our own parallel formal education.

As we come into the present, Indian people still have a high educational drop-out rate. We must face it, accept it, and address it, or else we cannot expect to participate effectively and to be leaders in the changing of society that is Canada today wherein nationhood and Aboriginal rights have emerged as major issues of Indian people.

References

Barman, Jean; Hebert, Yvonne; and McCaskill, Don. *Indian Education in Canada. Volume 1: The Legacy*. Vancouver, British Columbia: The University of British Columbia Press, 1986.

Batten, T. R. *The Non-Directive Approach In Group and Community Work*. London, England: Oxford University Press, 1967.

Buzan, Tony. *Use Your Head*. Vancouver and Toronto: Clark, Irwin, and Company, 1974.

Cardinal, Harold. *The Unjust Society*. Edmonton, Alberta: M.G. Hurtig Ltd., Publishers, 1969.

Cummins, Jim. "Anti-Racist Education and the Empowerment of Minority Students." In *Our Languages: Our Survival*. Proceedings of the Seventh Annual Native American Languages Issues Institute, edited by Freda Ahenakew and Shirley Fredan, pp. 35-52. Regina: Saskatchewan Indian Languages Institute, 1987.

Freire, P. *Pedagogy of the Oppressed*. New York, New York: The Continuum Publishing Corporation, 1970.

Frideres, J.S. *Canada's Indians Contemporary Conflicts*. Scarborough, Ontario: Prentice Hall of Canada, Ltd., 1974.

Indian Chiefs of Alberta. *Citizens Plus*. Presentation to the Right Honourable Pierre Elliot Trudeau, Prime Minister of Canada in Edmonton, Alberta, Canada, 1970.

Jackins, H. *The Human Side of Human Beings*. Seattle, Washington: Rational Island Publishers, 1978.

King, A.R. *The School at Mopass*. Toronto, Ontario: Holt, Rinehart, and Winston, Inc., 1967.

Knox, R.H. *Indian Conditions: A Survey*. Ottawa, Ontario: The Department of Indian Affairs and Northern Development, 1980.

61

Norma Gladue

I am a Cree Native of Desmarais, Alberta, a reservation north of Slave Lake. I plan on receiving an excellent education and achieving the goal I have set to become a therapist.

Editors' note — We received this letter from Norma Gladue, after she had rewritten her story:

I am extremely proud and sad to say that I've finally completed my story to be the piece I wanted it to be.

I am proud because it's a beautiful story and my heart ached every sentence of the way. I am sad because Little Crying Eagle is not a child (that's me) anymore. I've used this story as therapy while rewriting it, to accept what I couldn't change from my past. It has been an overwhelming experience. My past was staring at me day to day, and I could not do anything but face it with my feet firmly on the ground. As I've told you, I have quit drinking five months ago after nine years of it, and this story has brought me back to reality. That is my reason for rewriting it. I knew that I needed to release what I didn't have the courage to release from my mouth. The details, it's what haunted me for so long. What I find odd is that as I wrote I'd hear those screams echo in my mind over and over again, but it gave me courage to go on instead of being afraid to face and share it. It was very difficult but that's what I wanted. I wanted to turn a nightmare into something that people can learn from instead of being afraid. I find it beautiful. I can't believe that I, Norma Gladue, actually wrote this. It's beautiful, because it makes you "feel," not pity, but a learning hurt.

I am going to miss working on it, so many sleepless nights, crying, laughing at her accomplishments and happiness, "being the child that I never had the chance to be." I sound like a worried mother trying to keep her adult child to stay home long, don't I? What I find funny is that I am only seventeen and I feel so old, let's say about sixty-seven? Ha ha, I just can't believe that I've finally accomplished this goal, actually wrote it all right to the end. I have finally let go a piece of my past. That is what this is all about, after a decade of hell I've finally done it! I just can't believe it.

Broken Promises

The golden sun was setting just beyond the horizon, leaving a faint glow of gold upon the land — a land that the Plains Cree inhabited and claimed as their own.

Night was fast approaching as a six-year-old Little Crying Eagle hurried home from her secret place one mile north-east of the tribe's home. Little Crying Eagle loved life and all that the Great Mother Earth had to offer. She favoured traditional dancing the most. The elders relished viewing such vigour in one so young. They had all enthusiastically agreed that she would become a distinctive mate for a dignified chief one day. Little Crying Eagle believed that no harm would come to her as long as she remained the good girl she was. This was of no complication.

As she tread the moonlit path, she chanted the song that her mother had instructed her in the previous night. Each time she sang, it never failed to liven her spirits. Little Crying Eagle titled it "Little Angels."

> Little Angels dance in the night
> With no anger, with no fright
> But only with love and courage
> That will guide my soul from discourage,
>
> Little angels do not cry
> Little angels do not die
> Little angels only guide
> And dance to the songs of life.

She danced in flashing circles and burst into a fit of sweet laughter that lit her young and innocent face. If anyone was to have seen her laughing and dancing all alone in the forest, they'd have believed she'd surely lost her head and would have retrieved the shaman immediately, at once.

As her laughter subsided, she brushed the tears from her cheeks and resumed her way home. The camp was not much farther, her pace quickened. Little Crying Eagle wondered whether her mother would become angry with her for returning home so late in the evening, "I hope she won't be cross with me. In the future, I will be mostly aware of such things as when the sun falls."

Entering the campgrounds, Little Crying Eagle heard the soft sweet laughter of her mother. Instantaneously, she glanced in the direction the familiar laughter came from. Long, wavy, ebony hair cascaded down Raven Calls's back; the cream-coloured doeskin dress she was attired in luxuriously hugged her body.

Little Crying Eagle brought her hands to her mouth and muffled a giggle. She playfully ran toward her mother as her heart sang with loving laughter. She came to a sudden halt. The warriors and their mates were in full view. All eyes were set on Raven Calls. It seemed she was the centre of attention. Raven Calls spoke to one of the warriors as if telling him a secret. He entered his lodge and almost immediately he emerged with his drum. Everyone's exuberance was obvious to recognize as he began to beat a slow, steady mystical rhythm.

As she observed, Little Crying Eagle hid in the shadows; a drunken brave staggered by, hopelessly attempting to chant along with the drumbeat. Curiosity and bewilderment coaxed her to creep closer. Her pursuing eyes discovered Raven Calls once more. She was silently speaking with Blue Waters and Silent Wind. Little Crying Eagle was confused, for no announcements had been made for any festivities this evening or anything as such. She then realized Raven Calls was fiercely clinging to a tin cup. Slowly recalling the drunken brave, Little Crying Eagle was confused no more. It was definitely time for their weekly fill of fire-water. Dread and resentment washed over Little Crying Eagle as a great wave. She shook with disappointment.

It would be pointless to plead with Raven Calls to come home. It would be best avoiding any approach to her. Despair savagely tugged Little Crying Eagle's heart. She attempted to swallow the lump that formed in her throat, but there it determined to remain. She did not know what to do. To await for a drunken mother within the lodge was not worth the effort. To sleep at a friend's lodge would be humiliating under the circumstances. "Most assuredly I will not be within the warm furs of my sleeping mat tonight," she thought.

It took all her willpower to declare so, for she was tired and greatly desired to go home. She then decided to return to her secret place, thinking hopefully this will not become a routine she'd have to adopt. There was no other alternative. She had no place to go within the camp. Like a bolt she ran to their lodge, grabbed what fur she could and some venison for the morning. The creek near her secret place would quench her thirst. As she slowly walked away, the lodge seemed so destitute. "If only things were not the way they are and if only my mother. . .," she cut herself short, knowing better not to wish for faraway dreams.

Once again, she tread the moonlit path. This time, it was not with happiness and great joy as before. Now, salted tears stained Little Crying Eagle's face. Visions of her mother and the tribe laughing and making mockery at her made her feel like an outcast of the whole Native nation. The hurt agitated her hope that one day her mother would cease her drinking firewater for the sake of Little Crying Eagle and her well-being. To request of this would be asking Raven Calls to cut her right arm off. She concentrated to rid the thought of her mother, of the tribe, and of her aching loneliness. Little Crying Eagle could not dwell on the pain, for such thoughts could hurt her spirits.

Little Crying Eagle then turned her thoughts to a man whom she had known two summers ago. He had demonstrated to her how to produce a fire, the fire she had not yet succeeded in making. She did not know what had become of him. After that day, he had coloured his face and joined a party of men who had done the exact thing. A kiss and warm hug was all she'd received as he moved rapidly to his bay stallion.

As the warriors returned from battle, she was seeking him, but he was nowhere to be seen at all. The bay stallion was led by one of the warriors, a lifeless form laid across its back. The form resembled very much of the man she had known and who had protected her. Tears unashamedly streaked Loud Drum's face as he approached Raven Calls's lodge. Immediately, she came running out with an expression on her face that Little Crying Eagle could not understand. Before too long, she was quickly hurried away to her friend's lodge. Suddenly, Little Laughing Wolf found it extremely urgent that they continue their game that the arrival of the warriors had interrupted. She stayed at Little Laughing Wolf's for many days. That night of the warriors' arrival, Raven Calls had suddenly fallen ill. Blue Waters informed Little Crying Eagle that it would be best to remain within their lodge. "I wish to return to my mother. If she is ill, I want to assist nourishing her back to health," she stubbornly protested.

Blue Waters held firm, "Little Crying Eagle, this was of your mother's wish. She has requested that you remain here within our lodge. It is best for your health that this is so. This discussion has now come to an end. I do not wish to hear another word on this matter."

For many days, Little Crying Eagle was not permitted to call upon her mother. To this day, Little Crying Eagle does not know what the cause of the illness was. For many days upon her return, tears streamed like a river down Raven Calls's face.

Little Crying Eagle glanced at the full moon. She realized that it was not much farther to her secret place. She paused to collect some parched limbs. When she was positive she had a suitable amount, she progressed to her destination, "I will attempt to create a fire. If I do not succeed, I could claim that I've made an effort."

As she approached her secret place, she caught sight of a yellow object behind a windfall near her path. Little Crying Eagle was apprehensive to investigate in suspicion of it being a cougar. The thought soon cleared as her secret place came within full sight. She ceased her footsteps to view its beauty in the moonlight.

It was breathtaking. If she had known it held such a magnificent sight in the moonlight, she would remain much longer than granted. The long meadow was a few hundred paces, with the green grass going in all directions in the light breeze. The small creek leisurely flowed, singing a beautiful song in its own native tongue. Beyond the creek, a few dark bushes were waving a cheerful welcome beck to her. They seemed like people in the clear light of the moon. This was Little Crying Eagle's heaven, her only private and prized possession. Only she knew of its existence.

At the innermost of her heaven, Little Crying Eagle dropped to her knees and laid aside the dry twigs. She seized the two most arid and clumsily began to rub them against one another.

After quite some time with the strenuous task, she grew extremely exhausted and discouraged. Certainly, it had not taken this amount of time for the man. Just when frustration slowly came seeping in, a curl of grey haze emerged. With reddish fingers, sweaty palms, and low body heat, Little Crying Eagle for the first time ever officially had succeeded in building a fire. As a massive smile crossed her face, Little Crying Eagle's pride knew no measures. Now that she had a warm, fierce fire to keep away the predators, Little Crying Eagle was able to relax and feel at ease.

As she sat with her legs crossed in close proximity to the fire,

Little Crying Eagle was lost in the angry flames. Leisurely, a recollection formed, reminding her of the most painful experience she had ever endured in her brief life.

Raven Calls told her to retire shortly and announced that she had to part for Blue Waters's lodge. Raven Calls had committed to help Blue Waters with her tasks, for she was round with child and the time was approaching for the child to come into the world. She then kissed Little Crying Eagle, promising to return as soon as possible. She then bid her child a restful sleep and vanished from their lodge. Little Crying Eagle did not hesitate to do so immediately, for the day was fulfilling and filled with exciting activities.

Suddenly, Little Crying Eagle awoke in the midst of the night. The noise within the camp would have risen the unliving if it were a possibility. She thrust open the entrance flap and stepped into the cold night air. The grogginess immediately left her body. Little Eagle watched Raven Calls happily singing and dancing with a handsome, eligible warrior. There was no mystification in Little Crying Eagle's mind that Raven Calls had not swallowed a drop of fire-water. It was apparent that she had. Only the amount Little Crying Eagle did not know. She was aware of the fact that Raven Calls was very far from having a care in the world. As Little Crying Eagle stood and observed, she had no conception of what to do. She expected the least her mother could do was to come home and produce a fire for her child. Little Crying Eagle then marched off in the direction of her mother, highly agitated. She desperately searched for the words to say, but nothing in particular came to mind. She could blurt out, "Mother, why is it that you swallow fire-water more than you attempt to remain level-headed at least for one sun? The very least you should do is to build a fire for me. It is cold within the lodge. I hope that isn't too great of a request, since you are having a heavenly occasion."

Raven Calls gave Little Crying Eagle an aggravated glare, but that did not stop Little Crying Eagle from speaking out, "I believe that it is only decent that you manage to keep me warm. Father had informed me that it was only righteous to request fairness when it is not acknowledged by the other."

Raven Calls appeared to be extremely far from the vivacious one she had been. Her soft topaz eyes now darkened like roaring thunderheads. She spoke with clenched teeth and a mere whisper, "My child, your father has long since entered the spirit world. I highly recommend that you avoid mentioning his name and his past existence. Mark my words, Little Crying Eagle, it would be wise of you to heed each one. It would not pay to cross me. Do not inform me of words that I do not wish to hear. Is that understood? Return to the lodge immediately! I do not desire to see you for the remainder of this night."

Raven Calls appeared to be restraining from striking Little Crying Eagle. Her child's words had embarrassed Raven Calls amongst her friends.

Little Crying Eagle did not know what to do. The feeling of frustration was very new to her. For one, she knew she must defend her loving father's honour. All her fear washed away as she declined, "No, Mother."

Little Crying Eagle had not a moment to realize her error as Raven Calls seized her by the hair and gave her a swift backhand across her face. In a grated tone, Raven Calls commanded, "DO NOT disobey me once more! Go home before I remove your vile tongue from your head. Honestly, I sometimes regret the day I've given birth to you."

Little Crying Eagle stumbled home and hurriedly crawled under the stiff furs of her sleeping mat. She attempted to alleviate the stinging sensation on her face as she silently wept. As she drifted off, it still remained. She dreamt of the father she wished had been alive to embrace her in his powerful arms, to fulfill the need to be protected, and to be by her side. As she shivered in the cold dark lodge in her sleep, Raven Calls laughed and danced with the warrior.

As the memory drifted away, Little Crying Eagle realized that her fire was perishing. As she sat in near dark, she knew that the warrior she had known was indeed her father, "He is gone, but I will find him once more and we will live healthy, happy lives and, hopefully, we will persuade mother to quit drinking fire-water."

She could not understand death, for she was yet so young. Only time would heal her loss, a loss she did not know existed. He was out there in some distant place and she was going to find him. She then decided her secret place was where she'd wait upon his arrival and she would not permit him to leave her again.

She needed more twigs and solid wood to last her the night. She stood and walked to the nearest thicket. As she assembled what wood she could perceive, a twig snapped close by. For an instant, her heart raced. "That must have been a raccoon," she silently assured herself.

After reassuring herself a number of times, she had collected all that was necessary. Once more, a twig snapped. This time, it was directly behind her and just a pace away. This is definitely not a raccoon. The instinct to bolt seized her, but to her surprise she spun around. Before she had time to see what it was, something immense and rapid knocked her down. As she hit the ground, two rather large flat feet faced her. As she examined the man, she poked his feet to see if he was real. Surely this had to be a mistake. He had a pale face, obviously unlike her own. His hair was as golden as the sun and his eyes the colour of a grey haze. He was attired in clothing the colour of the night with a bright yellow stripe along the sides. Surely this was not buckskin at all. Suddenly, the astonishment ceased to exist as she felt outraged by this egotistical, overbearing form.

As she quickly picked herself up, she spat the dirt out of her mouth and craned her neck to eye him. She exclaimed, "In such an extensive forest, how is it that two can possibly be a crowd? You may be large, but not as you believe yourself to be!"

Her voice rang in the forest. His face turned red, and he broke into a fit of laughter. This confused Little Crying Eagle. Furthermore, she stomped her foot firmly on the ground and held both her hands on her sides. "Would you care to share a part of your amusement with me?" she angrily questioned him.

As he caught his breath, his facial expression transformed and he scanned her, full of detestation and malice. "Is there a problem?" she asked.

He pointed his finger toward the earth. Little Crying Eagle examined her moccasins, assuming that he was demanding her to give them to him, "NO, not on your breath. My mother made these especially for me. They were a gift, and all that I have to wear. My feet are much smaller than your huge ones."

Her hands flew to her lips as she hysterically laughed at his humorous demand. It took some time to control her amusement, "Ha ha ha. I am very sorry, ha ha ha ha, but this does not occur to me on a regular basis, ha ha."

He gave her a perplexed look. She then realized that he did not understand her tongue at all. He removed his jacket and spread it out on the ground. He spoke in a grating tone. His eyes shone like daggers that threatened to strike at any moment. She looked downward at his coat, then back at him. She began to ask him to repeat his words. Before she realized this man meant harm to her, his enormous, powerful fist crashed into her young face. With quivering lips and blood flooding from her nose, Little Crying Eagle dropped to the ground.

He came down toward her. She pivoted, evading his massive body. He fell on his face. She bound up and ran as fast as her short legs would take her, although she was tall for her age, but he was much too fast. The soldier grabbed her by the hair. She fell once more, blood and tears mixed on Little Crying Eagle's face. He pinned her down as he saw the tormented expression she wore. He then threw his head up to the moon and laughed like a madman. The predator was about to claim his prey.

Little Crying Eagle kicked, scratched, and did all she could to fight off this monstrous and crazed man. She fought with all her strength. Desperation screamed in her veins, hopelessness writhed up her spine as he took his knife out of its sheath. As he held it firmly against her throat, terror released the tension. She held onto his hair. The warning glare in his eyes told her she was fighting a losing battle, a battle that held her life on the line. He removed her clothing.

He did many things to Little Crying Eagle that she found extremely repulsive (beyond words). He gruffly commanded her to do things to him. She could not repress her tears as she begged him to stop. To this, he turned a deafened ear. "Great Spirit, what need does this beast feel from this. I feel so ugly and filthy. Does he not experience the exact shame as I? Why all the hurt? I feel so humiliated. Have I done what was forbidden?"

His face came above hers once more. It held great antagonism. She could not understand why she felt guilty. Suddenly, his hands were on both sides of her head so she could not move it at all. Little Crying Eagle did not dare to blink an eye. He screamed a few hard words to her and brought his mouth to hers at full force. Little Crying Eagle could taste her own blood as it flowed down her throat. She squirmed and tried to break loose. It was fearfully difficult to breathe. His hand came to her jaws. It did not take a great deal of an effort to pry her clenched teeth apart, she gagged on his tongue as he forced it down her throat.

"Oh Great Spirit, I beg of you, please make him stop. See my tears that fall like great rain. Please hear my silent pleas and cries that call for you. Protector of my soul, where are you?!" Little Crying Eagle could not restrain from crying loudly.

He looked at her; then, his hand came up and slapped her

repeatedly until she was too apprehensive to make a sound. Once more, it was deathly quiet within the forest.

This has to be a bad dream. There is absolutely no one in sight. Mother is savouring the taste of her most cherished fire-water, and I feel like a gross, evil, and horrid beast. That is what I am. All good thought was evil and bad. Maybe that is the way it has always been after all. Is he punishing me? "Great Spirit, are you there? If you are, please give me some sign that you are. Make him stop. Please make him stop! I am begging you with every inch of my being please make him stop! I will do anything, but please make him stop! I'll make it up to you, somehow, I can't take this anymore."

The pain. It seemed as if a thousand talons were ripping her to shreds. He compelled himself deeper. The agony was greatly strenuous. She screamed with pure raw agony. Her whole body felt as if it was atop furious flames. Little Crying Eagle could not withstand the torture. "Somebody please help me! Where are you! I am calling, calling for you, I need you . . . Great Spirit!"

She screamed in anguish. He was going faster and faster. The thousand talons had completed their task. The very centre of her being was left to mere nothingness. Little Crying Eagle was sure she was entering the spirit world as the darkness enveloped her. She cried out to gain consciousness. The soldier also screamed. Their cries echoed in Little Crying Eagle's ears as she drifted into unconsciousness. It was so, so dark and cold. The fucking, bloody insolent bastard fell asleep on top of her. The morning sun beat down on her without mercy. Many drums pounded wildly within her head, attempting to drive her mad. In time they may succeed. "If only I had died, if only I had died and gone into the spirit world."

She felt degraded, loathsome, and so alone. "I wish I was a cheap piece of worthless dogmeat. Not anyone will ever understand me. I will go to my platform where I will peacefully sleep, never knowing what it would have been like. I will hold my head down in shame forever. I am not worthy of any love. I am a beast, and I do not deserve the good that the Great Mother Earth bestows upon me!"

She lay limp as tears silently washed her face. In bitter frustration, she exclaimed, "You have no reason to explain why you did not appear, do you? You claim to be the Great Spirit and yet unbearable harm has come to me. You did not arrive when I've called for your aid! I do not want you to be in any part of my life! You've dishonoured all that I've freely given and have done for you. I have tried so hard to take whatever you had in store for me, but this is just too much. You, Great Spirit, are no longer in my life!"

A sudden calm arose within her. It was not a peaceful calm. Her soul cried out in desperation for comfort and loving support. Her heart forcibly demanded to repossess the exhilaration, the self-respect, and the love she so willingly gave. The expression she wore on her face revealed no emotions. Her eyes did not see the beauty of the land she possessed, and her heart did not sing with the angels amongst the skies. In the centre of her being, it held nothing, a great void claimed to remain.

With painful movement, Little Crying Eagle rose from the ground. The soldier had left his jacket. For many moments, her eyes fixed upon it. She had huge bruises on her upper arms and they covered her thighs. She could feel the blood dry on her face. She hoped there were no noticeable cuts or bruises.

In spite of the constant throbbing that covered her body, Little Crying Eagle knew that she must continue to endure the pain. She must return home before her mother awoke. Her lateness might provoke Raven Calls and give her reason to lash out on Little Crying Eagle.

She painstakingly pulled the dress over her head. As she dusted it off, a patch of blood on her moccasin immediately caught her eye. Little Crying Eagle did not know the meaning of this. Little Crying Eagle did not care if her body screamed in pain, if her body bled, nor would she care if it ceased to live. Compared to the amount of blood she had bled with degradation, compared to how rigorously her soul had been shattered, compared to the intense pain and humiliation she had withstood the previous night, no amount of blood could be equal to it all!

Little Crying Eagle could not conceive children. He had broken her womb. There would be no little feet walking within her lodge. There would be no little faces to look up at her for protection and comfort, to give her a strong sense of pride as they grew into fruitful, strong, and wise adults. Little Crying Eagle would not be the one she had been for many summers to come.

Little Crying Eagle walked to the creek. As she slowly washed her face, there were no dark bruises visible. There was a cut across her upper lip, but she could find something false to explain it. Little Crying Eagle walked to where she had built her very first fire. Where the fire once blazed with fury there lay only cold dark coals to whisper she had once been there.

She slowly limped her way home, with the fox fur wrapped around her shoulders. She could not find any explanation for her blood-stained moccasins. Many unanswered questions were sure to arise. With her head held high, a tear-stained face, and a broken soul, Little Crying Eagle trod the path that led her home.

The camp came within sight. A pang of resentment filled her empty heart. As she entered their lodge, Raven Calls questioned where she had been all morning. "I slept within a friend's lodge. Little Laughing Wolf offered when he'd learned you had been drinking again. Blue Waters and Loud Drum were not home either, so we kept Dawn Cloud, his baby sister," replied Little Crying Eagle.

The angry tone in her voice was difficult for Raven Calls to dismiss. She took her daughter in her arms and whispered an apology.

Many apologies cannot erase the memory nor the suffering she had endured on the account of her mother's drinking. Raven Calls looked her in the eye, as she became worried over her child, "Little Crying Eagle, what is the matter? You appear as if the Great Spirit has deserted you."

Little Crying Eagle would not answer. The fear and frustration confused her heart. "Nothing is the matter, mother. Everything is fine. I feel a bit ill and tired, but no further," she answered.

She could not risk anyone gaining knowledge of the previous night. She was afraid that they'd believe she was bad, too, as the soldier had. As Raven Calls looked down at her daughter she noticed a drop of blood on Little Crying Eagle's moccasin. Her mouth flew open in exasperation as she gave her daughter a questioning look.

Little Crying Eagle could not restrain the tears that needed to flow. She ran out of the lodge like the wind, just to get away from the mother that caused her great pain, to get away from the tribe that didn't hold any pride, just to get away from the pain.

She stumbled on a rock. Her face buried in the midst of the tall grass, hidden from the world, Little Crying Eagle released her pain and heart-break in long, loud, wailful cries that echoed throughout the land. Little Crying Eagle could be heard for miles, so full of hurt, so rich of total despair, so raw of sorrows. The tribe stood still, puzzled by the cries. Raven Calls search for her daughter frantically, but she was nowhere to be found.

As Little Crying Eagle wept, a golden eagle flew twenty feet above her, circling, calling, scanning, and for a long moment his golden eyes stayed on the crying child. It seemed as if it understood and cried with his namesake. It began to fly away. Then, he returned as if forgetting something. It dove down straight for Little Crying Eagle. Within a few feet, he flew skyward. He let out a piercing cry that echoed across the great skies as he vanished into the thick clouds.

Little Crying Eagle continued her weeping and as of that moment she vowed that not one soul would know of her secret. She would never love again. All that came too close would know great pain as she had.

Little Crying Eagle had no pride, no love and understanding. If the Great Spirit could not give it to her, then who possessed such powers as he? Nobody. As of that day, Little Crying Eagle began to construct her own sheltered dwelling. There was no love given, no love taken. It did not hold comforting warmth. It was ice cold. It was not for the weak, the caring, and the loving. In order for them to enter they will have to be strong in the mind, in the heart, but, most of all, in the soul. Her world was for the strong, the sorry, and the lonely.

It was a world for actresses, with their fake smiles and painfully crying souls. For ones who stand tall as their tears stain their faces and the true cries scream from deep within their beating hearts.

Lillian Guay

I am twelve years old and a Cree Native. I was born on 21 September 1977 in The Pas, Manitoba. I am presently living in Winnipeg, attending General Wolfe School in grade seven.

I would like to dedicate this short story to my grandpa. Special thanks goes to my dad, mom, sister, and brother.

The Mysterious Death

It was 19 February 1975 as death was about to overcome someone. This person had a feeling about her death, which she had told other people about. She was not scared about her death at all.

It was 15 February 1975, and a sixteen-year-old girl was put on the Winnipeg Grey Goose Bus by her mother. The last word her mother had said to her was "goodbye." Why? Because her mother knew that she was going to die, and she told her daughter that but her daughter never believed her.

It was February, Trappers' Festival. Her mom and dad had gone to the Trappers' Festival. They came back late. The mother had driven her husband back home in a royal blue, four-door car. The mother had rolled the car while driving back to town again. She crawled out of the car and walked toward town to the police station and told the police what had happened. The police officer had asked her to go to the hospital, but she refused. The policemen drove her home.

When she got home, she told her children to go to sleep. Before they all went to bed, the mother had said "goodnight and goodbye" to her children. During that night, she slept on the couch. By the next morning, the children had found their mother lying on the couch dead. The oldest son of the family tried to wake up their mother, but he was not able to succeed. The police were called to the house, and the mother was pronounced dead. Everybody related to the mother was notified by phone that she had died during the night while she was sleeping.

Relatives and friends gathered together for four nights and five days to have a wake for the mother. The funeral was held on the last day of the wake. The mother was buried that day. The father and his children had to face the fact that the mother and wife always will remain in their memories.

This was based on a true story in The Pas, Manitoba.

Louise Bernice Halfe

From the Saddle Lake Reserve, Alberta, Louise Bernice Halfe now lives in Saskatchewan. She is married and has two rainbow children, Usine and Omeasoo. She is a social worker, and her fingers create on paper and on speaking clay sculptures. She is a self-proclaimed hag.

Journal Entries

1

The sweetgrass is aged. It whispers beneath my fingers like eagles spreading their wings for flight. I am gentle, for it is a gift like everything else.

The wisps of smoke fill my nostrils. I inhale deeply and gently, fan the tiny flame. I lift my hands and caress the ghosts of smoking spirits, cleanse my ears and my eyes, and bid my heart to open in prayer. The sweetgrass scent is the pathway to heaven. With this, my prayers can rise to the Creator, but only if I pray with integrity and in deep humility. May the grandparents bless the prayers.

2

We went to a Round Dance last night. For hours, we danced in circles to the beat of the drums. I listened to the swishing, sweeping sound of moccasined feet and modern shoes.

My mother tells she had the spirits of the dead come into our house with the same sound because she neglected to put food away. They didn't frighten her. Instead, she gave them an offering of the food, cast it into the wood stove, and burned sweetgrass.

This dance is a spiritual dance, a union of the living in the present with those living in the life hereafter — white people prefer to call them the northern lights or aurora borealis. We call them the Spirit Dancers.

My husband was the only pale face in the land of brownness.
Of course, he's used to that, after fifteen years. More often than not
I'm the only brown face in the land of paleness. It took me years to feel
comfortable with this, and when I did the pale ones became uncomfortable around me.

3

Going into the sweat lodge is like going into the heart of the universe.
The darkness envelopes you, and you enter the unknown. All the stars
you see in the galaxy present themselves in the red heat of the rocks.
You then realize how little we are on the face of the earth and the only
comfort in walking into darkness is prayer.

4

Isn't it funny how much credibility Carl Jung has with his theories on
visions and dreams? My people have been having visions and dreams
for centuries, yet they are scoffed at. We are told that we are pagans and
that our rituals don't have meaning. Strange, when even the bible is
full of visions, dreams, symbols, and rituals.

5

Prince Edward Island memories (7 April 1989)

Remembering burning sand as it whirled, lashed around my legs and
face. The wind was whipping it in absolute rage. I feel it. It is my first
encounter with flying rocks, tiny spirits making themselves known. I
stand facing the ocean, viewing the foaming, rolling, thundering
waves. The ocean is powerful. It scares me. I walk away back to the
safety and shelter of the land, but I feel the spirit of the ocean still
clasping. My body will not yield. I command, propelling my spirit,
pulling, dragging it from the magnitude of the ocean. She reminds me
her power is beyond my comprehension, and it is not to be disputed.
I wish I had my sweetgrass and an offering of tobacco to appease her,
for I wonder if I have projected some disrespect, and her fury is a
reminder she possesses the power of the universe.

Pakak*

Flying skeleton
I used to wonder where
You kept yourself

I'd hear you rattle about
Scraping your bones

I opened a door
You grinned at me through a
Hollow mouth
Pierced my heart with your
Socket eyes

Lifted your boney hands
To greet my entrance, and I
With a soundless shriek
Ran

Upon my back you jumped
Clinging to my neck you hugged
My mound of flesh

For a thousand years you were
The companion who would not leave
A burden beyond endurance
Bones heavy

You knocked your skeleton
Skull upon my head
And I felt your leaden feet
I dragged and dragged until

The day I could not carry
Your burden more
I pried you loose
Bone after bone

We stood face to face
Pakak, your skeleton frame
All exposed
And I lighter than
I could stand

I fed you the drink of healing tears
And you ran your skeleton fingers
Down your face and on to mine

I gave you a prayer cloth
And weaved a blanket of forgiveness
And you covered us both
Skeleton and flesh

I gave you the smoke of truth
You lit your Pipe to life
Lifted it to your ghostly mouth
And to mine

My Pakak companion
A telling and frightening soul
My dancing skeleton
My dancing friend

We carry our bundles
Side by side
Hands held

---

*Pakak, the Flying Skeleton, is a mystical creature who lives in the evergreen forest. She/
he is of mischievous nature and frightful to look at. But when treated with proper respect
and given the gifts of tobacco and prayer, she/he in turn will bestow blessings on the
hunter of wild game. She/he is honoured in the Ghost Dance and the Give Away Dance.
Pakak is a Plains Cree spirit.

Pakak, like any other spirit, is a paradox. She forces us to look within and
confront and resolve our skeletons, the past that burdens and hardens our lives. To
ignore her appearance is to run from our own frightful personal lives. When we view our
skeletons and give them the food of respect, they strengthen our spirit, and emotional
and spiritual healing occurs. Our desire to live in harmony with others and with our
Earthmother becomes possible.

Spirits

The aorta throbs
splattering
red the sky

Comes the
night travelling
blood
swirling skirts
lifting
swishing moccasins

Swaying formless bodies
to the tempo of the
beating rawhide drum
shuffling deer-skinned feet
fluid bodies

An infant babe
released from that
umbilical tie
splurts blood

Covers hay and furred bed
wolf-mother rejoices
echoing the ancestral
chant

Red sky, night travelling
fluid bodies and infant babe
wolf-mother's blood
wolf-mother's voice

Dancing, dancing the union of
swirling skirts
moccasin feet
to that beating common lung

Sun-dog Mate

Pregnant for so long
agonizing, dying
to birth
The opportunity
never arose

The greased war
paint shone on the
Sun's face
Sun-dogs laughing
A cheering squat
All my own

Spread my legs
Push, push
A contraction here
A contraction there
Caught bare-assed
Again

Supposed to be ready
for the challenge
The call
And I struggle to give
birth

Greasy make-up
Smeared on the sun's
Sun-dog face
Laugh, cheer me on
Sun-dog mate

Valentine Dialogue

I got bit.

By what?

A snake bite.

Where?

In my spoon.   Gone er eea merchant.

Wholee sheeit.

Love, he dold me.

I have a pain in my heart.

Fuckin liar.

Hate all of dem.
Dhink day can hang dair
balls all over the place.

Cross my legs next dime.

Mudder says day all alike.

Snake in dair mouth.
Snake in dair pants.
Guess dats a forked dtongue.

Mudder says I'll never lift it down.
Fadther says I'm nothin but a cheap dramp.

Shame, shame.

Da pain in my heart
hurts, hurts.

My brown tits
they shame me.
My brown spoon
betrays me.
My spirit weeps.

Dired of dis crucifixion.
Dew ya dink confession will help?
Dew ya dink penance will clean me?
Maybe I'll be born again.

Guild guild.
Da pain in my heart
hurts hurts.

Durty priest
jest wants da details.
Needs to get his rocks off.
Not at my expense.

Fuckin men.
Dthey dink I'm a cheap badge
to hang on dere sleeve, as if
to make me public property?

A dongue in dair moudth.
A dongue in dair pants.
No nothin 'bout the heart.
No nothin 'bout my soul.

Day lookit my mouth.
Must be a nice mouth
cuz I see the demptation
in dair eyes.

And my mouth
wants
to feel dair wet lips.
Sheeit my body betrays me.

It's mudders fault.
Never told me right from wrong.
Fadders fault.
Always says mudder a slut.
Guess I must be one too.
Guess I showed dem.

Meet nice man one day.
Maybe brown.
Maybe white.
Maybe black.
Maybe yellow.

Won't show.
My body betrays me.
Won't tell
About the snake bite.

Hurt, shame, guilt.
Awas.
Ugly, ugly, not nice
battle scar.

Grandmother

A shuffling brown bear
snorting and puffing
ambles up the stairs

In her den
covered wall to wall
herbs hang
carrot roots, yarrow,
camomile, rat-root,
and cha cha moose e gun

To the centre of the room she waddles
sits with one leg out and the other hugged close

She bends over her medicines
sniffs and tastes them
as she sorts roots into piles

Satisfied
she selects the chosen few
grinds them on a small tire grater
Small mounds of powder collect
Her large paws take a patch
of soft deer skin
In it she mixes and wraps her poultice
until hundreds of tiny bundle chains
swing from the rafters

The brown, labouring bear
Nohkom, the medicine woman
alone in her attic den
smoking slim cigarettes
wears the perfume of sage and sweetgrasses
and earth medicine ties

Nohkom, the bear hag
healer of troubled spirits
healer of ailing bodies
queen of the sorcerers

She wears a red kerchief on her head
Long blond-white braids hang below her breasts
She hums her medicine songs

She bends and her long skirt drapes
Over her aged beaded moccasins
she brushes her potions off her apron
straightens and surveys her medicine chest

A long day's work complete
the bear nohkom ambles down the stairs
sweeps her long skirt behind her
drapes her paws on the stair rails
leaves her dark den and its medicine powers
in silence

Barbara Higgins

I am a Coast Salish Native from southern British Columbia. My people are from the Sechelt Indian Reserve on the Sunshine Coast. I now live in Yellowknife, Northwest Territories.

God's Man on Earth
or
First Communion

Religion was important in our family. At least, it was on my mother's side of the family. My dad could either take it or leave it, and most of the time he chose to leave it.

My mother and her mother were very strong, devout Roman Catholics. My grandmother spent tens of thousands of dollars adorning their church at the Indian reserve at Seashell. I can recall the Stations of the Cross that she had imported from Italy, the fine lace that she purchased for the altar, and many other little extras that she bought and donated to the church to show her love for her God.

Granny was an artisan when it came to making something beautiful out of virtually nothing. She used to weave baskets and other items from cedar roots, which she adorned with intricate designs made with cherry bark and other contributions from nature. Her work was so fine and wonderful that she never lacked for customers to buy it. People from all over North America and a few other countries collected her masterpieces for museums and private collections.

I suppose because of their influence, I decided that I would study to become a good Catholic also. When I was nine years old, I wrote to the priest at Seashell and asked him to send me correspondence lessons. This he did immediately, and thus it was that I began to study the Roman Catholic dogma very conscientiously. I don't believe he ever sent me an actual Bible that I could read for myself, but there were a lot of Bible stories that must have originated with the Bible. The lessons were always the regurgitated words of some high-ranking Catholic person who was supposed to have been inspired to interpret the actual Bible. I guess they didn't believe that we ordinary people were capable of reading the original for ourselves, even though the Good Book plainly states that its contents are not to be given to anyone's single interpretation.

Because we lived in an obscure little fishing village in the very centre of Nowhere, there was not a church of any denomination for us to attend. I know that my mom found this very difficult, having been raised in a Roman Catholic boarding school. I often saw her sitting on her bed, praying to some romantic mystic being that I could not communicate with because I didn't know how. She never made the sign of the cross or prayed in front of my dad, because he almost always sneered and may as well have said, "Bah! Humbug!" just like Charles Dickens's old Scrooge.

Of course, none of my brothers and sisters were vaguely interested in religion because of dad's attitude. I was the only weird one in the whole flock who had to see for herself what it was all about. When I think about it I guess I have always had to find out about things for myself. I am not saying that I could not learn from someone else's mistakes, because I can and I do all the time. It's just that sometimes I am certain that no one but me can feel or sense whatever it is I am looking for, so at these times I do whatever I have to do to get that first-hand experience, and then I just seem to know what I needed to learn.

Most of my friends thought that I was out of my tree when they learned what I was doing. They said that I was wasting my time and other such words of discouragement that only made me the more determined to learn all I could about the Roman Catholic church. I had a deep-seated need to get to know my Creator, and because of this need I studied in a dedicated manner and progressed very rapidly. I was like a person possessed. I couldn't learn enough about this Father-God, Son, and Holy Ghost, who were supposed to love everyone in the entire world if they would only embrace the Roman Catholic faith. I thought that was wonderful, and I told my friends and my teacher all about it. The school I attended was a one-room school with grades from one to eight. There were about forty students. I must have been a gutsy little brat, because I can remember standing up in school and preaching to the entire school about religion and their need to know God. The teacher didn't object to my preaching. She allowed me to speak my piece, and I did so on more than one occasion.

Even though my best friends would not listen to what I said,

I did not give up on them. A couple of them said that I was no longer any fun, because all I thought about was religion and God. They would try to remind me of all the fun we used to have together. They reminded me that I was the leader and that there wasn't much fun anymore since I got religious.

As I walked home from school, I thought about what the kids were talking about. I had to admit that it was true that I had always been the undisputed leader of my peers. Somehow, without anyone really knowing how it happened, everyone looked to me for quick decisions and A-1 alibis whenever we needed them. I was just good at these things. I had a natural ability to say exactly what most parents wanted to hear.

My mom once said that I could lie faster than a horse could trot, and I suppose, at that time, it was true. Why, I can remember standing in front of a mirror practising how to lie without allowing my facial muscles or looks to give me away. This was really important practice for me, because I always knew when my brother was lying by the tick that would appear in his left cheek. He could look you right square in the eye, but he couldn't keep his cheek muscle from giving him away. My older sister couldn't look you in the eye when she tried to lie. Like I have already stated, if it was possible to learn from someone else's mistakes, I was all for it. So I would stand in front of a mirror and practise telling lies without letting my face or body language give me away.

My mind slowly wandered back into the past, and I began to recall some of the escapades I had been involved in. I recalled that I had been late starting school because of World War II. There had been a lack of teachers, and our community, because it was so small, had to go without an instructor for a couple of years. I don't recall that this was any hardship for me because I was always an avid reader. My dad was a bookworm and taught me to read when I was very young. I consumed everything I could get my hands on, including comic strips, which I would read at my grandfather's house. I would then go home and relate everything I had read to my mother, who did not believe in reading anything as frivolous as a comic book. This didn't deter me in the least. I continued to reveal everything I read to her, acting out many of the parts in my funny little way. And I'm certain that after awhile she looked forward to having me come in and place my fat little bottom on the floor, the table, or the cupboard where she was working and tell her all about my latest reading adventure. She always laughed at the stories I told her about a dog named Napoleon. He was almost human, and I used to love to become Napoleon so that she could see what I was talking about. Even in those days, long ago, when I was so very young, I realized that my mother took life too seriously and I couldn't see where she had any enjoyment at all. I became so good at reciting and miming Napoleon episodes that my aunt nicknamed me Napoleon. The name stuck for quite a few years.

When my aunt joined the air force and she was stationed in Moose Jaw, and other far-off places, I used to write her little notes that I never signed. I just clipped out the long row of pictures at the bottom of the comic strips that were of Napleon in many different poses. She said that she always knew who the notes were from.

I began to think back to when I was eight years old, and the first time and only time I told my mother to "Shut up!" We lived near the beach on the left-hand side of Silver Bay. Grandpa, whom I always called Henry, and grandma lived on the same side of the bay, next door to us. Next door, in this case, was about a half mile away. It was low tide and I was down on the beach engaging in my favourite sport. I was trying to outsmart the eels, bullheads, and sticker bullheads that were plentiful on our beach. I had a large tin half-filled with sea water in which to keep them. I had a spear that I had made from a piece of kindling wood, with one of mom's best darning needles for a spear tip. I had also rigged up one of my hair nets for a drag seine, and it was with this net that I was practising when mom called. This was serious business, and it called for total concentration.

Mom was standing on a clothes-line platform that stood about seven feet above ground. She was busy hanging out the morning wash when one of my tattle-tale little brothers went up to where she was and told her that I had been rooting around in her closet and her sewing basket. I couldn't understand what the big deal was. It was low tide, and if I wanted to catch enough fish for my cat's supper I had to fish while the tide was just right. Couldn't they understand anything?

She called me again. I pretended I didn't hear her. Three more times she called, and I finally realized that it wasn't going to do me any good to ignore her. She was too persistent. I waded back to shore and looked up to where she was standing, my hands on my fat little hips to show my feeling of exasperation. When she saw that she finally had my full attention she said, "Come here this minute! I want to speak to you about snooping around among my personal things. How many times have I asked you not to poke your nose into other people's property?"

None of this cut any ice with me. How in the world did she expect me to learn anything if there were always so many rules to get in my way? How could she expect me to catch my quota of bullheads and eels if she didn't let me use a couple of darning needles and the · odd hair net now and then? Grown-ups can be so exasperating! They expect you to listen to them and learn all kinds of things, and when you finally do learn something that is fun they say you can't do it anymore. Well! I had had enough of this. The tide was low, and I had already made my spear and drag seine, so I didn't see what she was making such a fuss about. I looked straight up to where I thought her eyes must be, from a distance, and I said, "Mom, I have already made my spear and drag seine. It's too late to say I can't have a dumb old darning needle. I already hammered it into my spear shaft and the hair net has big holes on the side where I tied my string. They're no good to you anymore so what is all the hollering about?"

As I spoke, my head was wagging back and forth and my mouth was pulled to the left in a show of total exasperation with this mother of mine, who wouldn't listen to common sense. It all seemed perfectly clear to me. Even though my mom was standing up in the air about a hundred and ten feet away from me, I could see that her face was as red as a newly steamed lobster. "Now what's wrong with her?" I thought. "She is always bothering me when I'm having fun. Why can't she bug one of the other kids for a change?"

Mom dropped the shirt she was going to hang on the line back into the clothes-basket. She gripped the guard-rail with both hands and peered down at me. Taking a deep breath, she again spoke to me, and her voice was beginning to take on a decidedly unfriendly tone, "Carman! If you know what is good for you, you will get your fat little bottom up here this instant! Do you hear Me? You come up here this instant!"

As she spoke, her right hand was emphasizing each word with a short, choppy stabbing motion that indicated the ground directly in front of her. I began to feel a mite nervous, but I wasn't about to allow her to scare me with a few tricks of her vocal chords. Totally ignoring everything she said, I answered, "Oh why don't you shut up, mom? Can't you see I'm busy? You're always telling me to look after my dog and my cat. Well, that's what I'm trying to do, if you would just stop hollering like some coyote up in the hills! I'm fishing for my cat's supper. I already got ten bullheads. I just need more time."

With those flippant words, I turned my back on mom and began setting my drag seine again. Some yet-undeveloped instinct told me that I had better check out what mom was up to. I turned around, and there she was coming down the steps of the clothes-line balcony. All at once I didn't feel so sure of myself, and I called out to her, "Aw, mom, can't you even take a little joke? I was going to come up as soon as I caught a few more fish."

She didn't so much as acknowledge me. She kept coming down the path beside the house, and she was moving pretty fast for an old woman of thirty years. For the first time, I began to feel more than a little uncertain about my control of the situation.

Throwing down my precious drag seine like it had suddenly become red hot, I raced along the beach toward Henry's place as fast as my chubby legs would carry me. If only I could reach him, I felt I would be safe. He wouldn't allow anyone to lay a finger on me, and I had frightening hunch that my mom was going to lay more than a finger on me when she caught up with me. Perhaps I would have made it if I didn't stop to see where she was so many times. Each time I stopped to check she had gained on me by an unbelievable distance. I couldn't believe that old people could move so fast. I took off again, but my nervous energy worked against me, and I think I tripped over every piece of slippery green seaweed there was on the beach that day. My hands and knees were skinned and bleeding from falling on rocks and barnacles, but the sight of blood frightened me far less than the prospect of facing my irate mother behind me. Needless to say, she caught me before I reached Henry. I was only about fifty yards from sanctuary when she collared me.

She held me by my shoulders, and she just looked at me for about two minutes before she finally spoke. Her hair was in her face, her chest was heaving from the unexpected exertion, and her breath was coming in long drawn-out gasps. I think she was fighting back the urge to cry. I didn't let that bother me. I started in hollering and crying like she was half-killing me. She shook me a few times to try to quieten me down, but that only served to make me louder than ever. In no time flat, I had everyone who was working in the old saltry peering down to see what was hurting me. Henry, my dad, and all of the deck-hands came loping along the beach to help mom save me from whatever was hurting me.

I continued to scream as though I was in deep pain. When everyone arrived and asked mom what was wrong, she put her hand over my mouth and proceeded to tell them what had just transpired. She didn't leave out a solitary thing. Henry smiled his usual tolerant smile and told mom that I probably didn't mean one word of what I had said. I nodded my head vigorously, indicating that Henry was right. My dad was stone deaf, but he could read lips like he was reading a newspaper. He removed mom's hand from my mouth and asked what I had to say for myself. I hung my head in contrition, although I knew that I could have gotten away with my behaviour just by telling a few lies.

Even though I was only seven years old, I had an octogenarian's understanding of adults. I knew I could make them believe anything I put my mind to, but, thank goodness, deep down in my soul I wasn't really a bad girl. I didn't want my mom and dad to fight over me, and I didn't want Henry to get in trouble over me either. Always being a little ham, I fell on my knees and grasped my mom and dad around the legs and asked them if they could ever forgive me for being so mouthy. If they thought they had seen tears before that day, they were in for a real surprise. I let go with buckets of tears. I moaned and writhed and my entire body was wracked with sobs. And just as I knew he would, Henry said, "Can't you see that Bubs is sorry for what she said? Don't let her cry anymore or she will be sick. She didn't mean it. You know how full of life she is? She just talks before she thinks sometimes."

I slowed down on my wimpering to see what my parents were going to do. Maybe good ol' Henry had again saved my backside from a good tanning. I sneaked a furtive look at mom's face, and I could tell that she wasn't buying any of this. Daddy didn't look any friendlier either. Dad reached over and again took mom's hand from my noisy mouth. Mom just stood back and observed. Daddy made me stand up straight and look him directly in the eye, as he asked me why I had told mom to shut up.

The moment of truth had come, and I knew there was no way around it. My dad was an old guy of twenty-six years, and he was very wise for his advanced age and I knew it. Looking directly at him, so that he would be able to read my lips well, I began to explain my side of the story.

"You old guys don't remember how hard it is to be a little kid. I was only doing what you guys told me I had to do. I was fishing for bullheads, eels, and sticker bullheads for my cat's supper. You are always telling me to make sure I feed my pets. So that's what I was doin'. I only borrowed one of mom's needles and one of her hair nets. I was going to go up and see what mom wanted after I made one more sweep with my drag seine. There were lots of big bullheads swimming around, and I wanted to catch them before they went away. Anyway, I knew that little brat had went up and told mom that I had taken the needle and hair net. He's always tattling and trying to get me in trouble. You know how hard I try to stay out of trouble? Gene is always telling lies just so you guys will get mad at me; you know he never liked me!"

Instinctively knowing that my explanation was going to be found wanting, I again began to howl in a desolate fashion. Henry took out his big blue polka-dotted handerchief and wiped my eyes and nose. I clung to Henry and thanked him for loving me, even though I sometimes acted like a brat. He hugged me right back and said that he wished that all of his grandchildren were as full of life as I was.

Feeling that everything was beginning to work to my advantage, I sneaked a peek at mom and dad to see what their reaction would be to that statement. I thought they should be bursting their buttons with pride at having a special kid like me for a daughter. I began to wonder if they were both deaf. How could they not take their elder's word for it, that I was a special grandchild? I could tell by the look on their faces that this wasn't going to cut any ice with them. Then I made up my mind to be quiet and take a look-and-see-what-is-going-to-happen attitude.

After a couple of moments, I stopped crying, and my dad said, "Carman, what are we going to do with you? You know that it is wrong to sass your mother or to talk back to any adult. Don't you?"

I nodded my head in agreement, and dad continued, "Your brothers and sisters are not always telling on you. I doubt that they tell us even half of the mischief you get into."

Henry and the deck-hands all laughed.

"I can't allow you to grow up with no discipline. You have been a naughty little girl this morning, and I am going to have to tan your backside for you."

Holding me to his huge chest for a moment, he continued on, "I want you to know that this is going to hurt your mother and me more than it hurts you."

Having said his piece, he placed me over his knee and proceeded to give me a sound spanking.

What I will never know is why he said it would hurt them more than me. I can tell you that I didn't want to have to sit down on my scorching hot little bottom for at least two or three hours. As you may have begun to suspect, that wasn't the only time I helped to contribute to the grey hairs my mom was to possess later.

I remember one hot summer's day, when we had a whole bunch of friends over swimming at our beach. We were having a great time. It was wonderful to be young and full of life. As usual, mom was busy washing clothes while we swam. She never left us unattended for any great length of time, even though there were some older children among us. My older sister had two or three friends over, and they were all thirteen or fourteen years old, which seemed ancient to me at the time.

Anyhow, to get on with the story, I felt that we needed a little excitement to make the day "special." I was very big on special days at that time in my life, so I called a conference with all the kids, young and old, who were present. I asked them if they wanted to take part in a little excitement. Of course they all said, "Yes! What do we have to do?"

Getting everyone behind the huge boulder that was on the beach, out of mom's sight in case she came and checked up on us, I suggested that we have a bit of fun with mom. Some of the older kids were a little hesitant, but I quickly talked them out of that, explaining to them that mom liked to have a good laugh every now and then.

Our house, at this time, was up on a high plateau with a large rock bank overlooking the rocky beach on which we were all playing. Mom would come out to the rock every few minutes to see how we were getting along. There were a couple of other huge rock piles between her vantage point and the ocean. That is where we decided to have our fun. I gathered everyone around the place mom couldn't observe and instructed everyone to start screaming and hollering on my cue. The plan was to get my second youngest brother to pretend that a huge octopus had hold of him. It was easy enough to do, because there were lots of octopuses around there. My dad and us kids had caught lots of them right around that area. Of course, they were only fifteen or twenty pounders, not nearly big enough to carry away a little boy.

Having gotten everyone into position, I gave the sign and everyone began to yell at the same time. It was utter chaos! There must have been fourteen kids there, all yelling a different version of, "Help! An octopus has a hold of Steve."

Steve was screaming blue murder, and he must have had his whole heart into it, because he sounded absolutely terrified! A couple of us little darlings had a long stick which we were beating at the water with, hoping mom would think we were trying to beat off the octopus. Mom came tearing along the short path to her rocky vantage point, stopped an instant to hear what everyone was saying, and then she came running down the beach. She didn't even take the path. She made her own road right through the tame blackberry patch that grew thick below the rock cliff. She looked like a grizzly bear coming to defend her cub from some unknown danger. By the time she was two-thirds of the way down the embankment, the older girls began to run away. I guess they had more sense. They knew that mom was going to be hopping mad when she found out it was just a prank.

The rest of us kept right on yelling and beating at the water, and Steve kept on yelling for help. Well, mom must have got there in one minute flat. When she came around the last rock pile and saw that Steve wasn't in any danger, there was a look of relief on her face, and she came to a complete stop about five feet away from me. Everyone who was stupid enough to stay there was jumping up and down in excitement. Three or four of us little rascals were bent over and holding our stomachs because we were laughing so hard. I looked at the kids, and we all hollered through our laughter, "We fooled you! We fooled you! There's nothing wrong with Steve. We just wanted to see how fast you could make it down to the beach! You shudda saw the look on your face, mom! We really fooled you that time!"

Suddenly, we realized that she wasn't taking this joke very well, and the laughter was frozen in our young throats as we looked at her. She didn't laugh or say a word. She looked so very stern and serious, every kid on the beach headed for cover. They needn't have worried, because just as a compass points automatically toward true north, so did mom single me out. She began to walk toward me with a look in her eyes I had never witnessed before. It frightened the hell out of me, and I too retreated to a place of safety.

Fortunately, I was near the ocean's edge, and I headed for deep water as fast as I could move. I swam out about forty feet, just to be on the safe side, before I asked her what was wrong. I couldn't, for the life of me, see what she was getting all hot and bothered about. After all, it was just a joke. We were just having a little harmless fun. Sometimes, grown-ups are so hard to understand.

Even from forty feet I could feel the chill of her frosty stare. I found it difficult to paddle my arms and legs to stay afloat. I felt as though she had pierced me with an ice-cold stare that bored a hole right through my head and pinned me to the surface of the salt water on which I was trying to float. When she spoke, her voice was deadly calm and controlled, "You ask me what's wrong? Well, let me tell you what's wrong. What is wrong is that I have this totally thoughtless and wilful child that never gives a thought to the stress and pain she puts people through."

As I paddled around, I was immensely relieved to hear her talking like this. For a moment, I thought she was talking about me, but nobody could say those things about me. My grandpa Henry said I was the best little girl in the world, and I knew he wouldn't lie about a thing like that. I tuned in again on what mom was saying about some kid, "She organizes her friends and brothers to act like little hellions. As if that is not enough, she could have caused serious injury to her own mother. When I came over that rock bluff, I was thinking only of saving Steve from the giant octopus you kids were yelling about. I could have fallen and broke my legs or even my neck. What would happen to you kids then? Your father is hundreds of miles away up north, and it would take days for him to get back home. Who would have looked after the baby and all the chores I do every day? Who would have washed your clothes and cooked your meals?"

For the first time, I began to understand what she was talking about. I noticed that her hands, face, and legs were covered with deeply gouged blackberry vine scrapes. There was slowly seeping blood oozing from a dozen places on her body, and I recalled the way she ploughed straight through the centre of that humungous patch of blackberry vines. It was a large patch, probably ten feet high where she came charging through. The stocks of some of the plants were a couple of inches in diameter, and they had sturdy thorns on them at least a quarter of an inch long. They must have felt like knives when they carved through her flesh. Even though her voice was level and controlled, there were streams of tears running down her face. She ignored both the tears and the blood as she continued speaking, "Why can't you be like other children? Why must you continually be finding ways to get your brothers and sisters and yourself into trouble? If someone would offer me two cents for you today, I would take it and feel like they had overpaid me. Now, you come in here right now, because I am going to give you a spanking you will never forget!"

Having finished speaking to me, she began to look through the various pieces of branches and wood that the tide had deposited at the high-tide mark on the beach. I knew she was looking for a good sturdy stick to spank me with, and I hoped fervently that they would all look sturdy but snap easily when applied to my backside.

There wasn't a kid in sight anywhere. They had all retreated to safer ground without the slightest thought for me, all alone, out in the water. I wondered how mom could possibly be so sure that this idea had been mine. I was worried about getting a spanking, but I felt like I deserved it because of all the blood I saw running from mom's wounds. When I had planned this little escapade, I hadn't intended for mom to get hurt, and I felt that I was probably the worst little girl in the world. I swam ashore and submitted quietly to the disciplining hand of my mother. And true to her word, she did give me a whipping that I will never forget. Not so much because it was painful but because that was the first time I viewed one of my pranks from her point of view. I remember that I was responsible for my mom receiving some very serious injuries that day. I remember how bravely she came to the aid of her child. I think she would have walked through fire with her bare feet if she had been called on to do so for her child's sake. She didn't give a single thought to her personal safety. She only knew her child was in trouble and she was charging right down to rescue him from the humungous octopus we were screaming about. I wonder how many people would attack an octopus single-handed?

I think that was the first time I saw my mother as a real person. I was a wee bit in awe of her unselfish thought for self. Something away inside of me was repentant for the prank I had instigated. It would not allow me to push it away like I usually did. My heart could barely keep beating because of the remorse it felt. I could feel a hand squeezing it, and my breath was no longer regular. I felt like I would die of suffocation in a world that was full of air. I believe that it was this experience that made me decide that I should become a good Roman Catholic. I guess I thought that this mysterious "God person" would turn me into a good girl. After all, hadn't I heard granny say that God always answered prayers? Finally, after studying for more than a year, mom received a letter from the Father at Seashell, stating that I was ready to take my first communion during the Easter holidays.

We lived about fifty miles from Seashell, which was accessible only by boat. It was an annual event for my mother to pack up all us kids and go to the Seashell Indian Reserve for two weeks holiday. That was the only time during the year that she went to confession and received communion, which was very important to her.

I was thrilled beyond words to learn that I was now able to receive first communion. Actually, I didn't really understand what that meant, but if all good Catholics did it then I wanted to do it too. I could hardly wait for the Easter holidays to arrive — I wanted to be just like my mother and grandmother and become a devout Roman Catholic.

Gradually, the days passed and I found myself dressed for the service I had striven toward for more than a year. I was dressed in a white lace dress with a short white veil on my head. Granny wrapped her strong old arms around me and told me that I looked just like a little angel in my new outfit. I nodded my head sagely, because I too had thought that very same thing. Inwardly, in my heart, I thought I must be on the right track to becoming a "good Christian girl." Then, I wouldn't have to worry about being bad ever again. Somehow, I equated becoming a Roman Catholic with never being a bad person.

There were five pews of children ready to take their first communion with me. They seemed to know what all the rituals were about. I certainly didn't have any idea about such things, as this was only the second time I had been in an actual church. I sat quietly and prayed that God would understand that I couldn't participate in the ritual because I did not have the vaguest idea about such things.

I had noticed that the kids in the pews in front of me were going, one by one, through a doorway beside the altar. I wondered why they were doing that. Eventually, it was my turn to walk through that doorway. I wasn't a bit afraid — I believe that I thought I was fulfilling my life's destiny that day.

The doorway lead into a large, dingy room that smelled faintly of mildew. There was a tall, handsome priest standing there in his long black dress. He was not the priest that I had been writing to; he was someone new to the district and new to me. He was about thirty-five years old, with a husky build and curly black hair. He smiled at me with his large blue eyes, and I returned his smile. He seemed like a really nice person, and I felt a sense of relief. Even though I was fully committed to doing this thing, I did have a few reservations and fears.

He introduced himself as Father Camsell and he asked me for my name, which I told him with no hesitation. He then turned around on his right heel and entered a tiny room that resembled a clothes closet with a dark curtain on the doorway.

How very strange! I stood there, watching the curtain behind which he had disappeared. I wondered what he could be doing behind there. I couldn't understand why anyone would spend so much time in their clothes closet. I didn't hear any water running, so I guessed it couldn't be a toilet of any kind. I was becoming impatient, and I shifted my weight from one foot to the other as I kept my eyes glued to the doorway. Nothing happened.

After about three or four minutes, he pulled aside the curtain and asked me what was taking me so long. He was sitting on a little built-in bench, holding a cross with Jesus on it on his lap. I was completely dumbfounded. I didn't have the vaguest idea of what he was talking about. I shrugged my shoulders indicating that I did not understand. I was humiliated because I did not understand what was happening or what was supposed to be happening. When he noted that I did not know what to do, he told me that I was supposed to enter the other cubicle, kneel down, and face him.

Grateful for the chance to move out of his line of vision, I immediately did as directed. It was nice and dark in the little room, although the air smelled very stale to my nostrils. I could hear him mumbling or praying and after a moment he slid open the little door that separated us and nailed me to the little bench I was kneeling on with his icy blue eyes. He knelt there and watched me intently. He seemed to expect me to do something. I gazed right back at him, my eyes meeting his square on. Finally, when he became aware that I wasn't going to do anything, he told me that I was supposed to confess my sins to him. I knelt there mutely for a number of moments. I was thinking, "What sins? I don't have any sins. I'm just a kid, and kids don't have sins!"

With my eyes squeezed tightly shut, I attempted to make some sense of this development. Closing my eyes only made me more aware of this great hulk of a man who was sitting opposite me. I could see him even with my eyes squeezed tightly shut.

His breath was terrible. I found it revolting. It made me feel faintly nauseous. It smelled like sour onions and garlic, and I found the odour repelling. I wondered how long I was going to have to kneel there and look at him. I hoped that it wouldn't be too long, because I was going to try to hold my breath until this ordeal was over. After a couple of minutes he stood up and said that he was going to speak to my mother.

I remained where I was, not understanding what was happening. I was beginning to think that First Communion wasn't such a wonderful thing after all, if you had to endure this type of torture. My knees were tired of kneeling on the hard little bench, my stomach was still upset from the Father's rancid breath, and I wished I could get out of there just as quickly as possible.

When he returned, he said that my mother and he had decided that he should ask me questions about my sins. He inquired whether or not I would answer his questions. I nodded my head vigorously, hoping to end this ordeal as quickly as possible.

The conversation went something like this:

Father: "Do you know that here on earth I take the place of God? If you lie to me, it is the same as lying to God!" (I wondered why I hadn't read about any of this stuff in the books they had sent me to study. It must be right or mom wouldn't believe in it.)

Me: "Yes, Father" (nodding my head in agreement).

Father: "When I ask you a question, you are to think about it and then answer honestly. Can you do that?"

Me: "Yes, Father" (humble tone of voice).

Father: "Do you steal?"

Me: "Yes, Father."

Father: "What do you steal?"

Me: "Cookies and candies."

Father: "Do you tell lies?"

Me: "Yes, Father."

Father: "What do you lie about?"

Me (innocently): "Why about the cookies and candies of course. I always say that I didn't take them."

On and on went the questions. I answered every one, until he asked me a question that I had no inkling of what it meant.

Father: "Do you let little boys stick it into you?"

Me: "I'm sorry Father, but I don't know what that means. Would you explain?"

Up until this time, he had been sitting back on his bench. Now, he sat forward and impaled me with his eyes that seemed to be made of cold, blue ice. His eyebrows seemed to be drawn together like jet-black awnings over his eyes. His breath seemed to have fermented even more since we entered this cubicle of torture. I wondered why the Mother and the nuns didn't see that he didn't eat onions and garlic when he was going to be talking to people in these small boxes. I felt totally miserable. There was no way I could hold my breath and answer his questions.

As I watched him, it seemed that his neck was receding into his shoulders, giving him the look of a bird of prey. His stance reminded me of a buzzard, and he smelled as badly as I thought a buzzard would smell. Perhaps it was just my imagination.

Father: "I have told you that when you speak to me it is the same as talking to God. I take his place here on earth. If you lie to me, your soul will burn in hell for a million years."

As he spoke, his eyes never wavered from mine and his voice had taken on a steely quality that made me believe that he already knew that I was guilty of whatever he was talking about. I didn't utter a word. For once in my life, I was so frightened that I had no words to answer and I nodded my head vigorously to signify that I understand him fully.

By now, my hands were becoming sore from clutching them together so tightly. My knees were aching and my stomach was upset to the point where I would not have been surprised if I had been physically ill and vomited on the spot. But, still, I didn't know what to say to this emissary of God, who believed he had caught me in the act of some heinous crime too awful for me even to begin to visualize.

Father: "Do you let little boys stick it into you" (with much more emphasis)?

I closed my eyes and rested my head on the shelf in front of me. I rolled my head back and forth in complete desolation and agitation. I had been so proud to be taking my First Communion, and, now, here I was on the point of getting to my feet and running away. But, I couldn't. Mom and granny must do this same exercise. Mom looks forward to going to confession, so this must be all right.

I sent a torrent of prayers to heaven, asking God to tell me what "letting little boys stick it into you" meant. Granny said God always answers your prayers. I waited. I prayed again. I waited, but God did not answer me. I guess he was too busy to answer me. He probably had a lot of truly important prayers to answer and didn't have time for my insignificant little problems.

"Oh God! This is not an insignificant little problem. It is a huge problem. Please help me, because I don't know what your man here on earth wants me to say. Help me! Hear me! Tell me what it means, please! Granny and mom say that you answer all prayers. I remember the story about you answering prayer. I think it came from Jeremiah 33:30, and it said something like, 'Call unto me and I shall help thee.' Did you mean that promise for all of the people who love you or did you just mean it for the people you love? I had been waiting for a few minutes now, and you haven't even let me know whether you are hearing me or not. I'm afraid that if you don't help me, your man is going to be very angry at me and he might send me straight to hell. Please, God, help me!"

Of course, I got no answer, and I was confused. Didn't my granny and mom say that God would never let me down? I opened my eyes and looked at Father. He was bending forward, and the look on his face said that he was sure I had committed this sin. I began to reason within myself. If I did do this sin, then I should answer "yes," but if I didn't do it, then I should answer "no." But what in the world is IT? If I did this thing and I say "no," then I will burn in hell. Maybe I should say "yes," just in case I did it. God will probably forgive me for saying I did something bad, even if I didn't do it. Summoning all the inner strength I had, I looked the Father in the eye and answered in a small voice, "Yes, Father."

He must have been sitting there holding his breath for some time, because when he let it go it make a loud sound in the small room. He may as well have said, "Aha! I knew it all the time. I knew you were guilty by the way you acted so nervous and because it took you so long to answer."

I still didn't know if I was guilty or not, but I felt an immense sense of relief that this session was nearly over.

My penance was to return to the pew and say ten Our Fathers and ten Hail Marys. This was the first time in my young life that I had personally met God's man on earth, and I was so contrite and afraid that I said fifty of each. My knees were awfully sore after the extended kneeling, but I felt pretty good about myself. After all, was I not just like my mother and granny? Wasn't I learning to become an A-1 Roman Catholic? And, as everyone knows, if you aren't a Roman Catholic then you just aren't a true Christian.

About a week later, I went over to my cousin's to play. Eddy was my best friend, and we had lots of fun together. We could talk about anything, and we often compared notes on school, teachers, brothers and sisters, parents, and just about anything you can think of. He was swinging back and forth on what he called his Tarzan swing. It was a length of hefty rope with one end tied high on a sturdy branch of a gigantic cedar tree. The other end had a number of knots tied in it to make one large ball that he would place between his legs and swing back and forth on, emitting his Tarzan call every few minutes. The knot on which he was riding was about four feet above the ground.

I was leaning against the same cedar tree and we were discussing our recent trip to Seashell. Eddy had taken First Communion over the Easter holidays also, so we had a lot of notes to compare. This is roughly the way the conversation went:

Eddy: "You went to confession too, huh?"

Me: "Mhm-m-m."

Eddy: "Did you tell him your sins, or did he ask questions?"

Me: "Mom told him to ask me questions."

Eddy: "Did you like him?"

Me: "Sure. He's God's man on earth, so of course I like him."

Eddy: "I don't believe that."

Me: "He told me he was. Why would he say it if it wasn't true?'

Eddy: "I dunno. But I don't think God has a man on earth anywhere."

Me: "Well, what do you think, then? Why do we have to go and tell him our sins if he isn't God's man? Why do our parents go to Fathers, if they aren't good? I don't think you know what you're talking about this time." (As I made these statements, I was shaking my head at Eddy in a wise manner.)

Eddy: "Did he ask you if you lied?" (He never took his eyes off of me for a moment. He reminded me of Father Camsell.)

Me: "Yep."

Eddy: "What did you say?"

Me: "I told him yes."

Eddy: "You didn't? Did he ask you if you stole things?"

Me: "Mhm-m" (feeling smugly important).

Eddy: "Did he ask if you disobeyed your parents?" (All this time, he has not taken his eyes off of my face.)

Me: "Yep. I told him that once in a while I forget to listen to them."

Eddy: "Once in a while? You mean that you listen to them once in a while. Do you think he believed you?"

Me: "Why shouldn't he? I told him the truth."

Eddy ran down the complete list of sins. He left nothing out, and, just like the Father, he kept the sin I didn't understand for last. I guess that even little boys are always practising to become obnoxious grown men. He swung back and forth a few times, and then he again tried to rivet me to the spot with his beady brown eyes. I was beginning to wonder what his problem was.

Eddy: "Did he ask you if you let little boys stick it into you?" (His voice sounded rather detached and hardly interested in the topic, but he didn't take his eyes from my face even once. He didn't even blink.)

Me: "Yep." (And, I was still feeling self-satisfied.)

Eddy is now leaning down as far as he can, in order to better gauge my reply. I was feeling quite important to see that he was taking such an interest in my first communion.

Eddy: "What did you say? Did you really answer that old fart?"

Me: "You shouldn't talk about him like that. God won't like it and neither would your mom and dad. I told him yes."

Eddy: "What!? You didn't! You're just saying that to get a rise out of me!"

Me: "Why should I? Sure, I told him yes, and he forgave me."

Eddy: "I'll betcha don't even know what that means? If you did know, I know you wouldn't do that. How could you be so dumb?"

Eddy is now laughing out loudly. He looks at me again, and he breaks out into more howls of laughter. He hangs on with one hand and wipes at his eyes running with tears. He is no longer just swinging back and forth. The swing seems to be going up and down as well. If I wasn't so worried about what he was laughing at, his crazy antics would have me in hysterics also. He laughed so hard that he lost the strength in his arms and he could no longer hang on to his swing, and he fell to the ground and began to roll around, kicking his legs and arms like some zany cartoon character.

Me: "What's so funny? I don't see what's so funny! Why are you laughing at me? I don't like anybody to laugh at me. I thought you were my friend!"

My voice had taken on an injured note that even a deaf person could not have missed. That didn't phase Eddy in the least. He continued to hoot and holler and roll around on the ground. Every time he looked at me, he would break out into a fresh burst of hysterical laughter.

I was growing tired of his failure to communicate with me, so I picked up a long, springy cedar bough. I stripped all of the leaves off of it, until I had nothing left but a long whip-like implement. I swished it through the air a couple of times, and I heard it whistle in a way that suggested it would sting nicely if I smacked him with it.

Eddy had short pants on, so I walked up to him and began lightly flicking my whip at his bare legs. He let out a yelp at the first contact. He stopped rolling around in an agitated way and began backing away from me. I advanced after him, flicking the whip but not hitting him with it. Flick. Flick. It sang through the air in a most intimidating manner.

Eddy: "You wouldn't hit me with that! . . . Would you?"

He was beginning to feel just a bit wary of me. He wasn't sure whether I would let him have it or not, and I put the sternest look I could muster onto my face.

Me: "What does that mean? Why did you laugh at me?"

Eddy: "Why did you answer yes if you didn't know what it meant?"

By now, I am totally exasperated with Eddy for not letting me in on the joke and with myself for being so ignorant. I told him that I didn't know what it meant, but he kept after me to answer. There was no one there to ask. The Father wouldn't tell me. I prayed and asked God to tell me, and He wouldn't talk to me either. What was I supposed to do? He said that if I lied to him I would go straight to hell. I was scared. I didn't want to go to hell. He kept on looking at me with eyes that said I had done IT, so I though that he must know. After all, he is God's man on earth. I had rambled all of this off with such a rush that I was nearly out of breath.

Eddy was no longer laughing or clowning around. He had his legs drawn up under his chin, and he is hugging them with his arms — not because he is afraid of me and my switch but because for once in his know-it-all life he did not know or want to know how to answer my questions. He hung his head and clamped his mouth shut. I continued to harangue him with questions, which he refused to answer.

Getting nowhere, I dropped the stick and began to walk up the pathway toward home. I didn't look back. I just walked away with my head hanging down around my knees to display my feeling of rejection and dejection. I hadn't gone twenty yards when Eddy called out and asked if I was mad at him. I did not answer. I continued my way up the path.

Meanwhile, Eddy is beginning to get the idea that he has let his chum down and he doesn't want her to go home mad. After all, they have been best pals since they were just toddlers.

"Carmen, don't go home. Yer mad at me aren't cha? I don't know everything, you know? I'm just a little kid like you. I only know what Bobby told me about boys sticking it into little girls. I'm not even sure that it's true. Sometimes he tells whoppers, and I can't be sure that he's telling me what's right. He's a big guy, and sometimes he likes to embarrass me to prove how smart and tough he is. You know how he is?"

By this time, he has caught up with me and is entreating me to stop and talk about it.

My mind is really confused now. What in the world did he mean by boys sticking it into little girls? Sticking what in where? The world of grown-ups must be a very confusing and scarey place. Eddy and I sat right in the middle of the path, and he told me that he was sorry that he laughed at me. He said he didn't think I would get in such a huff. Being my usual self, I told him to forget all that rubbish and tell me what the Father meant.

He looked at the ground, and he began to speak with a lot of passion in his voice, "That old bugger had no right to talk to you like that. He asked me if I stuck it into little girls, and I asked him if he did when he was my age. He got real upset and tried to pull that God's man-on-earth stuff with me, but I wouldn't buy it. He wanted me to say twenty verses of penance, and I didn't do that either. I don't like him, and I told him so. He's not God's man on earth, he's just an evil-minded old fart that gets his kicks out of shocking kids. He said he was going to tell my mom that I was an evil boy, and I said that I was going to tell her that he was an evil man. He didn't even talk to mom, so he must have known he was no good for nothing."

Now, Eddy has a stick in his hand and he is making scratch marks in the well-packed earth on the road. I reach out and grab the stick to stop his nervous movement.

"Okay, I can understand that IT must be a bad thing, but what it IT? How can boys stick whatever IT is into little girls? Tell me! I want to know. I thought I was doing a good thing, going to confession and taking first communion so that I could grow up to be just like my mother and granny. Now, I don't know whether they know what they are doing or not. I don't know whether it was good or bad. For God's sake, tell me what letting little boys stick it into you means! If you're not going to tell me, then I'm going home right now and I'm not going to talk to you for a whole year! And you know that if I say I won't talk to you I won't. And it will be your own fault. You can get somebody else for a best friend. See if I care!"

Here, I stood up and made as if to continue up the path.

"OKAY, I'll tell you!" Eddy shouted.

I sat back down on the ground opposite him, and he began to draw pictures on the ground. My eyes opened wider and wider as full realization of what the Father was referring to began to sink in. Before that day, I had not even given sex a thought. But I sure had my scope of knowledge widened instantly as Eddy gave me my first biology lesson. He could not bring himself to talk about the act of copulation, but he certainly knew how to draw succinctly. I watched in stunned wonder as he made certain I understood fully. I had had no idea that the human body could act in such a way. I had thought girls were girls and boys were boys, and I never once thought of them having to fit together for any imaginable reason. When he was finished, he still could not bring himself to look at my face, because he seemed to be embarrassed for the whole male race.

I studied the picture, and I began to cry silent, hurting tears. My tears felt as though they were made of boiling water, and my eyes ached with the pain of crying them. I felt like my world had tumbled about my ears. My mom and granny must have known about this stuff. Why hadn't they told me about it? They should have known what kind of man that priest was before they let me go to him. How could he tell me he was a man of God and still treat me like I was a piece of dirty linen? How could he accuse me of doing such a revolting thing. I hadn't even held hands with a boy. I thought boys were for beating up.

Unbidden tears were gushing down my face. I didn't make a sound, but my body began to tremble and convulse of its own accord. I turned my face toward the sky, and, just like a wounded animal, I howled my agitation to the Grandfather Spirit, whom I knew would hear me and understand. I wailed long and mightily. Eddy was becoming frightened. He nervously put his arm around my shoulders to try to comfort me. He was probably afraid I would nail him for daring to touch me. Indeed, he had nothing to worry about, for I didn't even notice his efforts to cheer me up.

I felt that my life was shattered. I lost all of my innocence that day. I could see clearly that the Roman Catholic faith had large holes in its fabric, and I knew that I would never willingly set foot in another Catholic church. Eventually, I pulled myself together and Eddy walked me home. We vowed that we would never be Roman Catholics again.

Some time later, my mother asked me why I hadn't been studying the material the priest at Seashell had sent me. I shrugged my shoulders and told her that I had no need to go to church, for, as far as I was concerned, I was already better than God's man on earth. Even though I was only ten years old when this all took place, I had made up my mind about religion. I never did tell mom or granny why I wouldn't have anything to do with the Roman Catholic faith, because, even today, forty years later, the wound is still too fresh and new to even think of opening it for discussion.

Sarah Jerome

Sarah Jerome was born at Fort McPherson, Northwest Territories, on 6 September 1947 and is Gwichin (Loucheaux). With the encouragement of her grandmother Annie G. Roberts and her father John Telttihi Charlie, Sarah continued her education and graduated from grade twelve. After attending further education at Yellowknife, Sarah entered the teacher education program. After teaching for two years, she and her family returned to live on the land in the MacKenzie Delta region of the western Northwest Territories.

After the birth of her fourth child, Sarah decided to attend university and enrolled in the education program at the University of Saskatchewan, majoring in curriculum development, with a view to improving Aboriginal language development.

In January 1987, when her grandmother Annie G. Robert died, Sarah says she had to come to terms with her grief. The opportunity presented itself when Native literature professor Grace Jolly encouraged students to share oral stories with their classmates.

Sarah graduated in spring 1990 and lives at Fort McPherson, where she is not only involved with Aboriginal language development but also continues to write short stories about the lives of her people.

Granny

It was a cold January day when I sat in the living-room of my home, waiting for the phone to ring. I looked out the living-room window and across to the Richardson Mountains in the distance. My thoughts wandered back over the years to the times when granny Annie G. Robert was always there for us. She was the historian of the Teetlit Gwichin of Fort McPherson. I refilled my cup with hot tea and sat back down. I remembered the many visits I had had with her, often just to visit and renew her acquaintance with my children, who were her great-grandchildren. Other visits would be to cash her cheques or to go shopping for her. Whenever I made deposits for her at the Hudson's Bay, she knew the exact amount in her account. On some of these visits, she would sit up on her bed at the old folks home and begin to talk about her family and how life was in those days. On many occasions, she cried about the hardships she had endured and reminded me that we were so lucky to have all the modern conveniences today.

She was born somewhere along the headwaters of the Peel River, between Fort McPherson and Dawson City. She was the eldest of a family of six children. She remembered living totally off the land for all the basic survival needs. She mentioned travelling by dog packs in the summer to go into the mountains to hunt for the porcupine caribou herd, which was an important source of food.

While camping on the winter trail in the mountains the year granny turned thirteen, her mom fell sick and passed away. Granny had learned as much as a thirteen year old could learn from her mother, which were the simple chores around the camp. She was devastated by her mother's death. Being the oldest of the children, she would be required to take on the responsibilities of her mother. The first shock came when her father decided they had to move camp. It was the responsibility of the women to pack food, clothing, household implements, and, lastly, the tent. Before, she had been a bystander watching her mother perform these duties; now, it was her responsibility to do them. Not knowing where to begin, she stood outside the tent and began to cry, as her father disappeared down the trail. Eventually, one of the other women saw her despair and went to help her with the chores. When she was all packed and ready to leave, she thought of her mother's grave outside the camp. Another flood of tears began to flow, as she realized her mother was dead, never to be seen again. Granny had to learn to prepare and cook meals for the family, and she had to learn to clean and tan hides to make clothing for her father and her siblings. She grieved for years over the loss of her mother, while trying to take care of her brothers and sisters.

At the age of sixteen, granny was married to a young hunter by the name of Robert George (his name was reversed later). After they were married Indian style, Robert left her for two years. She continued living with her father to look after her brothers and sisters. Granny says there was another woman, but, to this day, we have not encountered distant relatives who claim to be Robert's children.

Robert and Annie G. had twelve children who were raised on the Peel River, just inside the Yukon Territory border. The place was known as Road River. Granny raised all her children on the land before contact, and after contact they still spent a lot of their time on the land. Granny tells about the time she was expecting a child and the people decided to move camp, as they were short on the meat supply. While on the trail, she went into labour. She put a caribou skin on the side of the trail, had her baby, put the baby in the sled, and continued to the next camp, where she helped to set up camp.

Gradually, granny's children married and moved to different hunting and trapping areas. We were fortunate; after mom married, she spent six months in the Delta with my dad and his family and then dragged dad to Road River to live with her parents for the rest of their lives. We had grandparents who influenced our lives and loved us very much. Looking back now, I realize that, of all her grandchildren, we were the luckiest, because we lived with them practically all year long. Granny was always available to help mom with her domestic chores. Often, she would come over and wash diapers for mom, or if fresh meat was brought in she would cut it up and make dried meat. Some evenings saw her mending shoes or clothing that was in need of repair. She took us along on her snare line to check for rabbits or to haul wood from the surrounding camp. After all but one of her sons were married, she continued to live at Road River with her husband and son.

In 1960, her husband George Robert (Senior) was taken to the hospital in Aklavik where he died and was buried. It was during the spring breakup and there were no modern airports in those days, so we were unable to attend the funeral. Prior to the death of her husband, a daughter-in-law passed on, leaving behind six children. Granny took in two of the boys who were younger and raised them during the summer when they were home from the residential school. She had a lot of amusing stories about those characters, whom I am sure were entertained many times through their ridiculous activity at the summer fish camp. At the spring camp across the river from the winter cabins, granny and mom would be busy working with meat or cleaning the caribou and moose skins that were brought in during the year. The men would be away hunting muskrats and beaver on the lakes, and, being children, we were a nuisance, getting in granny's way as she tried to work with the skins.

Those were beautiful days, when the ducks and geese from southern Canada would arrive and flock on the river. The melting snow created streams that went singing their way to the river. Sweets and junk food were not known those days, so on visits to granny we were given a piece of dried meat or a cookie. Of all the years that we lived beside granny, we never once answered her back when she reprimanded us or spanked us for wrongdoing. She had a great sense of humour; she was always teasing us and telling us funny stories.

Granny was a believer in the Anglican Church. She did her household chores from Monday to Saturday, and Sundays found us all gathered in her cabin or tent, participating in a Gwichin worship. Some Sundays while sitting in the house or tent, we would hear her singing Gwichin hymns at the top of her lungs. Although granny was illiterate, she memorized practically all the Gwichin hymns and sang to her heart's content. On those days, we dared not work; carrying water and wood, even playing loud games, were forbidden on a Sunday.

After the death of her husband George Robert, granny continued to live at Road River for the winter months, then moved to her fish camp ten miles south of Fort McPherson on the Peel River. In the fall of 1973, we were shocked to find that mom had cancer and had only a few months to live. We were so full of pain in those last days that if it had not been for the daily visits of granny I am sure we would have given up totally. She would tell us stories of her life experiences, which always ended with a lesson or behaviour that was expected of us. After mom's death, she reminded us of how we were to behave. Dad was coming home with the coffin, and when the plane arrived we were to be strong for dad. With those words of encouragement, granny left it up to us to meet our dad, composed and ready to begin the funeral arrangements. Granny took us under her wing, although by that time she was ninety-four years old. She was mentally alert and always inquired about members of the family. She had to know what each individual was doing, where they were, and how soon she would see them again. I did not blame her — there were twelve of us in the family.

While living in Inuvik during the mid-seventies, my trips home would always find me at granny's house to see how she was doing. Due to the many hardships in her life, granny always made these visiting occasions a time for shedding a few tears. Often, I would tell her I had not seen her crying for a while and missed it, therefore, I was back to see her shed a few tears. Immediately, granny would begin to laugh.

My husband and I moved back to Fort McPherson in 1979, which gave me the opportunity to relearn my native language. I understood the language but could not speak it very well at the time. I spent a lot of time with the elders of the community but mostly with granny. After mom's death, she spent one more year at Road River with us. Then, she was unable to go back. She moved into the old folks' home in Fort McPherson for the winter months but always returned to her fish camp ten miles south of Fort McPherson. In the summer of 1982, she lost a daughter who was the mother of eight and she took them under her wing. The following summer, after spending the month of August at Road River with my dad, I returned to Fort McPherson to prepare for the coming school year and work. Two days after I left, my dad died suddenly from a heart attack. Once again, granny was there to give us the moral support we needed. "Now, you are orphans," she said to us. "You will have to take care of one another."

Funeral arrangements were made, and granny was right in there on her wheelchair, singing in the church. I began to spend more time with her, getting her views on the many changes that had taken place over the years. She understood the news broadcast on the radio and knew of major events happening all over the world. When she brought up the subject, whether it be a flood, plane crash, or the Queen of England on her world travels, I would fill in the details for her. I was amazed that she was so knowledgeable of current events.

Granny celebrated her one hundredth birthday in 1981. We had our community radio station installed a year earlier, so we decided to celebrate the first anniversary of the radio station along with her one hundredth birthday. It was a memorable event for her, as she received telegrams from the Queen, the Prime Minister, Pierre Elliot Trudeau, and John Parker, Commissioner of the Northwest Territories, among other dignitaries.

In July 1983, the Settlement Council honoured granny Annie G. Robert by naming their new building after her. At the opening ceremonies on 16 July 1983, Prime Minister Trudeau, accompanied by his three sons, arrived in Fort McPherson. With the help of Richard Herysoo, legislative member of the Northwest Territories and Prime Minister Trudeau, granny cut the ribbon and officially opened the new building in her honour. Granny began to walk less often after that; she was helped around by her children and could still walk to and from the front door of the old folks home, but she had to rest after those short walks. She began to lose her eyesight, she said, but it surprised me that she recognized me whenever I walked into her room. Granny still made her summer trips to the fish camp, leaving in June and returning to the old folks' home in September or October. She was always reluctant to return to Fort McPherson, as she enjoyed the outdoors and the peacefulness of the land.

On our way to Road River, we would stop by her camp and inform her that we were going to our summer camp and the approximate time of our return. We were always advised to be careful and to take care of the children. During the eight years that I worked in Fort McPherson, before returning to university, I always informed granny of my travel plans. Her first concern was, "Who will look after the children?" Many times, I had made prior arrangements with my husband to be back from his trap line to baby-sit while I was away. One day, in the fall of 1986 when she was 106 years old, I again went to see her to inform her that I was travelling and would be gone for a week. She assured me that she would pray for my safe travel, then asked me, "Who will look after the children while you are away?"

I said to her, "If you are so concerned, why don't you take care of them?"

She began to laugh and said, "What can I do at my age?"

On returning to my community, I would go see her and inform her that I had returned safely. She was a granny, but most of all she was a mother. She had mothered her brothers and sisters. She then raised her own children. Later, she would take in two grandsons to raise until they went on their own. As our parents passed on, she was there to give us the moral support that we needed to continue on. She passed on the value system to us, but, most of all, she was there for us.

As I gazed at the Richardson Mountains, I thought about the time she said they arrived in Dawson City and set up camp on the outskirts of the city. The men went down to the city to look around, while the women stayed around the camp and did their chores. One day, Robert asked her if she wanted to accompany him to the city. Despite her fears, she decided to go. She said, "When we walked into the city, I could smell the scent of oranges." She had said this in Gwichin, except for the word scent.

I was so surprised that I said to her, "What did you say?" After repeating her sentence, I asked her what she meant by the word scent.

She said, "The smell of oranges was in the air."

I laughed at her. Here was a Gwichin elder who could not speak or write in English, and she had used a word I did not know was in her vocabulary.

In January 1986, I decided to return to university to get my degree. Granny had always encouraged us to get an education and was proud that most of the immediate family were involved in community activities and sitting on various boards. When I went to see her one day, she said, "I hear you are going back to school?"

I said, "Yes, Granny, I have decided to go back to school and get my degree."

Her next question was, "How long will you be away?"

I answered, "Three years."

"It's too long to be away from us and your community," she said.

I answered, "Granny, I will return in three years. Then, I will be qualified to work with the Gwichin language and I will be able to do more."

She said, "If you have to go and get your education, go, but take care of yourself and take good care of the children. Make sure you return to Fort McPherson." Those were the good times I had with granny. She always shared her experience with us, her comical stories, and her concern about the family.

As I went to refill my cup, the phone rang. I hesitated to answer the phone, as I did not want to know just yet. I finally lifted the receiver after glancing at the clock. It was 5:20 p.m. The caller said, "Granny just passed away ten minutes ago."

As I walked down toward the old folks' home, I thought to myself, "You were here with us for a long time, granny. You brought us through a lot of your experiences, you embraced us when our parents passed on, you shared your stories with us, and now we must let you go, too." With a sad heart, I continued on to comfort those who were grieving and perhaps give them some of the strength that granny had given me over the years.

Loretta Jobin

Loretta Jobin, nee Wuttunee, was born in the small prairie town of Battleford, Saskatchewan in 1948. Her parents, Gilbert and Lillian, were originally from the Red Pheasant Reserve, a short distance from the town of her birth.

The youngest of several children, Loretta spent many hours as a child reading and dreaming some day of becoming a writer. She was first inspired, at the age of eight, by the poetry of Pauline Johnson. Her favourite poem was "The Song my Paddle Sings."

After moving from Battleford with her family at the age of ten, Loretta lived in many different Canadian cities. She now resides in Edmonton, Alberta, with her husband Fred, and two children, Donald and Shalene. With the encouragement received from her family, Loretta currently is pursuing a career in journalism.

The Winds of My Youth

I never lived on the reserve, but at least once a year we would make the twenty-five mile trip in my uncle's truck to visit our relatives. It was hard to hear above the sound of the wind in the back of the pickup, but that never stopped us from talking. Every once in a while, I would turn to look in the cab to see my parents talking and laughing with my uncle. I was glad that they had allowed me to sit in the back with my older brothers and sisters. We counted the hawks circling in the sky and kept our eyes open in a contest to see who could spot the most coyotes or deer, but I liked best to watch the gophers scurrying in the fields. Mother always said she thought they were suicidal, for it seemed that they would wait until a vehicle was in front of them before deciding to race across the road.

When we reached the hills, the landscape behind us looked like an aerial photograph, and Ken spotted the old Indian residential building where our father had gone to school. I had often seen this large, white building from our attic window. It looked so forgotten, sitting on the hill in the distance, almost obscured by the tall poplars surrounding it.

"Did you know Dad was born in these hills?" Winston asked of anyone who might be listening.

"He was not!" replied Ken, who never liked to agree with anything our oldest brother said. "He was born on the reserve."

"Shows how much you know!" Winston shouted back. "The reserve wasn't even around when Dad was born," he added matter-of-factly.

I guessed that was true, for my father was quite old. He was born at a time when Indians still wore Hudson's Bay blankets wrapped around their shoulders and moccasins on their feet. My father had often told us that, as a small boy, he wore his long hair in braids and had a pierced earring dangling from his ear lobe. He also told us that he had seen the last of the buffalo roaming the plains. He was born in 1892, so if he said he saw the last of the buffalo I, for one, believed him. I believed everything my parents told me. Yvonne spotted the old fort in the distance, and this started us talking about all our relatives who we thought must have died in this area.

The steeple of the post office, the tallest building in our town, slowly faded out of sight. Shortly after, we reached the turn-off to the reserve and bounced around in the back of the truck as we drove over the bumpy roads. I stood up to wave at the children playing in the yards of the homes we passed. Most of the houses were small, and there was usually a truck or tractor parked in the driveways. It was early, so I knew most of my uncles would be working in the fields, bailing hay or threshing.

"Sit down Lulu, before you fall down!" Winston shouted at me.

I sat down, feeling bad that I had made him cross. I guess he was afraid I might fall out of the truck, but I was six years old and knew better.

We would have been made to feel welcome at each house we passed, but my father wanted to go straight to the house of his only sister. Ken was the first one out of the truck and raced up to my aunt and uncle, who met him at the door.

"Tansay," he said in his deep voice, while shaking their hands. He was ten and didn't like to be seen kissing, although that was what we were taught to do.

Yvonne and I laughed when Winston said, "Ha! That's the only Cree word he knows."

When the rest of us entered my aunt's small kitchen, I noticed the kettle already boiling on the wood stove. News travelled fast on the reserve, especially when visitors from town were expected.

I studied my aunt, who resembled my father, as she talked in Cree to my parents. They were both fair, and, although she was two years younger than her brother, her hair was bone white, while his looked like a mixture of salt and pepper. I watched as she reached into the cupboard for the cups for tea, and soon she was placing bannock on the table at which we sat. As she fried up choke-cherries in grease, I knew my parents' mouths would be watering, for this was a delicacy to them. It made my stomach turn, and I wondered how I could get out of eating. I knew it was bad manners to refuse the food put before me, but I hated the feel of the crushed pits mixed in together with the berries.

I said as humbly as I could, "No thank you, Aunty. I'm not hungry," although I was starving.

I felt that everyone knew I was lying, for mother had often told me my face was very easy to read. If they did, no one said anything.

Hearing a car door slam, I raced to the living-room window to see who had pulled up. It was my aunt and uncle with their seven children. They weren't really my aunt and uncle; they were just cousins, but because they were older that's what we were taught to call them.

I stared at my many cousins as they straggled into the house. Some had dark skin with big, brown eyes, others had fair skin, and one even had red hair and freckles. I don't know why I found this so unusual, for it was the same in my family. My father was fairer than my mother and even had green eyes. He always said the white blood that ran through our veins was strong. As I stared, I noticed the high cheek-bones, characteristic of the Indian race, prominent on every-one's face.

My aunt's neat but small house was crowded, and, after being warned not to go near the open well, we were sent out to play. I walked carefully as I stepped over the broken boards of the step and looked up to see my aunt's yard strewn with bikes. We had many relatives on the reserve, and as soon as we were spotted driving by young cousins had jumped on their bikes and rode through the fields to beat us there. Soon, I knew my uncles would hear of our visit and leave the fields to say hello and grab a quick cup of tea with my parents.

One cousin had ridden over on his horse and asked me if I wanted to ride it.

"Sure," I said, trying to sound brave.

But, I was happy to hear Winston say, "Honey, you're too little, you might get hurt."

That started my cousins giggling, for they had learned how to ride almost before they learned how to walk. Not only that, but sometimes they even drove their fathers' cars and tractors down the dirt roads of the reserve. When they started laughing and talking in Cree to one another, I was sure they were making fun of me. Winston must have seen the tears welling up in my eyes, for he said, "Hop on," while jumping on the horse. Ken boosted me up, and I held tightly on to Winston as we rode around the field on the other side of the driveway. I was scared of horses, because I had once been kicked by one of my father's Clydesdales that he kept in town. We never got to ride those horses, because they were used for pulling the wagon while he delivered water to the townspeople.

Later, Winston talked one cousin his age into going riding with him to a part of the reserve known as Pasquak. That was where he had been born, along with my older sisters Mary, Elsie, and Amy. The reserve was large and Pasquak a fair distance from my aunt's house. I knew he had to ride through fields and over hills, and by the time he got back I expected his clothes would be full of burrs and spear grass. If he took shortcuts around the sloughs, I thought he might also get wet and probably get into trouble with my mother. Or, if the horse stumbled in a badger or gopher hole, he might get hurt. "Be careful, Winnie," I said, just as he started galloping away.

I learned later when he returned from his ride that all that was left of the small house was the root cellar upon which it once sat.

I tired of trying to play with my cousins, who shied away from me. Yvonne was older than me and didn't like me hanging around her, so I went into the house instead. I sat down in a corner on the wood floor, hoping that no one would notice me. Anyway, I loved to listen to my aunts and uncles speak of old times with my parents. They were fluent in both Cree and English and often switched while speaking. My parents sometimes spoke Cree at home, especially when Mary and Elsie were home, for they could also speak Cree, and I guess I picked up a few words. I was glad when I heard a familiar word or phrase, because then I could figure out what they were talking about.

My father started telling the story about how he used to have to take his blind grandfather for walks as a young lad. He said the old man would be feeling the ground before him with his cane as he held on to my father's shoulder with his free hand. My father shook his head as he recounted how he would purposely lead his grandfather through all the gopher holes in sight and how he'd laugh when the old man stumbled and fell.

I smiled as I watched my old aunts dressed in their calico skirts, with bright kerchiefs tied around their heads. They would raise their hand to their mouths while uttering, "Mah!" in their disbelief at my father's naughtiness. Everyone laughed at his story, which set the mood for their favourite pastime. They were known for their story-telling as well as their teasing, especially my uncles, Gavin and Tom. How often I had watched my brother Ken stomp away after they called him "Little Mad Bull," because of his quick temper. Earlier, one of my small, dark cousins had bent her head to hide the tears after being called "a lighter shade of chocolate brown." Perhaps, they teased us in preparation for being called names by the white people, but, whatever the reason, we were used to it. We learned early that the worst mistake we could make was to get angry, for this only sent my uncles into fits of laughter and made them tease all the harder.

Uncle Tom also liked to tease my mother. She was his oldest sister, and he enjoyed getting her riled.

"Remember the first time Lilly had to give a urine sample to the doctor?" he laughed, while asking no one in particular.

"That's enough, Tom," my mother replied sharply, embarrassed at the memory of her naivete about the white culture when first moving to town.

Uncle Tom pretended not to hear her, and said, "Oh, dear! Didn't you save a sample each day for a month in a large bottle?"

"Wah, Wah, Tom!" my aunt cut in and, acting as though her next remark would erase mother's embarrassment, said, "She only saved it for a week!"

Uncle Peto interrupted the story to say, "I remember as a little girl you used to hunt down all the ant hills in the area and knock them down with a stick, Lilly."

Mother laughingly told them how she was mesmerized by the army of ants. She said she couldn't believe how the smaller ants could carry much larger captives on their backs with seemingly no problem and she would knock the large ant off with her stick, thinking she was doing the captor a favour.

"You always were a good hunter, Lilly," Aunt Hazel said, jokingly.

Uncle Lennox said, "It's true, Lilly was a good hunter," and then told how she used to shoot ducks and snare rabbits to feed her younger brothers and sisters when times were tough.

We heard often about how times were tough, especially during the depression.

"Neechas?" someone asked my father. "Do you remember that house we were helping you build before you got married?"

"Uh, Uh", my father replied. "That would have been a beautiful house."

I had heard this particular story many times. It was the largest house on the reserve and was being built on a hill, and it offered a grand view of the prairies below. My father had worked hard to buy the lumber and panes of glass for the many windows. The day before my parents' wedding, a freak cyclone ripped the shingles from the roof and shattered the windows, only moments after the men had found safety. They had no money left to rebuild.

My mother said, "I guess my vanity was nipped in the bud," as she recalled how they had to start their life together in the small house at Pasquak.

The room turned quiet for a moment at the recollection. Soon, the talk turned somber, as they recalled the many people who had passed away over the years. One uncle, they said, had buried four of his children after a bout of the flu. That made me sad. I liked better listening to the happy memories, especially mother's favourite, which was Christmas when the reserve was blanketed in snow. There was never much money for presents, she would tell me, but happy times were had wishing relations good health and wealth for the new year. She said it was so nice to drive down the road and hear the bells on the approaching sleighs jingle in the crisp night air. They would meet at a certain house and dance until the wee hours of the morning. Her father would play all the favourites, such as "Rubber Dolly," on his violin, and my uncles would accompany him on their guitars. I also liked to hear of the time when mother had barely enough time to hitch the horses and throw her four small children on a buck board to escape a grass fire burning out of control. The reserve held many memories for my parents — some good, some bad.

My father broke the silence by telling the joke about the Indian who went into the store asking for kiddely beans.

The white store owner said, "You mean kidney beans, don't you?"

The Indian looked at him in surprise and replied, "I said kiddely, diddle I?"

This started a round of jokes told mainly in Cree. If one were exceptionally funny and could be repeated in English without losing its humour, my parents would repeat it for my older brother, who by this time had come in the house. That is, if it were meant for young ears.

Long after the sun sank over the horizon, we would hop once again into the back of the truck. We would wave and shout goodbyes to our relatives and prepare ourselves for the chilly ride home. As we rode in the dark, we could see the shape of the hills and the scattered clumps of bushes silhouetted in the moonlight.

I never knew life on a reserve. When my oldest sister reached school age, my parents enfranchised, realizing the reserve could not offer hopes of a decent education for their children. Leaving relatives and a familiar way of life behind, they packed their meager belongings and moved to a small town.

Our house was on the outskirts of the town, close to the highway and the grain elevators. It was a wooden two-storey structure, with boards weathered grey from the many years of being stripped by wind, snow, and rain. Untrimmed caraganas bordered three sides of the front yard, and only a few patches of grass grew in the sandy soil among the weeds. The backyard faced the town, and from our attic window we could peer across the open fields into the hills and see the winding road leading to the reserve.

Bren Kolson

Bren Kolson, a Métis born at Yellowknife, Northwest Territories, on 28 September 1950, is of Chipewyan and Polish descent. Ms Kolson wrote her first poem at the age of eleven. Three years later, she was the winner of a literary contest sponsored by Molson's of Canada in memory of John Testo, a Dene trapper and writer. When she was fifteen, some of her poems were published in the local Yellowknife newspaper, *The News of the North*.

Ms Kolson went on to study business administration and journalism at Grant MacEwan College from 1971 to 1974, when she returned to the North to work as a reporter/photographer for *The Native Press*, a newspaper published by the Native Communications Society of the Western Northwest Territories. She travelled with and covered the Mackenzie Valley Pipline Inquiry, the Legislative Assembly, and northern Native politics before receiving a one-year scholarship in legal journalism, sponsored by the Canadian Bar Association. The Louis St. Laurent Fellowship allowed Ms Kolson to audit the law courses of her choice at Queen's University in 1980-81. Upon returning to the North, Ms Kolson worked with the Métis Association of the Northwest Territories in public relations and communications, until she went to work for the Aboriginal Rights and Constitutional Development Secretariat with the Government of the Northwest Territories as Land Claims Policy Analyst.

During this time, Ms Kolson continued to write poetry and prose, focussing on a two-year period of her life when she lived on the barrenlands east of Fort Reliance. She continued her involvement with various Native organizations and is currently Vice-Chairperson of the Native Communications Society of the Western Northwest Territories.

In 1988, Ms Kolson enrolled at the University of Saskatchewan and is currently in her third year in the English honours program. During her second year, she was awarded the Corbiere Lavell-Two Axe Early Award, sponsored by the National Native Women's Association and given to Métis and Treaty women intent on furthering their education.

Ms Kolson intends to attain a masters in communication, before returning to the North with her daughter Kiera-Dawn, where she hopes to work for the betterment of Native people interested in achieving a higher understanding of Native communications and their culture. She believes Northerners have a natural oral history that has not reached the greater Canadian audience, and she hopes to be able to assist those Native northerners interested in writing careers. Ms Kolson is currently revising a manuscript on her barrenland experiences and continues to write poetry and prose.

The Barren Journey Home

Leaving is sometimes survival.
But energies mustered, must make the journey home.

Tradition has me winding my way,
along half-paths — bumpy trails.
There are no people here, except the ones to whom I speak.
And they too — are not real.
They are past acquaintances, long dead,
friends of my youth, friends in my life.
Yet some survive.

Native to this cold and unwanted barrenland,
I have learned to take the fierce elements
and tame them by the windows of my eye.
They command me. I am indifferent to them.

Indigenous to this land I know,
I have seldom snared an animal,
if it was not for survival.
They have tried, though, to fix me,
in their motionless trap.
But I am human. I would not succumb,
to the wild wind's whip or the wilful wolverine.
I am fixed, in sanity, on surviving.

Legends of my ancestors do not leave me alone.
But legends about people survive.

It is my ancestors who said, "Trust the spirit of the land,
but do not trust the land to man."
And they have helped me.
These spirit men and women helped me to survive,
welcomed me into their spirit world,
while I surrender myself to the land.
Guided me, throughout and in, decision.
Used the signs on the land as augurs,
pointing the way to the right path,
and not losing myself to insanity or indecision.

But, teaching me how to survive
this barrenland of God and man's creation,
they have told me tenderly the time was ripe,
for aged souls to leave the land.
But I do not believe them this time.
They are failed energies,
while I am living and leaving legends to survival.
I will not make the journey home this winter.
I will leave my dogs hitched to the post
and make the journey home
in the spring.

Preview

Careless
and wanton images scramble the cells,
mobilize my mind.
Desire
is just a word with no emotion.
A stanza,
selfish and senseless to my Spirit.
Craving
is the shadow accomplice,
silently signals which way to wave and weave.
Dreams
are only sweetened by the senses.
Untouchable ghost,
ceaseless, to the movements of my brain.

Unknown
is the field of timeless touching.
So suffers
every martyr on the path.

Castaway
in a world of conscious vision.
Foreign
in a listless land of longing.
Satisfied
by the climax of our moods.
Safe
within the womb is coupledom.
Some times
the times are for reminiscent lovers.
Oft' times
the times are for Spirit wandering.

The Ride

Let's go riding in your daddy's Buick. 'Round the town tonight.
I'll give you some money to buy us a dozen
        and we'll drink a la biere delight.
Drop me off at the home-town inn, and I'll use this quarter I have.
I'll phone up the girls, tell them upwrap those curls,
        and we'll meet at the local cafe.
I don't want to meet Mr. El Jacko Creep.
        He's been giving me the eye, you know.
Let's just walk down this street, play hide and go peep.
        Don't give him the eye — then let's go.
Want a drag of this butt? Last one in the deck.
        So savour it long and slow.
Let's just sit in the car, listen to the radio stars,
        and see who comes out of the show.
Must have been a sad one. Look at their faces.
        No one here tonight.
Where do you think the party's at — ask him — outta town.
        We'll put on those old headlights.
Do you think Mr. Cutie will turn up soon?

Do you think he'll be with a girl?
He'd better not be — 'cause it's my turn you see —
 and my brother, he better not punch and roll.
So where have you been? It's an hour since I seen ya,
 gotta go pretty soon, don't ya see?
I promised midnight and it'll be one more fight,
 if I'm not in the house by the three.
Just one more beer? Are you sure you can steer?
 Better watch the road on the side!
Don't go so fast! That's better at last.
 You know I don't like to drive crazy.
So he promised a date for tomorrow night's slate.
 Well, lucky old you, here's the key.
Be quiet! They're sleeping, and here you've been creeping,
 dear cousin with cutie — not me.
Nah, I'm not mad. Better you glad than sad.
 There's a thousand fish in the sea.
Yeah, I know I'm still young. Just fourteen and one.
 But I already feel twenty-three.

Celebration: Drum of Life

Tah-tah-tah-tah, tah-tee-tah-tah-tah-tah, a-tah-tee-tah-tah-tah,
the life is beaten out of the skin.

The speed of the hoof on the lichen below,
the weight of the body flying the flow
of the herd, in a frenzied, swaying gallop.

The straggler, the calf, the limp of the lame,
struggling the hummock, broken down
by the strong who survive the barrenland crust.

The hunter, eye cocked in gravity around
the snap of the bullet that finds its
red-blood target in the heart of a majestic bull caribou.

Eye to brown eye, the prayer is said, one
for forgiveness, the other for thanksgiving,
to the same Creator; forfeiture for fortitude.

The hide, cut clean, the meat carved and carried
on the backs of survivors, to the cache stage,
staid; ready for eating.

The hide, staked in the ground; sun-dried,
then scraped to starch white, with the hair
cut away with a razor-sharp blade.

Soaked in lake water, wrung out with hands,
scraped to perfection, and swaying on the clothes-lines,
outside in the mid-March halo.

Tanned by tree wood, smudge of the fire,
and rubbed in the summer by the muscle
of the working hands; grinding softness.

Boiled bark, curve of the tree, spliced
into pieces to make the round of the drum
the taut hide will hold.

Stick of life, drum of hide, beating out
ancestral songs. Memories of life's defeats
and life's enduring will to go on and on and on.

Tah-tah-tah, tah-tah-tah, ah-tah, tah-tah.

II

A-high, high, hey-high. Hey a-high, high, high.
Hey a-high, hey, high,
man beats out life from the drum.

The old ways taken swiftly from Dene/Métis by man.
The weight of the burden in flashes of bad drink,
poor houses, and dying children.

The mis-Chief, the orphaned, the abuse of the will,
straining the pavement, broken down by the man
who keeps his foot to the throat of the city crust.

Stained survivor, eyes alert, balanced in gravity
between staying within or self-survival without,
the proud will of the government man.

Eye to some eye, no prayer is said, only favourite
catchwords and fast farewells, in the name
of the same self-Creator; fact for false fiction.

The face of man, cut clean, the body craving and carried
in the box to the bleak cemetary, without will,
ready and waiting for saving.

The will of man, strong, in the heart; four sun directions,
purified by the heat, with menace cut away
with razor-sharp defiance for his people.

Solitude of the lakes, washed clean the hands,
vision of perfection and sways with revival,
inside, during every month.

Mind working the muscle, hands grinding the callous
of the paperwork and the meetings and the assemblies,
to bring secure messages for the people.

Boiled meat and made bannock, strong stew and tea,
spliced into feasts for the celebration,
listening to the beat of the hide and the drum.

Man of life, drum of skin, beating out ancestral
songs and memories of this afternoon and the tomorrow,
of the children and life's will to go on and on.

A-high, high, hey-high. Hey a-high, high, high.
Hey a-high, hey, high.

Spirit Music of Misty* Elders
(For Mary Kolson, Florence Erasmus, and Dorothy Beaulieu)

"Hey, hey, hey, my girl, — where hahf you been?"
She said: "I've been to London Mama, to see the Queen."
"The Queen," she asked, "Why the Queen?"
She said: "To change an attitude to happy, from mean."
"But my girl, — whot did she say?"
She said: "The Queen wouldn't see me . . . said, 'a-whey, whey, whey.'"
"But my girl, whot did you do to make her thas way?"
She said: "Cause we were born of two worlds. Don't know how to
say, 'May I'?"
"Whot do you mean, my girl? I dohn un'erstan."
She said: "We're the daughters of the Métis. Don't have any land."

"I wan to tell you a storee, bou' lon' tine ago,
Whin your gran'mahther an' gran'fahther, like you, feel so low.
'Cause the Whi'man, he come, to take-it all ar lan',
Say sun peeples ar hahf-whi', ohthers mus' lihf in the Ban's.

Lon tine ago, beefore you are born,
Lihf har' on the lan', feesh-nets sun tine they torn.
But we know how to hun' and we know how to trap,
An' the lan' treet us gute. We know it like map.

Sun chil'ren get seek, no medi-sin then.
So we gihf them the muh-sic, deep down from whith-in.
An' soon, they get bedder. But sun chil'ren dieeee . . .
But Whi'man say school'ng will be righ', thas why.

So they take them there kits, beefor they are fif,
No bedder in beeg houwse. Still chil'ren they dieeee . . .
At the hans of the Sihsters, who feed them raw feesh,
Say they can hahf no more food til they lick thas las' deesh.

Sun tines kits they talk to e'ch ohther at nigh',
Wan' grah-mah and gran'pah . . . they cry 'cause they frigh'n.
But soon, they be hitt'n for ta'kin thas way,
An' they star to loose muh-sic . . . now noh-thin' to say.

They te'tch them there kits how to luf thas One Lor',
Whin they do not do this, get hitt'n with a boar',
An' soon, cun the tine thas they leaf thas there scho'l,
Know noh-thin of ar ways — becun Whi'man's fools.

Sun peeples work har', not get any lan',
So they stey in poor houwses an' they eat trash from canse,
An' they dreenk that bad medi-sin. They call it boose,
Loose the muh-sic of Elders. Got no way to chooose.

Sun peeple be happey. They lihf on the lan',
An' they talk whith the Speirits. It like they hol'ng han's.
Get sum kin' o' bless'ng fron way hi-a-buff,
They know in their har's how to gihf thas there luf.

An' the Speirits they tell them: 'Dohn lo'se the lan','
Or you gihf up your lihf a' the han's o' Whi'man.
An' they tell them be-leaf you can he'p your own selp,
It onlee whith gute medi-sin thas we he'p ar' own selp.

So my girl, dohn go there to see thas there Queen.
She dohn know us — dohn know lan' — 'cause she neh-ver been.
But you go see the Elders, they know how to speak-it,
They not make you mean and they not make you weak'n.

You go! See the Elders my girl. It's for shure,
They gihf you the muh-sic. It sun-thin' like cure.
An' dohn be af'id of no Whi'manse Queen.
It no gute to go there whin she neh-ver seen.

An' dohn you for-ght to than' them there Ones,
For they tet'ch you to dance in new kin' o' sun.
An muh-sic you hear — it be sweet like small bir',
But you lis'en and hair e'ery thin thas they word."

She said: "Oh Mama. I love you. I know you are right.
But will I be strong enough to see that new light?"

"My girl, you no bad one. You figh' for thas ligh'.
Cause you dohn get noh-thin if you dohn be-leaf righ'."

She said: "But Mama. How will we know that new light?
Will the Elders give it to me. I mean, the Music of Light?"

"You know my girl . . . it cun whin, we dohn know whin it cun—
Cause you be bedder whithin — an' it cun to jus' sun."

She said: "But Mama, I don't understand."

"You will my girl, whin you know whot is righ'.
Cause the Spirit of Elders is the Muh-sic of Sigh'."

* In old French, misty meant Métis.

Old Man's Home-made Brew

The phantoms of your youth
they come to haunt you in the night
when you are not asleep,
but slowly sipping on your home-made brew.

You walked a mile on Saturday, to fetch the wood
to put into the home-made barrel stove,
and watched the water you pailed
from the lake boil fast.

Pouring in the brown sugar, rice, and dry fruit,
you bought in town on Friday night,
you stirred the water in the jugs the
home-made brew would hold.

You cooled the water by the minute gauge
of time and frothed the yeast, until
the golden mythical God of your near-century
ancestors said it was alright.

A cup for him, a cup for me, a cup
to drink the spirits free, from the
aged souls to whom you talked,
as you drank your home-made brew.

A story of the time you lost your
favourite leader in a heated dogfight
over a bitch in heat, and you buried
them both on the barrenlands.

A story about the ladies in town,
and the money you paid to the barman,
and children, whose parents were too poor
to buy their own golden dreams.

A story about the last time you hunted
the caribou and the grizzly fated one
who stole the meat from the cache
of esker mound; it was only dirt and rock.

You spoke to Rose that night,
about the times of youth, and poured
an invisible friend a cup to sip, while
she watched you do a Métis jig.

Then, by the morning light, with no one
left to mourn, you laid your bowed
head on the pillow of feather
and rose to greet the phantoms of the night.

Tell-a-Tale Trapper
(For Louison Drybones)

Seventy-two-year-old stained tobacco teeth
tasted many bitter-sweet memories,
but he says his vocation is trapping.

Sixteen-year-old desperado's young Stah-stay-nee
mouth Chipewyan words of free Ber-bats-theo,
and he wants to be a hunter.
Bartered, borrowed, Hudson's Bay motto,
buys gun and shells, canned grub, sewed seasonal socks,
and he's almost ready for leaving.

Snuff washed beer, unfocused gaze,
juke-box tunes, scratched "last call,"
and his dogs and he are flying.

Land barren, oasis of trees, wind sways
the carry-all and boxes on one pack;
no one to talk to until Christmas.

Esker mounds, caribou trails, stream-fed fish,
bare hands, tossed bannock — for hunger,
and loneliness leans on a friend.

Chopping wood, chipping ice, candles, aflames
the colour of snapping stove sparks,
and he's fleshing a hide by the fire.

Whirl-a-wind snow, black midnight's dressed,
fifty below plus clutches cabin floor,
and he's asleep at his outpost camp.

Frozen from time, animal snare of rabbit and fox,
penknife to shook-hide, auction delight,
and he's trapped enough fur for the season.

A-Chah — twelve, caribou-slippered dogs run
master with land, prayer of Denendeh breath,
and he's gliding his sleigh through the bushland.

Snow drifts in sight, lakeshore of silhouette sunset,
distant straggling smoke, voices barely visible,
and he's in communion with holiday spirits.

Out-of-town dogs pegged, stakes, frozen ground
back-patting, smiling teeth of free home-made rounds,
and he's telling his tales to the people.

Feast of fine feather, frill of fair friend,
family, nieces, and nephews lighten laughter,
and his fur money is gone like the summer.

Twenty and twenty vision, and years fading fondly,
rest assured routine, relished with reason,
and he's making "one more" trip to the barrens.

Seventy-two-year-old strained soul survivor,
trapped many bitter-sweet memories,
but he says he was always the hunted.

Stah-stay-nee in Chipewyan means friend or group of friends.

Ber-bats-theo in Chipewyan means meat or is slang for grub (food).

Sewed seasonal socks are moccasins or mukluks.

A *carry-all* is the sleigh a hunter uses to carry material for trapping.

Bannock is a biscuit-type bread made from flour, salt, baking powder,
    lard or animal grease, sometimes sugar, and water.

Fleshing is taking the hide off an animal.

An *outpost camp* is a subcamp some distance from the main camp
    and is used occasionally when hunting or camping for a short
    period of time.

A-Chah is the word used to order dogs pulling a sleigh to go right.

Caribou slippers are sewed from caribou hide for the dogs' feet, to
    prevent them from being cut when travelling, particularly over ice.

Denendeh, in the Aboriginal language of the Dene/Métis of the
    Northwest Territories (Western), means "homeland" or "man's
    place" or "the home of the people."

Jean Koomak

I was born in an igloo at Arviat, Northwest Territories, in 1952. My father was a hunter, and the family travelled year-round by dog team to follow the animals he hunted. I went to a federal government school in Arviat for about a year when I was thirteen years old.

When I was sixteen, my parents told me to marry. I have nine children.

This year, I went to a women's upgrading class at Arctic College in Arviat to learn more about reading and writing in English, because I want to get a job.

Jean's Story

My name is Jean Koomak. I'm living in Arviat (Eskimo Point), Northwest Territories. The women work hard. We have to look after our children and our elders. We have to make warm clothes because our land is very cold. In summer, sometimes, it is hot. Our men, they hunt by dog team or ski-doo. In summertime, they hunt by canoe or all-terrain vehicles. That's the only way to hunt, and we have to have food. Our living is sometimes hard because it is very cold and there are very few jobs.

Emma LaRocque

I was born early in the dawn of 1949 in a small log cabin in the small Métis community of Big Bay, Alberta. The midwives were nohkom (my grandmother) and my aunt Eleanor, who was felled by tuberculosis before I could know her.

Writing is the art of bringing to birth the human condition in thought form. I remember when I first announced I was going to be a writer to my grade eight classmates, and everybody but my good teacher laughed. Then again, who knew what a "writer" was? We were the offspring of a great Cree oral literature. Writing was not what we did. Nohkom and Ama (our family term for my mother; short for Ni-mama in Cree) were superbly skilled storytellers. Ama was also a reader and writer in Cree syllabics. And, whenever she went to town she brought me comic books, even before I could read.

I try to do in English what nohkom and Ama could do in Cree. But I have spent many years in university, as a student and a professor. There is tremendous pressure to keep up with the Academic Joneses, so I have had to read and write scholarly articles, theses, and dissertations. Unfortunately, too many scholars apparently assume scholarly writing must, by definition, be pedantic, stifling, and soul-less! But I am Métis — I refuse to let conventional dictates of Western scholarship bury me in dry dust.

In fact, I see no necessary disconnection between being a scholar and a poetic writer, or a poet. While my essays, social commentaries, and research articles have been published (in their respective eras and mediums) since 1971, only a handful of poems have been previously published. Yet, I have been a closet poet all these years. The words of poetry are closest/closeted to one's inner being. And, just as good scholarship demands excellence, good poetry demands an excellent way with words. So, it is with some trepidation (a scholar and writer's fear of the revenge of criticism) — and with not a small sense of exposure — that I submit my inner being words to the public.

Needless to say, my mother's journey (as yet unwritten) has

profoundly influenced mine. I am still in the process of writing a collection of "Mom Poems"; when I am finished, I hope to have them published. Some of these poems appear here, and I dedicate them to the memory of Maggie D. LaRocque, for whom there will always be an ache in the heart. Kih-mi-tat-ti-nan, Ama.

Incongruence

A verdant, crooked path
So earth-soft
Framed by ash and poplar
Surprised by red berries
waving from the undergrowth
Enveloped by a warm, cerulean sky
Your beauty knives through me
as a cold snap in October.
I should be holding hands
With my lover
I should be picking berries
With my mother.

Coffins Fell from the Sky

It was not night
It was not day
It was just before the moment of birth
or the moment before death
    "Our living relationship is over"
    The lover said
and coffins fell
out of the blue
    "Your mother has three months — cancer"
    The doctor said
    and cobalt coffins fell
out of the flukey sky.

The Last Journey

As expected
We threw pawfuls of earth on her casket
Wishing her well
As unexpected
The N.A.R. train whistled a farewell.
The loneliest, damned whistle I ever heard.

– – –

Train, blow a long, lonely whistle
When coming down the railroad tracks.
My mother won't be there
To meet you,
Waiting for her wayward children
At Mile 213, Chard.

Communion

Under a hot summer sun
By a sloping hill
Misty, mauve blueberries
made me stop
To pick a few
In Loving Memory
of my mother,
the fastest berry picker around
so her children would eat.

"I will never forget"
I said in Cree
in Cree I know she hears.
I ate the berries
reverantly
and drank the wine of tears
Under a hot summer sun.

Commitment

My father
Bends low
His brown face
etched
with grief.

With veined hands
He pulls the weeds
He rearranges the rocks
That held the tarp down
That covers
The flowering mound
That covers
Her death.

47 years together
And at 82 his hands
as strong as the love in his bones,
So caringly, so angrily
does he rip those weeds
To make her place of rest
As neat as her house was.

If he could
I know he would
lift her
tenderly
out of there
out of solitaire
and hold her
and caress her
in the way of their youth.

Lingering

I don't know how long it was
perhaps till the tip of my nose
lost all feeling
from the cold window
pane
I was looking Ama
for your scurrying walk
coming from the well
carrying water
bossing Bapa to cut wood.
I was looking Ama
for your green tam
pink paisley blouse
blue polyester pants
northern woman's working clothes.

What was it that brought me to this window?
nine-year sound of coffin going down.
I was looking Ama
past my orphaned gaze.

Grandmother Seasons

Who strips this tree
from its grandeur of green
to its naked gnarled grey?

Who washes this leaf
from its deep Ireland shade
to its crackled musty maize?

Who molds her face
from its soft sapling brown
to its crinkling crossroads of beige?

Loneliness

Ah Loneliness,
How would I know
Who I am
Without you?

The Beggar

i met a boozed-up, begging Indian
on the proverbial mainstreet
ten years ago
when i had no money
i would have fed him
today
i slinked off
in my unfaded blue jeans
harry rosen plaids
and turquoise rings.

then
i stole a poem.

Eulogy for Priscilla

I
1977

through the reading
of a friend's poetry
I learned about you
about us

us who don't belong
us
us brown people

who get laid
in white coffins
by pale men in black suits
in deathcars
who complain
of costs and taxes
to lay us in that cold ground.

Priscilla
I never knew you
I never knew those
who gave you your name
But I know you
I know you.
You are a thousand Indian babies
who have been waylaid
before you could grow
before even your full time in the womb.

You are a thousand of us
us
us brown people
who will never see sunshine
nor touch the warm earth
whose youthful sounds
will never be heard
whose little hands will never
have the chance
to ornament the earth
with the fragrance of flowers
the colours of rainbow
pure water of thunder rain
and fire from the sun
To make it
    graceful
    ecstatic
    elegant
    primitive —
        yes! exaltedly primitive
    breathing
    for all the world to live.

Priscilla
I never held you
I never clasped the hands
of those who buried you
But I know you
And I know those cousins too
who died by fire
who lie beside you
in that yard of death.
You are a thousand of us
us
us brown people
who die by fire
who die by water
who die by waterfire
firewater
or however —
we die.
We excel in death.

Priscilla
I never saw you
I never saw the dry tears
of your ama and kohkom.
But I know you
I know you
and your kin.

II
1990

The pacifist protestant priest tried to pray
over the sound of a DC-8
what could he say
in his anthropology ojibwe
to this cluster of six
Anishnabe
silenced
by mad modern man
angry prairie wind

coldstone Canada.
Anishnabe
silenced
over the open grave
for another of their own.

My protestant priest friend
his pacifist duties
stealing his tongue
to say his anger
grieved out a poem
to tell me
They the Anishnabe had called her
Priscilla.

Priscilla
I never knew you
I never knew those
who gave you your name
But I know you
I know you in Cree
You are a thousand of us
us
us brown people
who get laid
in white coffins
by pale men in black suits
in black deathcars
us
us brown people
who get laid
in any ground
by brown toms
by white toms
in black robes
in yellow stripes
in blue suits
in blue jeans
Naked men of many clothes
who blame us
to lay us on that yard of death.

Priscilla
I never saw you
I never saw those
who grieved for you most
But I know you
I know you
You are a thousand of us
us
us brown people
who get waylaid
before we can grow
before even our fulltime in the womb
before our fulltime in innocence.

Priscilla
You are you were
before I was born
my nohkom Mary B
my auntie julie
my sister josephine
mothers of many children I cannot name
whose many-layered songs
will never be heard
whose hands will never
have the chance
to embroider the earth
with flowers of hope
rainbow colours of peace
pure thunderrain of freedom
and firejustice from the sun
To make it
    promising
    safe
    enfranchised
    just   peaceful
           O there is no peace without justice
    clean   breathing
          for all the gentlekind to live.

Priscilla
I never held you
I never held the hands
of those who buried you
But I know you
I know you
And I know those men kin too
whose stained hands I will never hold
who bury us too
whose death-stings make them
lie beside you now

Priscilla

You are a thousand of us
us
us brown people who die by fire
who die by water
firewater
gun fire
steelblade semen fire —
or however —
we die

all laid
in some coldstone Canadian ground.

The Uniform of the Dispossessed

Sometimes I forget
so I buy soft things
surround my hard-won world
with synthetics
pastels
cushions
and Zamfir.

Sometimes I forget
so I go to theatre
surround my hard-won world
with cafes
espresso coffee
truffles
and Brubeck.

Sometimes I forget
so I buy books and brandy
surround my hard-won world
with ceramic thoughts
with silk shirts
modular sofas of burgundy
that match
    that hide
    the sorrow of the past
    the sorrow of woman
    the sorrow of the Native
    the sorrow of the earth
    the world that is with me
    in me
    of me.

Sometimes I forget
the combatant who has deserted

But I get recalled
Remembering
The uniform of the dispossessed
and like a court-martialled soldier
I cannot evade.

Sometimes I want to run
But I can't —
    I can't
            I can't.

Sweeping

I read the books
I saw the looks
I stooped to the downward
sweep

of Canada's eye
lids

cast in lead
cast in red neck

But inside my head
I burst with dreams
In my belly
I roared
In my throat
I chanted
In the wombs of my mind
I made love
with words and earth.

In the beginning was the word
and the new   story
was the earth
and the new   earth
was image   nation.

With sweetgrass I

swept up
the down wards
with sage I
swallowed
the leaded eye lids·

Joan Lavallee

Originally from the Piapot Reserve, Joan Lavallee lives in Duck Lake, Saskatchewan. She is known by her Indian Ancestors as Starblanket Woman. She is a pipe carrier: Keeper of a Woman's Pipe. She works diligently with women in prison, helping them through sweetgrass prayers, sweat-lodge ceremonies, feasts, and pipe ceremonies.

Cree Spiritual Traditions

The medicine wheel is a symbol used by Native people in North America and stands for the Universe and all natural things of Creation and the Earth. It means unit and keeps us (Native people) together physically and mentally. We get strength spiritually from each other by being together in a circle. The medicine wheel also means that everything we do moves clockwise in a circle, the Earth, the Sun, the Moon, the Seasons. There is a joining of all these forces. This is why we as Native people believe in spiritual strength in all these examples. We recognize the power in all these natural forces.

The number four is very significant to the Native people, because most things come in fours. For example, there are four directions — north, south, east, and west. There are four seasons — winter, spring, summer, and fall. There are four races of people on the Earth and four colours which are important and that have a meaning — red, yellow, black, and white.

These are the colours of the four races of people. Different tribes in North America practise their own special traditions, but there are similarities between them.

We always borrow things from other nations, and this custom is still practised today. In the Cree culture, the colours we use in ceremonies and that have special meanings are green, red, light blue, and white. Green stands for the Mother Earth and all plant life. Red for the animals and people (we call the animals our brothers and sisters). Light blue for the sky and everything in the sky, and white stands for the Great Spirit.

Four is special also, because there are four land bases on the earth and four main medicines that are found in these four geographical areas. Sweetgrass is in the west, sage to the south, cedar to the north, and fungus to the east.

We called these things incenses, because of the way they smell and the uses we were given them for.

Sweetgrass is a purification ritual that is done before you talk directly to the Great Spirit. It is burned and the smoke cleanses the body and spirit in preparation for greeting the Great Spirit and in preparation for the sacred ceremonies.

It is used in a smudge with other incenses like sage or cedar or is burned in a braid. It calls the good spirits into the ceremony, and their presence helps the people. It is used in all spiritual ceremonies like the sweat lodge. Sweetgrass was given to the Native people as one of the special gifts from the Creator and is to be used in a good way for the people.

First published in "Fighting for Our Future, Regaining our Past." Prince Albert, Saskatchewan: Pine Times Productions, 1989.

Alice Lee

Métis poet, validated by Grandmother Spirit, living in Calgary, plans to return to university full-time to complete her degree.

confession

i remember
my first confession
i was five years old

there is a snake inside you
the priest said
i must get it out
so you will stop doing bad things

i remember
his hands
under my skirt
inside my panties
looking for the snake

the way he was touching me
made me hurt inside
but i was too afraid
to say anything

he said it was my turn
to look for his snake
he put my hand on him down there
i felt a hot hardness
i tried to pull my hand away
but he held it tight

i always sleep with a light on
the dark makes me feel
a heat
in my hand

child's play

the child sits on the toy shelf
watching the sleeping doll on the bed
the child knows the doll dreams
of a tongue
in her white throat
in the dream the tongue becomes
a red hot knife
cutting into the white of her throat
to escape the doll turns her head
into the soft white pillow
but the pillow has turned red
the night has turned red
there is no escape
the doll must finish the dream
the child sits on the toy shelf
watching

Sasha shaves the unwanted hair from her legs shaves the

Sasha shaves the unwanted hair from her legs shaves the
unwanted hair from under her arms her hand feels her legs
now smooth feels under her arms now smooth her hands move to
her breasts full firm her stomach flat her hands to her
thighs and stop there feeling the unwanted flesh Sasha
thinks of the appointment tomorrow with the agent from the
man's magazine thinks of the eyes of many men looking at her
body at her thinks of the eyes looking at the flesh Sasha
reaches for the knife the fish filleting knife newly
sharpened by her reaches for the knife and slices the flesh
from her thighs from her thighs from her

you left your body as a suicide note

you left your body as a suicide note
for us all
the fetus inside a postscript
the last time I saw you
was at the wedding
a brown madonna dressed in blue
you said you were colour co-ordinated
i wasn't sure if you meant
your heart matched
your brown face
your blue dress
or both
you pointed out your lover
dancing with his pregnant white wife
your eyes were one-way mirrors
reflecting only the couple across the room

lesson

the year i turned six i borrowed my father's double-edged
razor blade and drew the blade down across my braids again
and again the blade also sliced open my fingertips i
remember red ‸ ʾin i remember wondering about white pain the
year i turned six i began school i wanted to learn to read
the first day i learned that the teachers are white the
children are white in my new book Dick Jane and Sally are
white i learned new words at recess squaw mother dirty half-
breed fucking indian i hope i know how to read soon i already
know my colours

love medicine

i met a man
i fell in love with
if he did not love me back
i thought i would die

Kohkom
was a cree woman
a medicine woman

you have to be careful
with this
she said
it is strong medicine

she showed me
how to crawl inside him
and make him love me

today he died
i was still inside him

Kohkom
never told me
how to get out

Medicine Call

The medicine man in Duck Lake, Saskatchewan, wears his thick black hair in long braids. The rest of him is a 90s white shaman. He wears designer jeans and a military green shirt. His power is like his jeans — well designed and tight. He carries his medicine magic in a leather briefcase.

A woman is waiting. They walk toward each other. He holds out his hand to her. She takes his hand in her own. Her touch is firm.

"I've been waiting for you," her voice is low.

"Come sit on my car, and we'll talk."

He leads her to a white Mazda RX7 parked in front of the Louis Riel Hotel. They climb on the hood.

He casts a glance at her. A white woman with sun yellow hair and black roots. Black roots. He identifies her as a half-breed. He senses a sadness. A suffering. Her inner person is wounded.

Today the prairie sky is a lake blue. The sun hot. Looking at the bright light around her, she feels dizzy and pulls a pair of dark shades down over her eyes. Images of the past live in her head. Bone white buffalo skulls. The Battle of Batoche and a people's defeat. A mass grave at the Batoche cemetary. Her dreams of a hangman and a white cotton hood.

Her favourite game when she was a child was when her sisters and brothers would put their arms alongside each other to see who was whitest. She always won.

She gives him her offering — a package of cigarettes and forty dollars. She originally was going to give him twenty but the leather briefcase demands double. She remembers her mother's past offerings — a package of tobacco and five dollars.

She looks down at the key chain in her hand. A glass prism dangles against her keys. The prism catches light and transforms it into dancing shadows on the car hood.

"I went to school here you know. The nuns, those bitches! Once, I had to kiss a wooden floor for two hours for swearing. I got blisters on my lips.

"I have dreams. I even dream with my eyes wide open. In the night, tall owl men stand by my bed and call to me. Red, yellow, and blue scarves fall from the darkness on to my face and I can't breathe. I saw my brother laying dead in his coffin two weeks before he was killed in an accident."

He assesses her strength. He takes a cigarette from the package she's given him, slides down from the car, and buries it in the dirt. He lights one and stands looking at her while he smokes it.

"The cigarette I buried is a gift to the spirits."

She nods.

He chooses his words, "You have a gift. This gift is a grandfather, an Indian spirit. This has been passed down to you through your Indian blood. Your dreams are visions. I'm surprised to see this in you. It rarely shows up in a woman."

She's glad she's wearing her shades. Her eyes are angry. Forty dollars has bought her these words. She controls her voice, "Why is it a grandfather spirit? Why isn't it a grandmother spirit?"

He shrugs his shoulders at her.

She turns her face to the sun. Thinks maybe she should stop dying her hair and let it grow out. Maybe braid it when it gets long enough.

"Can you stop the dreams? Can you change the visions?"

"You can't say no to dreams and visions. You can't say no to the spirits. I was taught by an old man these ways. You have to find someone to teach you. You can start teaching yourself. Come to a sweat ceremony and cleanse yourself."

She remembers the sweat lodge when she was a little girl. She used to go with her mother. She would hear the sound of drums, of spirits' voices. She would curl up and sleep in the darkness and warmth of the lodge. It was a safe place to be.

She sees him look at his watch.

She closes her eyes. She prays. To whom? A grandmother spirit.

She opens her eyes. Watches him watching her. She slides off the car and holds out her hand to him. She takes his hand and holds it in her own, "Thank you."

On the highway into Prince Albert, she stops her car and rolls down the window. She takes a cigarette out of the package and drops it out.

"For you, Grandmother Spirit. A gift from me."

Annette Lee

I am a thirty-three-year-old Plains Cree from Hobbema, Alberta. My husband Robin and I have five children. My husband is a teacher. Some day I hope to finish my education degree and teach in Hobbema. I would also like to continue writing and some day write a book of my own.

A Change in Attitude

Few people in this world are able to see and know their most significant faults. Even fewer are able to correct these flaws. Most of the time — as is the case with me — a negative character trait comes as a sudden horrible realization. The need to correct this flaw becomes very important.

My early view was that I was shunned because of my skin colour. The way I viewed others, non-Natives, affected how they treated me, and I have had a hard time overcoming this attitude. Although there are valid reasons at the root of this problem, university is not the place to harbour this negative attitude.

Nine years ago in 1979, I started my degree program. My time at school, then, was brief and not very productive. I was negative, non-receptive, pessimistic, and shy, so I isolated myself socially. I withdrew from other students because I read negative signals in our day-to-day interaction. In response to my negative attitudes, people (students, non-Natives) left me alone, to wallow in my self-pity and misery. To some degree, I did enjoy this miserable state because, deep down in my heart, I knew I was right. It was my Native heritage and skin colour that made the difference to all of these white people. How wrong I was!

I was the one who had built a wall around myself, and I could not see clearly through the wall. The protective barrier I so carefully built was not easily removed.

This problem is called a "self-fulfilling prophecy." I felt

inadequate as a person, not as a Native person. I related quite well with other Native students, so my communication skills were not totally lacking. However, I confused the two issues — being shunned by non-Natives, but not lacking Native friends — and came up with an over-simplified answer, discrimination. I used this excuse to justify my sorry lack of self-confidence.

To some extent, this problem did stem from actual discrimination. Over-sensitivity magnified what I viewed as discrimination in university. High school is where my defense mechanism and negative self-concept significantly appeared. Before I started high school, I was a typical adolescent, cheerful, unassuming, and bright. Although the discrimination was both subtle and, sometimes, blatant, I would ignore it and try to mind my own business. Had I known at the time that most of what really occurred happened because I was not familiar to most of these students, then I probably would have fared better academically. Most of the teasing — sometimes cruel — was meant to test our strength and character as people (and not as Natives). Ironically, it was when we reacted to the teasing that it became worse.

Many Native people conducted their business in Wetaskiwin. The most visible Natives were the ones who possessed all of the negative attributes — the drunk, the thief, the uneducated poor minority. Naturally, we were not allowed to forget these people, and, as a result, we were looked down on. We were made to feel that it was our fault that these people behaved the way they did; if they had only known how much we resented their presence, too! The difference was that we saw a person and the non-Natives saw a Native.

Building a wall around myself was the result of this painful experience. Now, I can look back from a safe distance and see how I had become such an insecure, guarded person. I learned to justify my (self-inflicted) isolation by thinking it was a result of my Native background.

Interestingly enough, I did have a few non-Native friends — misfits, of course — and this should have convinced me I was a worthwhile person and that my being Native didn't matter. But this was not apparent to me for many years.

I did have enough pleasant social encounters in high school to make it clear to me that I was a worthwhile person, capable of making friends when I wanted to, but I chose to be negative and remember only the bad situations.

Many Native students could not and would not put up with

these negative situations. So, they quit school. Those of us who chose to stay learned to survive in order to complete our high-school education.

To a certain extent, I and other Native students were labelled. We were dumb, slow, and inarticulate social misfits. At some point, I began to believe this myself. My self-esteem when I was a student was not very good. I went the business route and took the easier course (even though I knew that I would never want to work in an office). Personally, I have nothing against business people, but I could not see myself working in such a small space. Worse than that, I could not visualize myself as being a secretary. Too many negative traits had been attributed to these professionals to make being an office worker my goal in life. However, to avoid embarrassment, I took the courses that didn't require much effort. In consequence, I received a very poor education. Those years in high school were basically wasted. If I had not felt sorry for myself, maybe I would have been a teacher by the time I was twenty-two.

I owe a great deal of my self-confidence to my husband. He is one of the most positive people I have ever met. He is also Native, but the difference is that Robin grew up in a city (surrounded by many nationalities). He also received a lot of positive attitudes from his mother. Robin never forgot that he was a Mohawk and that he was just as good as anybody else. The exposure to one so positive is very contagious.

I believe that I have become a mature adult in the past year. This also has a lot to do with my positive outlook on life. I have learned to ignore bad feelings directed toward me. My improved attitudes have helped me to overlook other people's faults. I may not be without faults either, and I hope others will accept me as I am because, after all, no one is perfect.

Realizing that my Native background was not a detriment any more has opened the way to many new experiences for me. I feel that I belong in university. Overcoming my worst fault has been one of the most significant changes in my life; it feels good to break free from such a negative self-concept.

Laura Lockert

Twenty-six years ago, I came into this world, a baby of Native ancestry. My mother was unable to care for me, and I was adopted. This adoption did not work out, and at four years old I was again adopted. The family that chose me to be their daughter lived on a farm in Saskatchewan. These people cared for me, teaching me the values of life, and picking me up after my many falls. This family taught me to love, and it was through their love that I found my purpose in life. I was very lucky to have a solid basis for my adult life.

I have been married for eight years to a wonderful man who has also found his purpose in life. We have a beautiful six-year-old girl. Our home is in Regina, Saskatchewan.

"Voices of the Wind" was written to reflect the lives of our dads, John and Tony, who devoted their lives to farming. They are no longer with us but have left many memories as their children begin a new generation of Saskatchewan farmers.

Voices of the Wind

She sat alone at the kitchen table, desperately trying to piece together some of her life that was slowly slipping beyond reach. Without John by her side, she could no longer find the strength to salvage the world crumbling around her. It seemed as though it was only yesterday, when they would share their morning coffee break and together find answers to whatever problems may arise. His seat was empty now, as was the rest of her life. Even her dreams were gone, never to occupy her thoughts again.

She got up to put another log on the fire. It was the little fire in the stove that brought the only significant feeling of warmth to the house. My stove, she remembers, was a gift from John. He bought it when they sold the first load of wheat off the quarter by the lake. Oh, he was so proud the day they brought it home from Wilson's store. He even had to bring Mr. Wilson along to show me how to work it.

"Look Ma!" he said, "It's the top of the line. She even got a place for me to dry my mittens."

Each winter morning after that, he'd come in from choring and put his mittens in the "warming nook," as he called it. He'd then warm his cold hands over the crackling fire and wait for the morning coffee. Even when they bought the electric stove to keep up with the times, her stove from John still warmed the little kitchen on those frosty winter mornings.

Suddenly, the noise of the tractor shattered the silent winter air. She was startled by the interruption and quickly rose to go to the window like she had done so many times before. She raised her hand to wave at the figure on the tractor. The harshness of reality suddenly pulled her back. It wasn't John! John was gone and would never be back, she told herself. The activity was only the auctioneer preparing for the sale. They had told her to wait awhile after the funeral, but the bills didn't stop coming nor did the bank stop calling, just because her husband had died. They were all like vultures, she thought, the quicker they can close in, the sooner the kill. She found herself staring at the line of machinery. Each piece brought special memories to mind. She knew the equipment would all be viewed and sold. John truly valued his hard work, and you could see it in the condition of the machines. She also knew that as the implements would leave the farm today a piece of John's life would go, too. She wanted them to go, so there would be nothing left to taunt her memories.

John had always said, "It will be a sorry day in hell before I'll let them sell my life on an auction block!"

What would you have done in my place, John? she wonders. If only we had talked about one of us going. We were always too busy trying to make a life for ourselves.

She took her coffee into the living room to finish packing. As she sat on the couch, she looked up at the picture on the fireplace mantle. Somehow, she had neglected to pack it, silently hoping it too would disappear with the other memories. The third of December would have been their thirtieth wedding anniversary. This picture of a youthful young couple now held painful reminders. John had asked that she keep it out in full view, to remind them of how far they had come since their wedding day. His face had beamed with youth that day, as he carried her up the steps to begin their lives together. Her uncle had been quick to capture an image that had held them so strong for twenty-nine years. The house had been filled to the rafters with friends and relatives that day. Somehow, their plans to have a quiet wedding had been discovered. Everyone felt they couldn't have new neighbours settling in without a proper welcome.

"Where are all those friends now?" she silently asks.

Gone, she remembers, or too busy trying to hold their own lives together. The Simpson family down the road had to retire. Now, their oldest son farms the land. Then there was the Browns; they lost their farm three years ago. She recalls the tears as they said their goodbyes.

Sam Brown had held John's hand and said, "You're strong, John, fight them as hard as you can should they come knocking on your door!"

The Williamses, too, had left. They lost their crops three years in a row. First, it was the hail, and then was the unforgettable year of no rain. They were all such good people, she recalls. She knew farming held no favours for good or bad people, and with changing times the farmers had needed to take on more land. The smaller farms slowly disappeared as they were cultivated into one huge piece of land. It was now too far to walk from farm to farm like they had previously done. Everyone stuck to themselves, now, and when you did see your neighbours it was in the local store, but you were usually too busy shopping to talk or your husband was waiting for a part he'd asked you to pick up. Even their best friends, Bill and Marge Foster, stopped coming around like they used to. Marge had told her last year they were thinking of retiring.

"We just can't keep up anymore," she had said, "a little house in the city is an offer we just can't refuse."

They had shared so many good times with these people. There wasn't a weekend that went by without there being a barn dance, a church social, or some kind of neighbourly gathering. But each year the gatherings got smaller as the problems of farming got larger. Finally, the gatherings disappeared completely. Saturday nights were now spent looking over bills and trying your best to balance a tired budget.

The auctioneer's chanting voice interrupted her reminiscent thoughts. It is time, she remembers. She had faithfully promised John as he died that, should they lose their farm, she would still hold her head high and not let them see her pain. Now, she would go out and hold her head proud, knowing they had been the best farmers the land would allow.

When she got her coat, she noticed a car parked up the road from the farm. They are looking at the land by the lake, she thought. That land had once been her favourite place, but it was there they had found him, that first day of harvest. She had gone to the Sunday morning service, leaving John behind to take off the field by the house. She had wanted him to come. But he had said, "Ma, I ain't got time to get all fussed up right now. I gotta get that crop off."

She understood his answer, and when she drove out of the yard, she stuck her head out of the window.

"John, you be careful!" she yelled.

That afternoon when she got home, the field by the house was finished. There was no sign of John, but she had heard the hum of the combine somewhere off in the fields. He had mentioned to her that the wheat by the lake was testing dry. He probably was out there, she figured. She remembered John had asked her to repair his never-ending pile of ripped coveralls, so she had spent the rest of the afternoon mending, finally finishing up around five o'clock. Realizing supper would be late if she didn't get busy, she had gone to the kitchen to make John's favourite meal, cabbage rolls and perogies. He always requested a special meal the first day of harvest. It gave him a little taste of the feast they'd have when it was all over. She had finished preparing the meal around seven, and there had been no sign of John. Remembering they had picked a batch of choke-cherries, she sat down to begin the task of picking them over. Off in the distance, she had heard a vehicle coming up the road. She got up to go to the window, thinking it was John. There was a sense of urgency as the truck sped up the hill. When the truck came into view, she realized that it was not John but Bill Foster. She had run out to meet him and it was the look on his face that told her he was the bearer of bad news.

"Bill!" she said, "Is it Marge?"

"No, it's John!" he replied. "Get your coat, turn off the supper, and I'll tell you on the way to the hospital."

When she jumped in the truck with Bill, emotions controlled his voice, as he began to explain the tragedy that had descended upon them.

Bill had broken the table on his combine and had come over to ask John for help. On the way up the hill, he had spotted the combine down by the lake. He drove down to talk to John. When he approached the stopped machine, he could see John slumped over the controls. He stopped the truck and ran up the steps of the combine.

He knew it was a heart attack and quickly dragged John down the steps to the half-ton.

"He was in a lot of pain," Bill said, "but he still wanted me to cover the hopper before we left for the hospital."

Bill had told her that John didn't think he'd be coming back. The two men had arrived at the hospital as quickly as Bill's old half-ton could get them there.

Those last few miles seemed to run on forever. When they finally arrived at the hospital, the doctors were quick to tell her John had hung on till now in hope of seeing her. They expected the next few hours would be his last. She sat with him one more time, and together they looked over their lives. Together, they laughed at the happy times, and, together, they cried, remembering the bad times. They also remembered the love that had kept them so strong. Their hands were clasped tightly in each other's, and they talked no more. Words were not necessary; their eyes said all that was to be. She held on so tightly, until she felt his grip lessen; she closed his eyes, leaned over, and gently kissed him, realizing his face no longer held the lifelong strain of farming. Instead, she now saw a hint of that youthful man who had carried her into a life she would never forget.

The funeral had been small. John had asked that his body be cremated and his ashes spread over their land. Bill and Marge had been with her and together they returned John to the land he loved so much.

The next day was to be as painful as John's death. She had mentally prepared herself for the reading of John's will, but, now as she remembers, it wasn't nearly enough.

"There is nothing left," they told her. "John owes more than I think you're ready to hear."

"But he always made the machinery payment!" she replied.

"It was not so much the machinery," they argued. "John borrowed for the land you bought six years ago and hasn't made a proper payment since."

"I don't understand!" she said. "We always pulled a good crop in, except for two years ago."

"Yes," they had said, "but your profits went toward bigger bins, better equipment, and paying the interest on other small loans. Your farm was small and you were using more money than you were making. With the accumulated interest on the loans and the price of grain dropping, we had no choice but to tell John it would be his last year if the farm didn't show some kind of profit," they told her.

No wonder he was so anxious to get the combining started, she thought.

"But he was in his fifties. How could you possibly do such a thing!" she fought back.

"We are sorry," they said, as if to excuse themselves from any guilt, "but we have a notice to foreclose on the property the first of next month."

They told her she would be notified when all the accounts were settled. Then she could come in and pick up whatever monies she had coming to her. They didn't expect it to be much, but they thought she could get a little apartment in the city. It was difficult for her to accept, as these people told her what she could do for the rest of her life. She left the bank that day, only a shell of the woman she had once been. But, today, as she walked down the steps toward the people who would bid on her life, she held her head high.

The auction went fast, like she had expected, and it wasn't long before the last item on the block was the combine. They all watched her as the final bids opened and closed. She stood firm while the last part of John's life was auctioned and sold. Finally, the voice of the auctioneer stopped her from remembering any longer.

"On behalf of Mrs. Peters, we would like to thank you for coming out," he said, "but, before you go, Mrs. Peters has asked for a few minutes of your time."

The auctioneer bent to offer his hand as she climbed up on the truck. She pushed it away.

"I haven't given up yet!" she whispered.

"Dear friends," she began, "I thank you for the support you have shown John and me today. Without your attendance here today, our lives would have left this community as quietly as they came in. It is through your eyes I spread my message. John and I, like all of you, have worked long and hard on this land. We never took time off for sickness or play. We never had enough money or, for that matter, time for a vacation. We lived and dreamed farming. By city standards, we were the perfect employees, totally devoted to our jobs. But for some reason, we don't qualify for unemployment during the hard years, or the endless winters. Nor do we qualify for welfare when we can't afford to put a decent meal on the table. Farming, as you all know, is a life built on an uneven scale of chance. There are no guarantees as we plant the seeds in the spring. This is probably why we spend so much time here, waiting for the first seedlings. It is that tiny seedling that continues the balance of our lives. Now, the world markets have even found a way to make our profits half of what they should be. Still, though, we trudge on! We find new ways to survive. There is no one but you that can fully understand the hardships of farming. Nor is there anyone like you that can understand the pain and humility we feel when they take away our meagre existence. John and I were not ashamed. We know we tried our best in every possible way. If any of you should have the misfortune of losing your farm, remember you have not lost the right to be proud. Pride, to farmers, is something we don't have time to admire. When we do, it is usually lost with next year's crop. Stand tall, my friends, and remember to fight for what you believe is right."

It was with these people she found the understanding she needed. Her eyes swelled with tears as she left the truck. Once she had said her goodbyes, she returned to the temporary protection of the house.

They were all gone now, and it was getting late. She had promised to have her belongings packed by morning to take to the little apartment in the city. Her heart was empty, and she took no time to carelessly pack whatever she could into the boxes. Outside, the wind had come up, and she could feel the silent fury of a winter storm brewing. She got up to look into the darkness and watch the white fluffs of snow cluster around the light in the yard. The snow blanketed the yard in a freshness she hadn't felt in many months. The winds of the storm whispered softly into the night, and she listened closely as the calling voices seemed to beckon her to join them. She peered through the window to get a glimpse of the shadows and could hear the youthful voice of her husband. He wants me to join him, she thought.

"John where are you?" she called.

"I'm here," he answered, somewhere off in the peaceful night.

A smile came to her tired face as she looked around the empty room. There is nothing here for me now, she thought as she opened the door. Outside, it was now an utter confusion of white. She walked down the steps and the door closed abruptly behind her. It was as if she was not to return but, instead, was to join the voices of the storm. She turned for one last look and walked off into the serenity of the night. She would join hands with the spirits of the prairie winds, and, together, they would search for John. Maybe, some day, they would find each other and come to rest in the land they loved so much.

No one knows the hardships of farming better than a farmer. They fully devote their time to collect whatever the land may bring. They fight the governments and the railway closures to save not only their profession but also their lives. Their fight is getting more complex as the world turns to service those of high technology. But still they fight, as it is this fight that will eventually determine the basis for their existence.

Julia Manitopyes

I was born on the Muskowekwan Reserve and stayed for some time on my mother's reserve, Poor Man's Reserve. I will be completing my degree at university. My grandmother was Maryanne Favel.

My Kohkom

My grandmother, named kohkom in Cree, was my guardian when I lived with her on the reserve. I can still remember her sitting in her wheelchair. She looked so fragile in her overflowing, flowered dresses. Her head was always to one side, as she contemplated, or, sometimes, one crooked finger would anchor her head. Her hands were clasped together at times as she sat. The fine lines etched across her face would move as she talked or laughed. Golden penny leaves shimmered behind her as she sat outdoors in the fall. She would look so peaceful, and there was no movement except the leaves. She'd catch me staring at her, and, with a twinkle in her eye, she would call me over, handing me one of her flowered leaves to keep adding to my collection.

Kohkom's home was in the centre of all my other relations' houses. Her house, at times, was noisy with lots of talking, laughing, and joking. Silverware clanged together as the table was being set for a meal. The little kids would stand around her. One day, one little boy asked her why her fingers were all bumpy and crooked.

She replied, "My pills got stuck inside my fingers."

She had arthritis.

My kohkom astonished me at times. One evening, my friends came over. My grandmother noticed that they had been drinking as she scrutinized them from the window. When one of them came to the door, kohkom swung open the door, holding a broom in her lap and yelled at them, "Get out of here and never come around here when you've been drinking."

Another time an old man, Big Joe, came down the road, an unwanted visitor. Kohkom thought the door was locked. Meanwhile, Big Joe was slowly opening the door. With her sewing in her hands, kohkom took her needle, jabbed Big Joe in his hands, and watched him scurry down the stairs.

Kohkom's favourite outlet time was when she watched soap operas. She used to love watching "Another World" on television. One afternoon, when Iris Carrington, an actress, was stirring up trouble on the soap, I heard my kohkom muttering, "Damn trouble-maker."

My grandmother had very good eyesight. My cousin Vivian decided to take kohkom for a walk along the back roads. A few minutes later, I heard kohkom yelling in Cree, "Watch where you are going, and get me out of here."

My cousin, who has bad eyesight, had jammed my grand-mother's wheelchair, which got tangled in a bed of barbwire by the road.

Kohkom was born in 1899, which made her seventy-two years old at the time these events occurred. She was aware of things, people, and events. She was an articulate person and still is today.

One moonlit evening, my aunt and I were strolling down the road to visit a friend. Suddenly, out of nowhere we heard horses' hooves. To our left, we saw a white horse flanked by two black horses galloping toward us. We ran toward home, scared and shaking. Inside the house in kohkom's bedroom, we saw wafts of smoke emerging from the mattress. We dragged the mattress outside, tipped a barrel of water over it, and ran back in the house to check on kohkom and the children. Kohkom had accidentally tipped her candle. To this day, I feel that the horses had chased us home so we could save kohkom before it was too late. She was protected.

Sweetgrass is burned as an offering to the Great Spirit. To see kohkom praying while wisps of burned sweetgrass surrounded her, I felt comforted. Everyone within kohkom's circle felt comfort, even the newest addition. When the baby tries his first steps walking, kohkom encourages the baby to come to her by saying, "Come to kohkom."

She would make the baby say, "My kohkom, my kohkom."

Angela Maple

I come from the Standing Buffalo Indian Reserve in Saskatchewan, situated forty-five kilometres north-east of Regina. I am married and have four children. I write poetry and short stories that relate to Indian people. I spent many years in a residential school, which was very rigid and strict. Individuality was never recognized. Because of this, feelings, emotions, and opinions were suppressed, so writing became an outlet for expression.

The Cherry Picker

August was the month when the choke-cherries ripened and, like any other crops, they were harvested and prepared for winter use. The harsh spring weather produced such a poor crop last year, but Mother Earth was good this year and there was plenty. Marie intended to pick enough for two families. Her mother was frail and did not have the energy for such an activity. Crushed choke-cherries were such a delicacy for her people, especially in the winter months.

The hot August sun pushed the temperature high, making it a record. Mother Nature's splendour beamed with every colour imaginable. Her sky was clear and crystal. Birds chirped and fluttered from tree to tree, filling the air with nature's music. The berries hung in clusters like grapes, forcing the trees to bow their limbs. Soon this beauty would begin its change; the berries would have to be picked before it began.

Marie prepared herself and her four-year-old daughter Ginger for their afternoon excursion. She gathered pails and filled a container with ice-cold water. Her car packed, she drove. She decided to do her picking in the park. There was a dirt road leading up into a coulee that campers used; it was here she decided to park.

Her daughter scampered out of the car, delighting in all the pretty flowers around. Marie stood for a moment, admiring the little girl and realizing just how precious the child was to her. She could not imagine what life would be without her. The little girl called to her mother to come and see the butterflies. Marie hated to spoil her fun, but she wanted to start picking. She called to her daughter to help with the pails, and then they would look at the butterflies

Marie walked toward the bushes along the hillside, checking trees for the best place to start. She realized there had been many ahead of her, for the biggest juiciest berries had already been picked. Only the smallest and the ones infested with insects remained. She decided to look higher in the coulee for more of the choke-cherries.

As she slowly moved up the hillside, she could hear muffled voices. She assumed they were campers or others who were picking as she was. Her daughter was close behind and had already gathered a variety of flowers. Each new one she found brought more giggles of delight to the little girl. Marie had no fear in this garden of beauty and allowed her daughter to run and play freely.

She could see a station wagon ahead that was partly hidden by the bushes. A man came out of the bush near the car; she sensed he was of middle age. He carried a small white pail and another object she could not make out. She glanced around, because an uneasy feeling began at the back of her neck. She could see no one except her daughter, who was now near the bottom of the hill. She looked back toward the car just in time to see the man disappear back into the bush. The uneasy feelings grew stronger, yet she kept moving up the hillside. It was as if she were pulled by a magnet.

Suddenly, she stopped. Everything was too quiet. She could no longer hear the voices. Even the animals had become silent, as if sensing danger. She could not hear nor see her daughter, yet she could not seem to make herself call out her name. Her heart started pounding rapidly. She glanced furtively around but could see no imminent danger.

She looked back toward the car. Suddenly the man reappeared, coming into full view. He was smiling, yet it wasn't really a smile. It was more like a sneer. He started moving toward her. She soon realized what the object in his hand was. Sheer terror overtook her. She was frozen in her footsteps.

The axe head was smeared with blood. The pail and his white shirt were splattered red. She screamed, but no sound would come forth. She tried to run, but her legs would not listen. The stillness was deafening, yet she was sure her pounding heart could be heard for miles. The man was almost upon her now. Each step was bringing him closer and closer.

Ginger's screams brought Marie to her senses. She realized the danger before her and started to run. The edge of the coulee seemed a thousand miles away. She could hear his heavy footsteps behind her, hear his heavy breathing. She was sure he would catch her any moment. Her voice broke. She screamed at the top of her lungs, "Ginger! Run! Run! Go get help! Somebody help me!"

Ginger peered around the edge of the bushes. She saw her mother running toward her with the man chasing behind. She thought this was a game — a game like those her mother sometimes played with her. When Marie wanted to hurry, she would say, "Let's race!"

The little girl laughed, too excited to listen to what her mother's screams were about. She turned and ran.

Marie was terrified but quickly turned to see where her attacker was. He wasn't as close as she had thought. The man ran with a limp. She felt herself falling. As she hit the ground, her pails went tumbling. She screamed in pain as her ankle twisted. She tried to get up and run. She stumbled and fell again. She turned and faced her attacker. He was but a few feet away. He towered over her, raising the axe to strike. She could see the fresh blood dripping off it. She screamed with all her might.

She sat upright, her heart pounding. Her clothes were damp with perspiration. It took a second to realize what was happening.

It was the nightmare again!

Diane Maytwayashing

In 1965, I was born in Portage La Prairie, Manitoba. My family and I lived in Winnipeg since I was the age of two. I am the eldest of all my siblings, which are two younger brothers and a sister who is the youngest and eight years my junior.

Today, at the age of twenty-five, I live my life as a single parent with one child. My daughter Jacquelyn is five years of age.

The University of Winnipeg is where I attend school, and my goal is to achieve my bachelor of arts. Along with several terrific friends, my boyfriend of two years and I have started our own business. My first real love is writing, which I work at constantly in a personal journal every day, in letters to many friends throughout Canada, and, in the little spare time I have, I write everything from a novel to short stories. To write a poem sometimes takes ten minutes or ten days.

My life is busy and enriched with joy, happiness, and good people. I live a fruitful and fulfilled life. Every day, I continue to work to reach for the stars and to reach the peak of living. My dream is to be a rich and successful woman.

Conversation

Wait, wait for a call
Light up a cigarette, turn to stare at the wall
Wish the telphone would ring
It will not be long, it will be soon
Listening to the radio, on plays a sad tune

In the beginning, just another
Suddenly, to realize the need for each other
Began to call the more
Fell in love with a voice even more
Called from a street phone, gave away the clue
Should there be one day, our lives to share

Could not understand what is on our minds
Question ourselves, what is real love

Sensitivity would not be found in another
Could it be the trait comes in a family type
Losing the home is a strong fear
In our lives, we take these great chances
Someday to be in each other's arms
Too difficult to resist the loving charms
Let us make our dreams come to a reality

Time will tell, the telephone may ring
And my telephone lover shall announce
For our lives together to begin

Horror Movie

Earlier this evening, I watched a television program — a movie. Unfortunately, this movie was a true story. I held back my tears, although it was very difficult to do so. My heart bleeds for this poor woman and her child. It scares me to believe such tragedy exists in our world. It scares me even more to believe that it could happen to me. I read about these tragedies in the paper, in books, and watch it on the television in the news and in movies, and hear about it on the radio and on the street.

I remember, long ago when I was a young child, my mother, my aunt, and I were standing next to a hospital bed. The woman lying on this hospital bed had massive bruises throughout her entire body and wrapping around her chest. I could not recognize the woman, until my mother and my aunt began speaking to the woman. It was another aunt of mine. I could not say a word to her, because I was too young to quite understand. What I do remember was my badly beaten aunt telling my mother and my aunt how severe her injuries were. Several broken ribs and a collapsed lung is what I could recall in the conversation.

As a teenager, I still could not understand these tragedies. One day as I just came home from school, my mother gave some shocking news to my ears, by saying that my girlfriend was just beaten to death the other day by her common-law husband. My own mother could see my grief and pain. I took a walk to sort out my thoughts and that's the day I began to have some knowledge of the abused woman.

The movie in many ways opened my eyes. In this movie, a woman is constantly beaten up by her husband. She is always running away from him. He tracks her down and continuously finds her. When he finds her, it's the same threats — hurt and kill. Many times, or shall I say all of the time, she calls the police.

What do they do? Not a thing. Why? Because it's just a family dispute. With the police, well this sounds very familiar each time. Why does it look as if the police are very ignorant to these types of violent crimes? It just makes me so angry that I wish I could stop these tragedies from happening to all women.

In the movie, he finally catches up to his helpless wife. As she begins to run away, he grabs her by pulling her hair and hysterically stabs her back many times until she falls to the ground. He stabs, slaps, punches, and kicks her body. She looks like a helpless rag doll that's being destroyed. The sick bastard had slashed her right across the neck, as a policeman, a few neighbours, her child, and friends looked on in panic and none of them helped. He jumped on her head a few times as she lay there covered in blood and paralyzed. Her injuries were: a broken neck, approximately seventy stiches along her neck, and fifty stitches from her mouth right to her cheek. She survived, but, today, she lives her life paralyzed on the left side of her body.

What are we women to do about these monsters? These monsters tell us that they love us, then we hopelessly fall into their traps. We give them everything, our love and beautiful children, and they give us hurt and pain and take away our precious lives.

War Movie

As I sit here and watch men kill men, women, and innocent children, I weep — blood-thirsty bastards, these young men become in a war. In a small village, a young Asian girl, she looks about eleven or twelve years old; she is raped by four ugly, bastard, pigs — soldiers. A young Asian man, his head is bashed off with a rifle for no good reason. There is one soldier who writes a lot, and he wonders why and what he is doing killing other humans. He's emotional and sensitive. Of course, there is the bully soldier, the crazy individual, who not only kills what is called the enemy. The bully also kills his so-called fellow men. Every day, some go insane. Every day, some cry, and there are some who forgot or unlearned to cry. The dead soldiers are thrown into a large hole, just thrown in this massive hole, and a large truck filled with dirt comes along to fill the human hole. The so-called sensitive soldier then says to himself, "In a war, we don't kill the enemy, we kill ourselves, because we become the enemy to our own self."

And the movie ends with this particular soldier flying away to safety and to home. There is a large printing that appears on the television screen, and it reads, "Dedicated to those who fought in the Vietnam War."

I wipe my tears, blow my nose, and lock away my personal fears. But, I can't help thinking of this past, so many years ago and yet not so long ago. I begin to think of my precious child, her future and her children's future. And all I could do is pray that there will never be a war in my child's lifetime.

Crying Out

Yesterday, I thought I heard an animal cry out in agony, as if it were in a tremendous amount of pain. It sounded so frightening and threatening. I began to feel my heart beating faster and faster, the blood racing and rushing rapidly throughout my body. I walked home as quickly as possible. Just as I reached the apartment building, I was able to catch my breath and calm down.

Inside of my apartment, I sat down on the sofa to relax my body from the shock. I thought hard about the eerie sound, and I could hear it faintly in my mind. I made myself a cup of coffee and turned on the radio. The dial on my radio is always situated on my favourite classical music station. A very strange piano solo came on. I walked across the room, and I slowly opened the patio doors. I stepped outside and, suddenly, sheer horror came over me. Shivers ran up and down my spine. I could feel my tears, my warm tears on my stiff cold face. Such a horrible and sad feeling had just come over me. I stood on the patio, I looked up at the sky, and I could see that the colours of it were the colours I was feeling. The sky was the colour of a warm blue, and some parts of it were a disturbing grey.

My heart felt as if it had fallen down to my stomach. I could not hold back my tears beginning to fall from my eyes once again. A lump in my throat was uncontrollable, my jaw was now becoming numb, and the muscles on my face twitched. My knees felt very weak, and my entire body felt so heavy that I could barely hold myself up. I put both of my hands on the railing to get a grip and to balance my limp body. In great agony, I cried out like a wounded animal. My pain was deeper than my flesh. It was an animal I heard, it was I who cried out in agony.

To this very day, I sometimes wonder if that frightening cry I had heard earlier was some kind of warning. I believe it was, because when I look back I remember in that time of my life I sometimes felt great emotional pain.

Sunshine and Rainbow
(For Jacquelyn)

You brighten and colour my life

When you are with me
I feel the warmth of love
Like the warmth of sunshine
Sunshine coming in through a window

When the rain is pouring down hard
When lightening is flying through the air
There's the loud sound of frightening thunder
It's the horror I can no longer bear

You are that bright ray of sunshine
Coming out through the clouds
You are that colourful rainbow that is there at the end
                    of the storm

My sunshine, you brighten up my life
My rainbow, you colour up my life
My child, I love you and I need you for life

Linda McDonald

I am thirty-two years old, born and raised in Watson Lake, Yukon. Obtained a bachelor of education from the University of Alberta. Taught for several years, returned to university (Carleton) to work on my master's degree (still in progress). Presently working for Health and Welfare Canada, Medical Services Branch. Also, I am President of the Yukon Indian Women's Association and am involved in other committees and boards involving Indian education.

I am a Kaska (Athapaskan) and a member of the Liard Indian Band.

Adela Stone Watson-Chedudi

Adela was born in the mid-1880s in the Toad River area in northern B.C. Adela was the daughter of Old Stone, a well-known Kaska leader and medicine man. The Stone family was a large one, and they used extensively hundreds of square miles in what is now north-eastern B.C. and south-eastern Yukon. The Stones enjoyed a good yet difficult life, as they had the freedom to move about the land they knew so well.

In the 1920s, things began to change for Adela's family. She lost many of her brothers and sisters and other close relatives to influenza, whooping cough, and tuberculosis. The few remaining family members began to disperse to areas north as far as Ross River and south to Fort Nelson. Adela moved to Lower Post, where she met Frank Watson in 1912.

Frank was a prospector from Tahoe City, California, on his way to the Klondike goldfields. Frank did not make it to Dawson City. He married Adela and built a log cabin on the banks of the Liard River a few miles from Lower Post. A few years later, they moved to Winded Lake, one mile north of the present-day Watson Lake airport.

Adela and Frank had four children: Asnow, Edna, Bob, and Alice. Adela and Frank raised their children according to their traditional lifestyle. The children became adept in hunting and trapping skills and were expected to assist their parents from a very early age.

Frank died of pneumonia in 1938, in Fort St. John, B.C. Adela remained at Winded Lake, as did her children.

Adela saw rapid changes in the area in the 1930s and 40s, with the construction of the Alaska Highway, the building of the Watson Lake airport, and the influx of many southerners. As the town grew and non-Native influences were thrust upon Native people, Adela continued to live according to her Kaska values. She spoke Kaska at all times and spent many hours relating stories of her youth to her grandchildren. Even in her nineties, Adela set rabbit snares, chopped wood, and sewed moccasins.

Adela worked very hard all her life and did not ask anything of anyone. The fact that the Indian agent designated her as non-status because of her common-law marriage to Frank Watson did not concern her. In her mind, she was always Indian, always a Kaska, and, most importantly, a mother, grandmother, and great-grandmother.

Few people in the town of Watson Lake, with the exception of the old-timers, knew of Adela. Her name does not appear in history books, nor is she acknowledged anywhere in Watson Lake.

However, to her family she remains the great matriarch; one who survived hardships and epidemics and resisted the force of an encroaching foreign people and culture. In spirit, Adela is still very much alive; her strength and resilience is a legacy, a reminder to her family to remember who they are and where they come from.

Adela passed away in the Watson Lake Hospital on 23 March 1987.

First published in *Shakat*. Whitehorse, Yukon, Summer 1989: 40.

Their Time

I heard you went to visit your gramma the other day.
She was glad to see you,
and greeted you with open arms and a smile.
"I'm glad to see you grandson, where have you been?"
"Oh, I'm working now, gramma. And you know how it is,
I have no time."

She fed you rabbit stew and bannock.
You ate quickly and told her she was a great cook.
You were still chewing your last piece of bannock as you
dashed out the door.
"See you, gramma!"
Her tiny figure stood in the doorway and watched long
after your truck disappeared around the corner.

Weeks flew by and became months before you reappeared
on her doorstep.
After she fed you, your gramma started to tell you a story.
She said, "Did I ever tell you about the time your grandpa
and I . . ."
Her words were lost somewhere between her mouth and your ears.
Your thoughts were elsewhere, a different place
a different person.
When she finished her story, you stood up and said,
"Gee, gramma, that was a good story."
She answered, "I wish I could see you more often, grandson."
You nodded and said, "Well you know how it is, gramma,
I have no time."

Last week, we lost a great person.
Your gramma passed on to a new life.
Our whole village showed up at her funeral,
to show their respect.
I saw you standing by her grave, your head hanging down.
You did not say one word, and yet I knew your thoughts.
They rang out loud and clear and shook the poplars and
the willows and echoed in the valley.
"Oh, just one more day gramma, give me just one more day
with you.
Let me hear one more story, gramma, and see your smiling
face, one more time."
The truth tore at your heart, and caused your tears to flow,
they fell to the ground and mixed with the freshly turned
gravel at your feet.
No more time.
I know your sadness, I know your sorrow.

It happened to you, it also happened to me, she was my grandmother, too.
What is important?
Your time.
My time.
Whose time?
We must never forget — their time.

Leonora Hayden McDowell

Age seventy-one, widow, nine children, non-status, retired. Artist, writer. Raised white, Cree souled. Little to be said. "Where Eagles Soar" says it all. I wait the day.

Where Eagles Soar

When my soul is ready to
Leave this poor shell
Of shrivelled skin and aching bone,
My last request to go back home
Where tall trees grow and eagles fly.
Back to Hills and Kyrie's nest
My crying soul seeks by to rest.
Spread my ashes on Four Winds' Peak.
Kyrie will come. . . . Together we'll seek
The blue beyond. Let my soul
Soar with the eagles when I die.

I am Cree

My lips touch on the water;
It moves with sensuous flow.
My hand I place on out-thrust rock.
It warms with phosphorescent glow.
I twine my arms with branch of tree
And feel life's tremble.
              I am Cree.

The moon I worship
And call each star by name.
With grass and breeze I play
A laughing, running game.
Great manitou gives with grace
Each thing a spirit and a face.

I am Cree.

Old Neep-a-Wa Dies

Between the Moon of Wild Rice
And the Geese-going Moon
I shall return to my people.
The way has been long, and
My paddle heavy in the water.
Red leaves hang on the sumach
Like fur on the little red fox.
South wind has gone behind the mountain.
Northern warnings call geese to come.
I am weary . . . my people wait.
Around the river bend, beyond the ridge of pine
Time hangs suspended.
Old paddle, thin canoe, and I go Home.

Windsong

My People talk to the winds . . .
Winds of the four seasons;
And voices of the winds come back.
The West wind like moccasins in the grass,
East wind a rain-drenched crying child
Lost in the canyons of a Pass.
A strong man, Giant of the North,

Drums big talk, fierce, and wild,
But South wind, soft from over the hill
Chinook, chinook, tender and mild
Sings a sage-brush lullaby . . .
   Windsong of my People.

Chinook

In the lodges of my people
Time was heavy. . . . Winter's fleeting
Was too slow. The hills, like steeples
Of the village church below
Lay inches deep with winter snow.

Restless are the spirits of my people,
Chained by North wind's icy grip,
Too chill to hold, yet not so bold
To venture in the path
And face the last of Winter's wrath.

Beyond the dawn, and over the hill
Came sweet Chinook, young child of Spring,
Her breath soft-scented of the sage
That grows so old and sere with age;
The gift of life eternal its heritage.

Out of the lodges came my people
To live, to breathe again,
And like the sage, once dull and grey
To grow with Spring into the day
When winter's cares will wear away.

Give Me the Spirit of the Eagle

Lift my spirit to the midnight heavens
That I may feel sweet timeless space.
Keep in my heart a sky-borne vision,
Keep my body filled with grace.
Let my spirit be free as Kyree,
Strong as the span of her wing.
Let me be fearless of effort to fling
My spirit to the blue unknown.
Let me be akin to Kyree
And dare to reach into the wind.

Heartbeat

When nights are long, and sleep
Is far away, time is like
A thousand miles of footsore road.
I lie upon the dew-damp earth
And hear the heartbeat of
The roots beneath. They keep
A rhythm of their own — a chant
Like that the tom-toms made,
And I find surcease to the ache of
Solitary, and bless this peace.
This beat of Nature's pulse
Became a measure kept
By those who lived so long
Ago, and chanted by the
Camp-fire glow. Now I need
Their comfort, so I heed,
And hear the tom-toms
In my heart.

Ann McIver

I was born in West Germany. I am a nursing student and will graduate in the fall 1990. I started writing in junior high for the school paper and entered writing competitions throughout junior high and high school. I hope to make writing a second career.

The Eagle

As the sun rose, its first rays softly danced on the dew-covered forest. The breeze softly blew through the forest, making the leaves move as if they were shivering from the dampness of the dawn.

Slowly, a head poked out of the door of the canvas tent and stopped to listen to the welcoming call of the animals. The young man stepped out of the tent on to the damp earth, scratched his head, and pushed back his dark hair from his face. He looked back into the tent and asked his mother if he could start the fire.

"Yes, gather some twigs and watch the matches, that is all we have. Oh, Daniel, fetch some water, too."

With pail in hand, Daniel headed to the small lake for water. He knelt on the edge and filled the pail and stopped to look at his reflection in the water. How his hair had grown. It would soon be time for another haircut before school started. Oh, how he hated the thought of going back to that convent and those mean nuns. He remembered when he spoke Cree, the nuns would wash his mouth out with soap and water and tell him to never speak that language again and that he could only speak English. Daniel shivered at the thought and realized he should return to the tent before his Mom came looking for him.

He listened to the crunching sound his footsteps made as he walked through the field. Daniel liked to make the crunching sound turn into drumming, and then he would sing his song that he made up for Mother Earth. Soon the drumming stopped and he started to wonder why. Daniel heard the cry come from above — the cry that one rarely ever hears. He slowly looked up through the clearing of the trees and watched as the eagle circled overhead. Daniel put the pail of water down and raised both his arms toward the sky.

"My Brother, what can I do for you?"

Closing his eyes, Daniel heard the voice in the wind.

"My Brother, I am bothered by thoughts of my people losing their way of life and beliefs. Walk with them and help guide them through the hard times and help them enjoy the good."

Opening his eyes, Daniel saw the eagle rise out of sight.

"I will, my Brother, I will."

Clare E. McNab

I am Métis (also treaty through marriage). I am thirty-two years old and a mother of two children. My past experience has been mainly in the health field as a community health nurse. In the last seven years, I have become very interested and involved in traditional health and healing.

I have recently expanded my awareness through art and writing. Mostly, I do them for my own pleasure and expression. When I write, it is from my heart, so I do not consciously control the structure or lines.

The Porcupine Quill Saga
(On Being a Traditional Indian)

Part 1

After visiting my friends and relatives on the reserve, I renewed my resolve once again to learn how to quill. My husband's cousin's wife is a creative and artistic woman. When I asked where she found the quills used in making earrings, she said, "Whenever we travel, we carry a gunny sack, and when we see a dead porcupine on the road we put him or her in the sack and bring it home."

Sounds easy enough.

As I commuted about sixty miles to work, I thought my chances of coming across a dead porcupine were pretty good.

How right I was.

One day, I was driving from Muskowekwan Reserve over to Gordon's on the back road. I see ahead a lump on the side of the road.

My heart quickened, here was my chance.

Her words echoed through my head, "If you find one, they have about four thousand quills, enough to last you a lifetime."

I pulled up to a stop and got out.

On the side of the road before me was this round hairy object. No quills . . . well, maybe he threw them.

Upon closer examination, there were many quills but all lying down and covered with coarse hair.

To my dismay, as I reached out to pick him up, my hand began to quiver. My stomach rolled once.

"Come on Clare. Don't be silly. This porcupine is dead."

Damn. I couldn't bring myself even to touch this dead thing, let alone put it in the trunk of my car.

With all my energy, I scraped around the head with my shoe. A few quills fell out, so I scraped some more. I zipped home with my loot — twelve quills.

Part 2

A lady at work told me she had something for me to read. As usual, I totally forgot. A few months later, she asked, "What did you think of that article?"

I'm having trouble even remembering what she said it was about.

"Oh!" she says, "It's about quill work. I'll bring it again and show you."

So the following Monday, she brought it. I had some time to read, so I read through it. Hmm . . . interesting. I quickly copied it (at work, of course) and put it in my purse.

When I got to my desk and sat down to really read it, WOW!, I *need* some porcupine quills. I live in the city now, so it is a bit more difficult to find dead porcupines.

One day after Toastmaster's, I was talking to my friend and actually showed her some quill-work pictures. She said, "I travel a bit, I'll keep my eye open for you."

She had to run, and I put it out of my mind.

Another lady at work was arranging for the sale of a canoe carrier for the car (we had just bought a canoe), when I mentioned my need for quills.

"Oh, we planted some trees at our cabin, and the porcupines have been eating the soft small leaves — the trees have almost died, so my husband's nephews are going to shoot the porcupines. I will tell my husband to save them for you."

"Great, I would really like that" (just as long as I don't have to touch them!).

"What do you do with them?"

"Well, you can skin them, and then you just keep the hair and the quills."

"Oh, my husband can skin. I'll ask him to do it for you."
Now, all I have to do is wait.

At the next Toastmaster's meeting, my friend tells her tale of the porcupine. She and a friend were going out to Regina Beach, so she put a garbage bag in the trunk. Sure enough, on the way out, she finds a dead porcupine. She stops the car, and she and her friend get out.

"Now, Clare told us to pick it up underneath — it is soft and has no quills there."

She tries to lift it, holding it under the head, but it is HEAVY. Suddenly, all this comes together, blood . . . guts . . . death. She can't do it. (Thank God, what would I have done with it?) Her friend decides to give it a try. She gets poked with three quills in her finger. They both get back in the car. Her finger begins to swell. My friend grabbed it and sucked on it, and the swelling went down.

The porcupine stayed on the road.

What next?

Part 3

While relating my story to friends, they asked me questions about porcupines. Here we go!

1. Do baby porcupines have teensy porcupine quills?
2. Are baby porcupines born with quills?
3. Once porcupines throw their quills at another animal or object, do they grow back?
4. How fast do porcupines walk or run (or waddle)?
5. What do porcupines eat?
6. Why do porcupines cross the road?
7. Some statistics
    a) How many porcupines die each year in traffic accidents?
    b) How many dogs require care of their faces to remove quills?
    c) How many porcupines have narrow escapes from traffic accidents?
8. How do porcupines make love?
9. Where do porcupines live?
10. Do porcupines have any friends?
11. Do porcupines have relatives?
12. Do porcupines bathe (i.e., go swimming)?
13. Do porcupines talk?

Well, it finally happened. After Uncle Louis's funeral in Swift Current, on 20 January 1989, I was driving around the lake (Lac Pelletier) with Mom, Dad, and Uncle Joe. Guess what's lying on the road, close to where Mom lived as a young girl (fitting, somehow). We borrowed a box from Joe and Cookie LaSalle. and my Dad put the frozen porcupine into the box. WOW!! I can't believe it! My dream is about to become reality!

So I put the porcupine in the trunk of my car and bring it home. Mona and Enola are set to help me out and come over Monday after work. Enola asks, "Is he still frozen?"

"Yes."

"Well, we can't skin it, because the skin will crack." (She is our "expert" on skinning.)

I brought the porcupine in the box, put it in a garbage bag, and kept it in the house to thaw.

The next night, only Mona is able to make it. I scrape off the table outside (two feet of snow with Christmas lights frozen in it), cover it with newspaper, take the porcupine out of the bag and the box, and throw him on the table. We will have to work quickly, as the sun is setting.

Where is Mona?

So I grit my teeth, grab the knife, poke into the soft throat, and start cutting toward the bum. GROSS! Slowly, I work the knife, pulling back the skin as I cut. Finally, thank God, Mona comes. She gets right into it, bare hands pulling on the skin and hoping it will separate from the body. I got poked several times by quills. We exchanged knife and scalpel (of course, Biology100) as we skinned.

Mona says, "What should we do about this?" pointing to the front leg.

"We don't need the arms. Cut around them," I tell her.

Laughter — what porcupine has arms?

Finally, it is skinned. We have left a lot of quills on the neck and head and lower back and tail. We put the carcass back in the box, back in the bag, and put it under the table, in case we need it later.

I put the hide into the scrub pail and go into the house. I quickly make supper, while we put shampoo in the water and let the hide soak (don't ask, I was told to do it).

After supper, we are up in the bathroom, with the hide, trying to pull out the quills. Some come out very easily, others have to be ripped out. After two to three hours of pulling, we have two ice-cream pails full. The hide is still less than half done. We are very tired. I put the hide in a box and put it outside, in case we need it later.

The quills had to dry and were mixed with hair. I laid some newspapers on our card table and spread them out, poking myself several times in the process. My hands hurt, my knees hurt, my back hurts from bending over the tub. A common comment, "There must be an easier way."

The next evening, I sat by my quills sorting — four different sizes, hair for roaches, and the fine hair into the garbage. After two hours of sorting, I have done one very small corner of the table. There must be an easier way.

Mona offered to help sort, I packed up an ice-cream pail and sent it to her. I still have a table full of quills to sort. I gave it one more try, about two hours again. Still it made no noticeable difference. Already, I must have sorted close to a thousand quills.

Last week, Thursday, I was getting ready to work. Ivan got up, scratching and pounding his chest (jokes!). I am just about ready to leave, and he says, "What about those quills, when are you going to do something about them?"

I said, "I've been working on it, it takes a long time."

He says, "Well, hurry up or they'll be in the garbage. I don't see why you didn't leaving the f-ing thing on the road in the first place." What could I say? I slammed the door and went to work.

I taught a group at R.J. Davidson, and I made them make quill earrings. The class was a success, except for a few men who didn't want to do women's work. Their loss, and the group, and mine.

And it continues . . .

Discrimination and Prejudice

I've been having mixed feelings lately.
I have been blessed with
unusual looks.
For years I used to find myself
plain and, on bad days, ugly.
Why wasn't I given the
beautiful dark hair and good
looks of my older sister, or
the fair thick hair and
blue eyes of my younger sister?

Here I am in the middle.
Hair that is not dark or light.
Features that are mixed, large
nose, high cheekbones, fair
skin, double chin. Eyes that
can change from yellow to
green, the black spot inside
very small or very large.

How I hate the word "Moonias."
It is said with a sneer.
Laughter, poke, "I thought you
were 'mooniaskwew.'"
I have to work very hard
to be accepted. Why can't I
be me?

Deep inside I feel tempted.
To hell with these Indian
and Métis who are so petty
and discriminate against one
another. You have too much
education, you'll never fit in.
Who made you an elder?
You are not qualified to
talk about that.

Where do I fit? As I
went home a few weeks ago
and drove alongside the lake,
I had a feeling of incredible sadness.
I could feel my grandfathers and
grandmother there, with no
one left to need or ask for their help.

When we reached our old house,
I had fun exploring
the hills and the buildings
with my two children. Whatever
spirits were there were soothing
and reassuring. This was where I belonged.

I picked some rocks,
so I could take some
of that feeling with me wherever
I may go.
I know who I am.
I just have to stop proving
it to everyone else.
 DAMN!!

Granny Comes to Visit

When I was about seven or eight, my granny came to visit. It was Christmas. Our family was very excited to see our granny, because she lived in Edmonton. In my whole life, I had seen my granny three times.

Mom told us many stories about her life as a child and how her mom was then. She had fine qualities — pride, cleanliness, fierce independence, and inner strength. She sounded full of life, exuberant, and exciting. She was the best jigger in the country, and, at house parties, other Métis people would stand aside and watch her. She fought with her in-laws, her husband, and French people in the nearby community to have the best for her children. She was a seamstress, so even when times were hard her family was well dressed. She would bead my grandfather's tobacco pouch and his winter gauntlets, which he invariably lost or sold.

My mom also had many of the qualities that she used to describe in her mother, so we were eager to be close to this fine person. My mom hadn't seen her mom for fifteen years and had only made contact two years ago. Most of their communications were by letter for those fifteen years.

The day of her arrival was stormy. She came by bus and mom and dad went to town to pick her up. They brought home a wizened, soft, elderly lady (she was fifty-one). The years had not been kind to my granny.

I was disappointed in my granny. The fine woman my mom had described was gone. In her place was this small shell.

I still wanted to be close to my granny. We took her to town to visit relatives. When it was time to pick her up, I got to sit beside her. I remember being astonished to smell liquor on her.

My granny was an alcoholic. She was consumed with finding her next drink. When she was sober, the fine qualities would peek out, only to disappear when she took one drink.

After that Christmas, my granny returned to Edmonton, where she died in February. I have wished for the rest of my life to have had a granny. If I had to choose one, it would be the one my mother used to tell me about.

Today, I have found other elders to respect as my grandparents. The vacant hole I felt for years is slowly being filled with the wisdom and love that I had missed out on.

Robin Melting Tallow

Métis, this word immediately brings to mind a duality, a combination of cultures, traditions, and life-styles. I am on a personal journey of discovery, learning to realize, integrate, participate, and accept all aspects of myself. I am coming to terms with "Robin," weaving my culture throughout my roles as student, career woman, wife, mother, and friend. I am absorbing, developing, and growing each day. This is who I am, this is Robin Lorraine.

The Patchwork Quilt

Sometimes, late in the evening, my husband and I would lie together in the darkness of our bedroom. It was never completely dark, because I was afraid of the dark, and each night my fear would become a point of dissension between us. However, he would eventually relent, and I would turn the closet light on. If I closed the door all the way, there wasn't enough light, and if I left it open there was too much and he couldn't sleep. So we would compromise, and I would prop the closet door open with his cowboy boot. After our customary disagreement was settled, we would pull the comfort blanket over us, right up to our eyes. The blanket was really a patchwork quilt made for my husband by his mother for his thirty-ninth birthday. Our girls had christened that precious quilt "the comfort blanket," because it had brought them comfort on the days they were sick and during times of sadness. With only my eyes visible, I would snuggle up to him, resting my head between his shoulder and his arm and we would lie quietly, lost in our own thoughts and dreams. Eventually, we would take turns talking. Usually one of us had something on our mind that needed discussing, and I would always feel so safe in his arms under that blanket, with my three inches of light gently playing on the bedroom floor. Our hopes and fears found refuge in that room from ridicule or laughter. Sneaking a look at that dusky room from the shelter of my bed, I could see the outline of the desk in the left-hand corner of the room, and I would feel pride because I had saved for months to buy it for him and he was overjoyed to have a private place all of his own, and to the right I could make out my old stuffed lion sitting on the laundry basket and my tired old red Teddy bear limply propped on his back. They were the only possessions left over from my childhood. I was relieved to have some sort of visible evidence that I had once been a child and that it wasn't just some trick of my imagination. Lying there beside him it was hard to believe that I was not a young woman any longer. I felt robbed. Childhood had stolen by me so quickly that I could hardly remember it. I could scarcely believe myself at times. I had actually begun to day-dream about grandchildren. I didn't want to be a grandmother, not yet, anyway. Imagine some cute little creature calling me granny. However, I do believe that the maternal instinct has a mind of its own and that this entity had begun to toy with my heart and soul. I longed to hold a tiny, bundled, sweetly powdered form in my arms once more. But, a crazy thought struck me and made me giggle out loud (which caused my husband to give me one of *those* looks). How could I tell my grandchildren that I was afraid of the dark. This was ridiculous. I could just imagine them taunting me, "Granny's afraid of the dark, granny's afraid of the dark!"

OK, I thought, so I am getting slightly ahead of myself. Maybe I can still squeeze in a few more years of being Mom and that "sexy lady" (some days). Looking at my husband's profile, I felt a warm tenderness surge through my body and I realized that I really was too young to make love to a man by the name of grandpa. Now, if only the kids will co-operate!

Marlene Millar

Marlene Millar was born on 14 October 1949. She is married to George, who is the feed manager at Millar's Feed and Fertilizer and with whom she has three children, Sandra (age nineteen) and Jason and Dale (age sixteen). Until the age of six, Marlene Millar lived on Mistawasis Reserve in Saskatchewan. She is now involved in mixed farming, running a new and used store and upholstery business, and free-lancing for the local paper, *The Northwest Eagle*. Her post-secondary education is in sociology (government administration of social services).

The Death of Wooden Leg

The defense lawyer thrust the plaster skull at Sarah Spiritmaker's face.

"How long did you know Philip Bear? When did you last see him?"

Sarah gripped the sides of the witness stand and stared at the gaping mouth and hollow eyes of the skull. She closed her eyes when she saw the gash in its bony forehead. The interpreter repeated the lawyer's questions and awaited the Cree medicine woman's reply.

The lawyer placed the skull beside the wooden leg that lay on the exhibit table. This man who wore a white scalp talked for Daniel Darkwater, accused murderer of Philip Bear. Philip was known to the Indians as Wasee-ki-can, which means Wooden Leg. He was given this name as a child after he lost his leg in a bear trap.

The interpreter began to speak, "She says that she had known Philip Bear all her life. The last time she saw him was about a year ago, your Honour."

The judge leaned forward and spoke to the interpreter, "Tell the story in her words."

"She and her man, Alec Beaver, were picking cranberries on the shores of Muskrat Lake. The berries were so plentiful that red juices ran off their moccasin rubbers. They filled all the containers they had brought and that's when she spotted a fish crate in the reeds. She says she thought they could wash it out and pick more cranberries to sell. They needed the money to buy groceries. She sent Alec in to get the crate but he wasn't strong enough to free the crate from the sandy bottom."

Sarah listened to the Man of Words tell her story. The white man's language sounded guttural and strange. The man who wore the white scalp had spoken in a thunderous voice and had pounded Wasee-ki-can's wooden leg on his table.

The interpreter continued, "She goes on to say that she paced back and forth along the shore, disgusted with Alec's efforts. Then, she noticed an old wooden boat drawn up on the shore, half hidden with brush. She persuaded Alec to help her drag it to the water's edge. Then she climbed in, parted the reeds and paddled with her hands out to the crate. Sorry, your Honour, I can't understand her mumblings, something about . . . yes . . . women get the dirty work."

He stopped and wiped his forehead.

Sarah listened to the people laughing in the courtroom. Were they laughing at her or at the skull and wooden leg of Wasee-ki-can? She saw Daniel Darkwater smile at the man that had held Wasee-ki-can's skull, his fingers stuck through the gash, parading it before the courtroom. This foolish man did not seem to understand it was dangerous to play with the spirit's possessions. Daniel must know that Wasee-ki-can's spirit would seek revenge.

Sarah remembered that day at Muskrat Lake when she had paddled out to the crate. She, too, had been unable to pull the crate free but had managed to tear up a board that was nailed across the top. She had peered into the crate but couldn't see anything. She had leaned forward and sniffed cautiously, the smell of decay was strong and pungent.

She had reached carefully into the crate, touching something that felt like cloth. She had grasped a corner and tugged it out. At once, she recognized a blanket she had made for Wasee-ki-can the year before.

She remembered the cold fear that had settled on her heart, but she had to know the truth. She had reached into the crate again, her hand searching inside the blanket. She had pulled out something soft and fuzzy . . . a handful of human hair. Sweat formed on her brow, but she had reached in again and groped along the blanket until she felt the wooden leg. Aiyee! Wasee-ki-can!

Alec Beaver told the court how he decided to snowshoe into
the trapper's cabin to help Wasee-ki-can and Daniel bring their
winter's catch across the Muskrat River before spring breakup. They
had planned to store the furs in a tree cache until they could return
with a horse and wagon in the spring.

He had snowshoed many miles before he sniffed a wisp of
wood smoke from their cabin. The trees thinned out to a small
clearing in the centre of which sat the weathered cabin. Alex stopped
and cupped his hands to his mouth.

"Tanseh. Wasee-ki-can. Daniel."

Strangely, no one answered, but he could see smoke spiralling
from the stove-pipe. He snowshoed to the cabin door and stooped
to untie the laces and lean the snowshoes against the wall. He
pounded on the cabin door and stood stomping his feet to shake off
the snow. He heard muffled sounds and rustling noises within the
cabin, but no one came to the door.

"Hey, what da hell you guys do in dere?"

Alec lifted the latch and slammed the door back against a chair
that tipped to the floor. Daniel was hanging a blanket across the
bedroom door and turned to glare at Alec.

"Alec! What da hell you doing here?"

Daniel edged toward a rife leaning against the table.

"What you do sleeping dis time of day, Daniel? Why you not
answer da goddamn door? You bushed or something? Where da hell's
Wasee-ki-can? He out trapping or maybe he not feel well?"

Alec started toward the blanket, but Daniel blocked his way.
"Wasee-ki-can not here. He go duder north. I thought you go wit
him."

"I don know what you talk about. I see Wasee-ki-can before
the snow flies. He tell me come here before breakup and help haul furs
out."

"Hah, maybe Wasee-ki-can tink he don want you on his trap
line. I don want your help needer."

Alec slammed his fist on the table.

"Wasee-ki-can is my frien. He don say tings like dat. You go
to hell."

"Get da hell outa here."

Daniel grabbed the rifle and aimed it at Alec.

Alec hurriedly backed out of the cabin and pulled the door
shut. He quickly tied on his snowshoes and followed a path that led
from the cabin to the river. Standing on the riverbank he saw the path

continued on to a large hole cut in the ice. On the ice near the hole was a fish crate. Alec was about to investigate when he heard a rifle behind him.

"I tole you already, you sonuvabitch, get da hell off my trap line."

Daniel fired a shot that kicked up the snow at Alec's feet. Alec turned along the riverbank and headed for home.

The jury heard further evidence from a pathologist who testified the hair and blood found in the cabin were those of one Philip Bear. The murder weapon, believed to be an axe, was never found. All circumstantial evidence pointed to Daniel Darkwater, but there was no proof to warrant a murder conviction. Daniel Darkwater was found not guilty.

When the Indian village learned that Daniel Darkwater had been set free, they gathered in front of the medicine lodge to counsel with the medicine woman. They squatted in a semicircle around the entrance in which sat Sarah Spiritmaker. She listened to their complaints.

"White-man law is hard to understand. Dey throw old Eli in jail for being drunk, but dey let dis murderer go."

"Man who wears white scalp plays wit words like a dog play wit dead muskrat."

"Dey show no respect for Wasee-ki-can's spirit. Dey take his head off and play wit his leg."

"Daniel Darkwater lie. He say he not kill Wasee-ki-can."

"Daniel is bad man. Maci-manitou."

They looked expectantly at the medicine women but she sat unmoving and silent. They all felt that Daniel was guilty, and they wanted him to be punished. But she didn't speak, and slowly they filed silently away into the settling dusk.

Sarah Spiritmaker sat for a long time in deep thought, sighing often. Finally, when dark was upon her she rose to her feet and entered the medicine lodge. She went to a circle of stones in the centre and began building a fire. She sat, warming her hands and staring into the flames. With a sad shake of her head, she rose and opened her medicine pouch.

She choose the dried leaves and herbs carefully, then gently placed them in the centre of four small cloth squares, each coloured to represent the four spirits and powers of the universe — red for the spirit of fire and the powers of good and evil, blue for water and the powers of truth and justice, black for the earth and the powers of life and death, yellow for the sun and the powers of peace and harmony.

Sarah reached for a small box that lay near the circle of stones and withdrew a few strands of jet black hair and placed them with the herbs. Then, folding each corner of the cloth over the potion she rolled the bundle tightly and wrapped a bright red string around it several times. She placed the bundle in a medicine ball tied with leather lacing around her waist and began the ceremony.

She did not leave the lodge for three days and three nights. The villagers dared not walk near the lodge, and in those three days even the children were strangely quiet. They listened to the medicine woman calling the spirits, her chanting lasting long into the nights.

The smoke of the dry wood of the underbrush blended with the fragrance of herbs and sweetgrass, spiralled from the lodgepole and lingered in the village. The old ones sat crooning in their tepees, rocking themselves to an ancient rhythm.

Three months passed, and the leaves began to wither and die. Some of the villagers had seen Daniel Darkwater in a nearby town and reported that he looked more and more aged, as if he were deathly ill. His walk had become stumbling and heavy.

One day, Daniel came to the village and went to the medicine woman. He stood inside the door flap, fingering a parcel he was holding in his hands. Sarah Spiritmaker was squatting in a corner of the lodge, drinking tea from a tin cup and munching on freshly made bannock. She chomped off each bite and chewed it with a slow grinding motion. She sipped the tea with a smacking slurp. When she was finished, she wiped her mouth and brushed off her fingers. Only then did she motion Daniel forward.

He slowly crossed the short distance between them and squatted down before her. His hand trembled when he held out the parcel. After a moment's hesitation, she took and unwrapped it. Inside was a beaded leather pouch containing a wad of tobacco, cigarette papers, and matches. She rolled a thin cigarette from these makings, scratched her thumbnail across the head of a wooden match, and sucked on the cigarette. She exhaled a cloud of smoke with a low hissing breath and shook out the match. Daniel leaned forward eagerly.

"You like my gift."

She nodded slowly but she did not speak.

He continued, "I don feel so good. I tink maybe you help me

feel better. People say you make bad medicine for me."

"My medicine good. You make bad medicine, Daniel. Crooked words make bad medicine."

"I bring gift you like. Maybe you make medicine for me?"

He leaned forward, his eyes intent upon her face.

"Daniel, only you can make medicine dat make you feel better. You must make your crooked words fly straight, den you feel better."

"Why must I speak? What is the need? Wasee-ki-can is dead. He is dead while I am alive."

"His spirit wanders and cries for the truth. Have you not heard Wasee-ki-can calling to you, Daniel? He cannot rest until you answer."

Daniel's shaking hands clutched his ears as if to tear them from his head.

"I don hear anything. I didn't do nothing. Why must I suffer?"

"Look at me, Daniel Darkwater, and speak the truth now. Did you kill Wasee-ki-can?"

Daniel met her gaze, and his mouth opened, but his tongue seemed thick. The intensity of her gaze held him spellbound, willing him, warning him, to tell the truth. With terrible effort, he tore his gaze from that power and hung his head. Daniel would not speak the words that lay in the stillness of the medicine lodge. He finally rose and left, pain contorting his face and resignation in his steps.

During the following winter, Daniel collapsed on the town street and was taken to the hospital. The doctors were unable to find a reason for his malnutrition. They fed him special diets, but he grew steadily worse. He lay on the hospital bed, clutching at invisible enemies. Finally, in his delirium, he called out, but no one understood until the Indian man in the next bed spoke up, "He calls for Spiritmaker."

"Spiritmaker?" The nurse sniffed. "Spiritmaker indeed. Please tell him we do not allow alcohol in this hospital."

The man's relatives came to visit that day and when they left they carried Daniel's message back to the medicine woman, and she came.

She sat silently at his bedside, the only sound his tortured breathing. Then he spoke in a hoarse whisper, "I wish to make crooked words fly straight."

She nodded slowly, and he continued.

"I hab big fight with Wasee-ki-can. Trappin been good and we tink to buy lotsa tings. Wasee-ki-can like team and wagon to bring out our furs next season. I tink he jus like to ride to town like big shot and pretend he is white man. I say no, we buy new traps and rifles."

Daniel began to cough. The medicine woman raised his head and gave him a drink of water. He lay back, and she wiped the dribble from his lips. She sat back and waited.

"We didn't talk no more. We push and hit each other many times den we fell on da bed. I jump up and grab de axe and swing it at his head. He didn't move no more. He jus lay dere and look at me, look at me tru all dat blood. He wouldn't close his eyes."

The medicine woman leaned forward, touched his fevered brow, and smoothed back his hair.

"I sit dere wit him all dat night, holdin his hand. Wasee-ki-can be my friend too. In da morning, I wrap him in dat blanket he like so much and put him in da fish crate. I take him down to da river and chop a big hole in da ice. Dat's when I hear Alec coming, so I run to da cabin and hang blanket over dat door so he not see da blood. After Alec leave, I push da crate in da water and shove it under the ice. Dat be da las time I see Wasee-ki-can."

The effort of speaking had exhausted Daniel, and he lay gasping for breath. The medicine woman went to the sink, dampened a cloth, moistened his lips, and wiped the sweat from his face. He seemed to take comfort from her touches, and his breathing became quieter. She leaned over him and whispered in his ear.

"Rest now, Daniel Darkwater, truth is no longer a burden."

The nurse at the station watched Sarah Spiritmaker leave his room.

The ceremony of the wake began in the village the next night and continued for three days. On the third night, the men built a great fire that touched the night skies. The villagers gathered around the fire and parted to allow Sarah Spiritmaker into the circle. She walked to the fire and withdrew a small bundle, tied with a red string, from the medicine ball that hung from her waist. She offered it to the skies, then threw it into the fire. It burst in the roaring flames and showered the night with sparks and fragrant wood smoke.

The rawhide drums began to beat, and the villagers began to chant, their feet shuffling to the mournful sound of the death chant. Their voices reached into the darkness and guided two spirits into eternal peace and harmony.

Loretta Miskenack

I am forty years of age and a Métis. I am the mother of three children, and a grandmother of a little boy. I was born in High Prairie, Alberta, and am now living in Dawson Creek, British Columbia. I started writing short stories when I was ten years old, and it wasn't until seven years ago that I began writing poetry. I enjoy reading and writing very much, and I am hoping to have a book of my poetry published one of these days.

Valley of Mist

Through a valley
Flows a mist
Filled with hearts
That know no rest
Hearts that live
As the raging seas
Filled with anger
No appease

And in this valley
Flows no light
To store the heart
With love and sight

And in this valley
Hearts cry out
In agony
Because in this valley
Only darkness lives
And anger grows
As many leaves
On a tree

SkyBlue Mary Morin

One of the featured writers of an anthology of Native writers, *Seventh Generation* (Heather Hodgson, ed., Penticton, British Columbia: Theytus Books, 1989), SkyBlue Morin was born in Isle-a-La-Crosse, Saskatchewan, a Métis settlement. Since finding her Native roots as that of Cree ancestry, she has begun to use her Indian name with pride. She walks a spiritual path in life and gives thanks to the many blessings from the Creator, her writing being one of them.

The Woman's Drum

So long, the Woman's Drum
has been quiet
while Women looked to Men
for the Teachings.
Now, the realization comes
to seek Women
for the Sacred Teachings
of the Creation.

Women, search out
the Sacred Teachings
of our Grandmothers.
Take up the Drum
sing the Women's Songs
of the Healing Ones.

So long, the Woman's Drum
has been alone
kept in the back of minds
silent in the Spirit.
Now, comes the time
to pick up the Drum

to sing the Healing Songs
of the Women's Way.

Women, sing out
the Healing Songs
of the Women's Teachings.
Take up the Drum
sing the Honour Songs
of the Traditional Ones.

Too long, the Woman's Drum
has been silent.

Bonding with Mother Earth

Women sit upon the moss
cleansing their bodies
of monthly bleeding
to bond with Mother Earth.

They used to sit in lodges
for revered privacy
to relish their time
with the Earth Mother.

Afterbirth was returned
to the Earth Mother
to bond with whom
we had come from.

A child's umbilical cord
was buried in Mother Earth
to bond the child
to its true Mother.

Such bonding made us one
with the Creation
and gave understanding of
the Sacredness of Mother Earth.

A Sioux Sweat

The door to the South,
the light of birth.
Nearby an altar
where the buffalo head
awaits offerings of tobacco,
then the Sacred Fire
where the Rocks glow red.
The Lead Woman
enters the Sioux Lodge
in the direction of the Sun.
We women follow her
to the womb of Mother Earth.
Inside, she sits by the door
to the other side.
We take our places beside her
round the Circle Centre.

The water is sprayed
on the Seven Rocks,
Grandfathers of Life,
All Seeing.
The heat warms the Body,
the Heart, the Soul.
The Cedar sprinkled
on the Grandfathers
awakens our senses.

A Sioux Song is sung
by the Lead Woman,
joined by others
who know the song
in this Spiritual Singing.
I try to sing along
to Know the words.
Prayers for the People
Love and Peace,
then the door is opened
We welcome the fresh air.

Then, the Second Round
more water on the Rocks,
the Sacred Sioux Song,
the Prayers for the People
Good Health and Happiness
the heat intensifies.
The pores pour forth
heat dries the vocal cords
the door is opened
steam rushes out.

Now, Seven more Grandfathers
with red-hot centres
are placed in the centre circle.
They see our weakness.

The Third Round
more cedar on the new Rocks,
more water on the Grandfathers,
the Sacred Sioux Song,
Prayers for ourselves.
The heat envelopes the body
the body pours forth
its illness.
The door opens
and we welcome the Pipe.
Those clean from drugs
and alcohol
smoke the Sacred Pipe.
The Smoke is good
refreshing, energizing.

The Fourth Round
the door closes,
once again, darkness.
The water is poured
on the Grandfathers,
the Sacred Song sung,
Prayers in silence.
The heat scorches,

so hot, it's cold.
~~We are humbled.~~
The mind pushes out
all sickness,
we are cleansed.
The Ceremony ends.

The Lead Woman
leaves first,
we follow her
in the direction
of the Sun.
Out of our Mother
the Earth,
we are reborn.
All My Relations.

Spiritual Singer

Few hear the Songs
sung ceremoniously
for the People's strength
to keep the Indian Way alive.

Still fewer see the Faith
songs of Life
for the People's struggle
to keep themselves alive.

Spiritual Singer, song maker
tilt the head upward
releasing songs of life
to the Great Mystery.

To greet the new day,
The morning Song.
to honour the Grandfathers,
the Stone Song.

To greet the Ancestors
at the Sun-dance,
the Sun-dance songs,
praising the Creation.

The Ancestors' Spirits cry
through another's singing
to save the Earth Mother
and guide the Sacred Eagle.

Spiritual Singer, drum singer
tilt the head upward
releasing Song Prayers
to the Great Mystery.

Hear the Drum Speak

Hear the Drum speak.
Let it remind you
of days with the Old Woman,
the Visions she saw
the Dreams she had.

Hear the Drum speak
of days of learning
to smoke the Pipe
of burning Tobacco
and Sweetgrass.

Hear the Drum speak
of days we Fasted
for guidance
from the Creator
and in gratitude.

Hear the Drum speak . . .

Ahow, Holy Woman

Ahow, Holy Woman, Revered One.
We must go beyond the Man's tradition
of the subservient Woman.
Men have Power as they stand beside Women.
Mother Earth nurtures Men, as she nurtures Women.
But the Women! So Powerful are they
during the Sacred Moon Time, they are kept
from the Sacred Ceremonies in their honour.
Fears they will take Power
from Sacred Objects and Ceremonies.
Others say, Women are so Powerful
they could hurt themselves.
Yet, Women remain Sacred through this,
so in tune with their bodies, their minds,
their hearts, their Spirits.
Ahow, Holy Woman.

An Honour of Creation, the Sun-dance Lodge,
Ceremony of Life and Sharing
with Mother Earth, community, others,
giving thanks that Rebirth has come,
the Earth purified bringing forth.
Ahow, Holy Woman, Ancient Speaker
at the Sacred Sun-dance Pole.
The Men speak, now, in your absence.
The Virgin at the Sun-dance Pole,
like the Earth Mother
ready to bring forth Creation, is forgotten.
We must go beyond the Man's tradition
of excluding Women.
Women sing the Mourning Song
to bring down the Sacred Tree of Life
for the Centre Sun-dance Pole.
They mourned for felling the Sacred Tree
but, for the people, for Earth's re-creation.
Women rode the wagon that carried the Pole.
Now, the men ride the wagon, in the lead,
while the Women walk behind their shadows.

The Sacred Sweat Lodge, the Womb of Mother Earth
Men and Women go to Her for Rebirth,
for Knowledge, for Guidance, for Strength
to follow the Spiritual Teachings.
It is the Woman who lights the Sacred Fire
for heating the Sacred Stones of the Sweat Lodge.
It is She who guides the Men and Women
to enter the lodge in a Sacred Manner;
for, Woman is the Earth Mother
from whence Life comes. Ahow, Holy Woman.
Now, the Men prepare the stones for the Sweat.

The Sacred Pipe brought to the First People
by White Buffalo Calf Woman is of Creation.
The bowl of red pipestone shaped the Womb
of the Sacred Earth Mother.
The stem carved from the Tree of Life.
Just as the Men are Keepers of Pipes,
the Women are Keepers of the Pipe.
They have their Women's Ceremonies,
just as the Men have theirs.
The two can work together,
but one cannot replace the other.
This would cause imbalance in Life.

The Vision Quests, for Women, too,
to seek guidance from the Ancient Ones,
to become visionaries,
Women fasted in solitude.
From Spirit comes the name for the Soul,
who you are, what you are to do.
The final quest for Knowledge,
the Death Song, to be sung with Honour
for the purpose of dying
as important as the purpose of Life.
Ceremonies, like the Feasts
remember those in the Spirit World
who lived out their special visions
by endlessly and lovingly serving others.
How greatly they entered into Death.

Ahow, Holy Woman,
Feasts have been made in your Honour.
Let's sing the songs for Revival
of the Old Sacred Order,
when Woman was Revered.

Sacred Falls

It was a two-mile trek
into the dense jungle growth
from a round clearing
into a fast-running creek
over round smooth slippery stones.
One had to bend low
to get into the dense jungle path
while stepping carefully
yet stumbling over tree roots,
into a path of tall jungle plants
and a path pink from fuschia flowers.

Out into a clearing
dwarfed by immense rock cliffs,
where previous waterfalls had been
could be heard the Sacred Falls.
Another running stream to cross
wider steps to take
over faster moving water
and larger rock boulders.

There were the Sacred Falls
drowning out the sound
of human voices
spraying a cool mist
and plunging with power
to the waters below.

I held the Cornmeal to the skies
in meditative prayer.

Where is the Maid of the Mist,
the Keeper of the Sacred Falls?
The Cornmeal fell from my fingers
spreading itself among
the pools of water.

Many times I have returned
to those Sacred Falls,
to bathe in its showering mist
and envelop in its white light.
The white light of energy
energizing my mind, body, and spirit.

Charlotte Nahbexie

I have lived on the reserve, in cities, and in the farming community. Everywhere I go, I see the injustices that mankind does to one another. We need to set aside our prejudices, that look only at the outward person, and start to draw together in a communing of the inner spirits of man. There is good in all, if we but take time to look.

I am thankful for my four children, who have allowed me the freedom through their support to explore and grow, and for R.J. for his much needed encouragement. I am a member of the White Bear Band, located in southeastern Saskatchewan, but I am now living on an acreage near Wolseley. My kids and I raise and train Arabian and Appaloosa horses. I am thirty-five years old and enjoy the personal freedom that only living life to the fullest can give you.

Freedom

Streets of grey — cars — steel,
Spirits numb — cannot feel.
Leaden tears — apartments' eyes,
Too many souls — to hear their cries.

Build around me tall — a fence.
My soul is longing, won't you dance?
Forget those skies — azure blue,
Golden sunlight — grasses hue.

Why reach forth — cry — complain?
Teach my Soul — can you explain
To my children, to my true heart,
There will be no trill of a meadowlark?

Blood lies deep upon these streets,
Unconcerned under People's feet.
But each drop shed is paid to me
For it is Spirits now set free.

Again they step on grass — rich — green.
No longer suffering painful dreams.
Free from prison walls, they are
Spirits now at last soaring far.

Truth

Drums beat — beat — beat —
Voices lifting away defeat.
Feet step out the message clear,
We are survivors, what need we fear?

Mother nurses young son to breast,
Dreams him braver, in search, the quest.
Father watches him, eyes aglow,
Family fire-stones mask the cold.

My son, my son, as you lay sleeping
Grandfather breathes upon you, keeping.
The steed you'll ride is strong and wise.
He'll take you, reach for distance skies.

Drum beat — beat — beat —
Voices lifting sing of defeat.
Feet step out a message clear,
We have lost, and now we fear.

They came upon us as we slept.
Their guns killed us as we fled.
My son, my son, your cry I hear,
But I can't help you now Sweet Deer.

Silence

Traffic stops
Children's cries
Women's screams
As husbands die
Silence.

Sirens pulsate
Echo back
Families ache
Streets black
Silence.

Dead end
Lights dim
No friends
To love him
Silence.

Bars steel
Hard and cold
None feel
Ears hold
Silence.

Dry eyes
Hearts sleep
Spirit dies
His Spirit weeps
In silence.

Fields open
Horizon bare
Grandfather dreams
Rocks stares
In silence.

Evelyn Nelson-Kennedy

Evelyn Nelson-Kennedy is a university student. She started writing after she had read other Native writers. She hopes her writing encourages other Native people to tell their stories.

Our Modern Powwows

Every summer, powwows are held throughout many reserves in Canada and the United States. The first in our area is hosted by the Roseau River Reserve. Roseau's powwow has become synonymous with the coming of summer and the beginning of a new season of dancing. Native people eagerly await these gatherings as a time to get reacquainted with old friends, to make new ones, and to celebrate their Indian heritage. I wonder, sometimes, why I get to so few of them.

The most spectacular part of the powwow is the grand entry. The Canadian and American flags and the staff of eagle feathers are carried in by men of honour, the chief, and other dignitaries. Young and old rise to their feet, men remove their hats, and as the drum begins its hypnotic beat a hush falls over the crowd. Pride is reflected on the faces of the dancers and onlookers. Even the children are unusually quiet. The procession begins with the men's traditional dancers, followed by the colourful men's fancy dancers; next come the grass dancers. The women are led in by the traditional and fancy shawl dancers and, then, the jingle dress dancers. The order is continued with different age groups — boys, girls, and younger children. The song is prolonged until all the participants have entered the circle. With the hundreds of dancers, the air is cloudy with dust and feathers. The grand entry pageantry never fails to fill me with awe. For a small moment, we are all one people joined to our past by the magical beat of the drum and the singers' chants.

Yes, the grand entry is truly an awesome experience. How can anything that follows compete with it? Powwows have become so well organized. The hundreds of tents, trailers, and tepees in the camp-grounds attest to the splendid job the advertising people have done. Concession stands encircle the dancing area. I remember, once, even seeing carnival rides. Why did that upset me so much? I guess because it was one more proof that powwows are becoming more of a profit-making, carnival-like event rather than a celebration.

Back when powwows were becoming popular, after a long lapse, I remember one powwow that only had one small drum at the centre. There was no arbour to cover the spectators (perhaps because there were no spectators, only participants), there were no concession stands, and there was only a handful of not-so-colourful dancers, yet I remember a face filled with happiness. Binaseek was an elder from our reserve, who was not particularly respected by the young people. She walked with a limp and talked only to herself. The old people said that she had been severely burned in her youth and had never been the same since. Her withered right hand was evidence to the truth of the story. Binaseek had made a belt for her dress. The brown piece of cloth was wrapped around her waist, decorated with oversized buttons. Her stockings lay wrinkled at her ankles. The children laughed at her pathetic attempts at sewing. Binaseek, oblivious to the pointing children, danced around the drum with a look of pride and pure enjoyment radiating from her wrinkled face. When I think of what a powwow should be, I think of Binaseek and the look on her face at the long-ago celebration.

Little things at powwows bother me — the MC's blaring voice over the speakers while the songs are in progress, the selling of everything from bannock to T-shirts emblazoned with the sad faces of old Indians. At times, I know it isn't these petty happenings that irk me but rather the reflection of myself that I see in them. I am a mixture of the old and the new. Like the powwow, I have changed. I have progressed in the white-man's world. I wonder, at times, at what cost? Sometimes, I would like to see just a little of what Binaseek must have felt that day.

Leaving Home

My life was changed when I was six years old. My older sister Gene was deathly ill with tuberculosis and, after the rest of my family was tested, the Indian agent instructed my mother to get Gene and my younger sister, Marilyn, ready to go to the hospital. Our mother worked for days, making clothes for both. Mom had chosen shiny green material and lacy white trim for my little sister's dress. As I watched her peddling on her Singer sewing machine, I stroked the luxurious cloth and asked if there would be enough for another dress. I remember feeling very jealous of Marilyn's shimmering green dress.

On the day of departure, I watched the commotion with detached curiosity, until all eyes were on me. The Indian Agent had made a mistake. It was I, not Marilyn, who had TB. My mother frantically looked for something decent for me to wear to the hospital. Although the details of that horrible day are vague, the confusion and terror that I felt will be with me always. I understood that Gene was ill and needed hospital care, but I could not comprehend why my parents would want to send me away, since I felt perfectly fine.

As I walked into the hospital with its long unfamiliar hallways, I could smell the antiseptic that tried to veil the smell of sickness in the rooms. I clutched my father's index finger. This gesture had always given me a feeling of security, but it failed me that day. The nurses took the pink jacket with sleeves that were much too short for me and gave me strange pajamas to wear. My pleas were to no avail, and as my parents attempted to leave the room I leapt from my bed to the next bed and clung to them, screaming my protests. Even if I had known then that it would be three long years before I would return home, I could not have screamed any louder or clung any harder to my parents.

In the hospital, I spent a great deal of time daydreaming about my family. My parents had not abandoned me, but it was difficult for a six year old to comprehend the economics of raising eight children in those hard times. It was especially hard to understand, when the families of the other children came every Sunday with many delectable treats and presents. Many times, I imagined my father rescuing me from the uncaring nurses and the noise of crying babies. Still, their first visit was a shock to me. A year had passed after that eventful day when I finally saw my parents.

"Stanley! Marjorie!" I called out, as I ran into my father's arms.

I had not forgiven them for their betrayal. Even though I longed for them, I could no longer call them "mom" and "dad."

It would be a lie to say that none of my memories of the hospital were good. I adjusted and grew accustomed to my environment, and when the day arrived for me to return home it was like a dream. The week before my mother's arrival was unreal to me. At times I had to shake myself to believe it was true and not one of my imaginary daydreams. Only when I walked into our house and met my new baby bother, John, did I really believe I was home again. Never could I have imagined any baby as beautiful.

Shawna Lynn Danielle Panipekeesick

I am sixteen years old, from the Sakimay Reserve, near Grenfell, Saskatchewan. I started writing short stories when I was twelve and poems later. I am working at a day-care centre and want to become a child care worker at Ranch Ehrlo Society in Pilot Butte, Saskatchewan.

Me

You can judge me by the colour of my face,
You can judge me because I'm not one of your race.

You can strip me of my beliefs and my pride,
But there's a fire inside me that will never die.

So, I'll tell you once again.
I'm damn proud to be an Indian.

Wanted: Someone Who Cares

Who cares enough to accept me as I am,
Who does not condemn me for my shortcomings,
Who helps me to learn from my mistakes.

Who cares enough to respect me as an individual
with the right to learn and grow at my own pace
and in my own unique fashion.

Who will stand by to help when I need it,
but will release me from my own guilt,
and help me find constructive ways to deal with reality.

Who will encourage me to explore the world about me,
Who will open my eyes to beauty and my ears to music,
Who will listen to my questions and help me find answers.

Who cares enough to help me achieve my full potential,
and who has faith in my ability to develop into a worthwhile person.
Could this someone be me?

Lise Pelletier

Editors' note — We have lost contact with Lise Pelletier. When she submitted her material to us, she wrote:

I am a thirty-year-old single parent with two children. I have been writing since I was fairly young, and I also am seriously considering finishing the book I started to write three years ago. This book is more or less an autobiography of my life. It is about growing up on an Indian reserve until I was apprehended by welfare and placed in white foster homes, a detention centre, and the provincial jail, and, then, being sent to the Kingston Prison for Women at the age of sixteen. I spent time there until I was twenty-two. It is also about what it has been like trying to make it on my own with two children to raise alone, and I hope that by the time I finish writing the book I will be in university.

Life as it is in Pinegrove Correctional Centre on a Monday Morning

I awake to the sounds of the cell doors being buzzed open. I lie in bed, wondering to myself if it's a good idea to get up today. I pull the covers a little closer to me, trying to sink lower in the bed. It's Monday morning here in Pinegrove Correctional Centre. What a rude awakening — if there ever was one.

I jump out of bed looking crazy like. Dress myself with half-closed eyes. Not caring what I wear today. One morning, I wore my sweat-shirt on backward to the dining-room. It was good enough for an early morning chuckle.

I stumble out of my cell into the bright fluorescent existence. I feel my steps to the bathtub. I wash my face six times with cold, cold water. There! I'm considered to be awake in every sense of the word.

I slither on down to the grille to pick up my medication. Now, if I could just psyche myself into thinking that I've just swallowed some happy pills, I've got it made. Whew! What a buzz . . .

I head out into the direction of the dining-room, not wanting to wake up anyone who's having breakfast. I smile to myself, thinking about some old bygone joke. Over my second cup of coffee and a twelve-minute cigarette, I contemplate the day's forthcoming activities.

I listen to the PA system paging the sleeping bodies to their work placements. I wonder to myself why it is that everybody seems to forget where their work placements are on Mondays. Maybe we just do it to make sure for ourselves that we know where we're going.

Hey man, I don't need no PA. I'm always too busy going places to apply for one. Some days, I go for walks all over the country. Down Main Street in Winnipeg, Yonge Street in Toronto, 8th Avenue in Calgary, Granville Street in Vancouver. It doesn't matter to me where I go, just as long as I don't have to be here all day.

Just yesterday, I was out on the reserve picking berries. This time, I didn't even have to worry about the mosquitoes attacking me. It was so good to be back home, to peacefully breathe in all the sights and sounds that I'm missing so much.

I wonder sometimes, though, if everybody would feel left out if I told them that I've been going for walks without asking them to come along. I haven't been down to the beach for a few days now. Maybe I'll let them tag along today. Hey, we could always have a picnic, too. Lie back on the sand, hear the ocean's roar, feel the sunshine, listen to the seagulls playing, sighing softly to catch your breath . . .

At 9:45 a.m., some disgusted voice screams out, "Coffee time." I pull the reins on my imagination. It almost sounds dangerous to go have a coffee now. Oh no! Someone must have found out it's Monday morning.

As I walk into the dining-room, I scan the area very briefly. No signs of danger here. I almost feel very alienated from this expressionless moving flesh. Could it be that they're all down at another beach without me?

I pour myself a coffee. I begin my analyzing. Looks like everybody is really playing hookey from reality. I wonder some more if everybody realizes that I have a strange tendency to watch the unseen actions they try to display so discreetly. Over there, someone is asking what day it is.

Yikes! They've found out it is Monday morning. Oh no! Life is so rough here. I think it's time we all leave town.

"Okay, gang, grab your bathing suits. Let's go to the beach."

Monday morning will have somehow passed on its own.

In There, Out Here

It seems like not so long ago when I was inside there, too. Waking up at 7:00 a.m. every morning to another day of cell doors banging, the PA system blaring endlessly, uniformed bodies everywhere, florescent lights glaring down, loud conversations that never made sense, and the constant feeling of being so alone in a world that seemed so unreal.

The hurting, the desperation, the loneliness embraced me in a hold that almost suffocated me. The pain of being imprisoned so far away from my family and friends never once left me. Late at night, there were tears — always crying out, but never being heard. Then, the feeling of being afraid and never knowing why. Feeling powerless. Desperate. And overcoming it with a raging violence inside me that I vowed never to let surface.

Yeah, I was in there and made it out of there. I lived in that world that I used to dream so hard at night wouldn't be there in the morning when I woke up.

Now it has been nineteen months since I heard those cell doors close behind me. Nineteen months of good times and bad times out here — and times when I felt I couldn't make it another day. Every day has become like a struggle. Having to take care of two young boys on my own is sometimes not easy.

Waking up late because I read too long last night, missing medical appointments because I had taken the wrong bus, cooking and preparing three meals a day, making creative sandwiches out of peanut butter, bologna, and ketchup, wiping noses, tying shoelaces, reading the story of Bambi for the thousandth time, learning a new word in baby talk every other day, trying to do laundry amidst the yelling and screaming and crying of two little boys who just want to go home, watching Fred Flintstone yeb-a-deb-a-doo all over the television screen, trying to wake up quietly, only to fall and stumble over some toy left in the hallway, kissing some stupid-looking Teddy bear good night, taking one whole hour to finish my first cup of coffee, sitting and waiting to fix some broken toy, or to tell another fairy-tale story . . .

It's worth it in so many ways to be out here. But I have not forgotten where I once was not so long ago. The echo of prison doors slamming closed wakes me up to the reality that I am ready for any challenge that today has to offer — that will help me stay out of prison another day.

Patti Penny

I am a young Native woman of the Saulteaux tribe. My place of birth is Broadview, Saskatchewan, and I was raised in my grandmother's home on the Sakimary Reserve. I enjoy reading, writing, doing small illustrations, and learning about my Native traditional culture.

On Being Traditional

I have always thought that I was a "traditional Native woman," up until recently. I went through life believing this was a true fact. Because of my Salteaux ancestry and the colour of my skin, I naturally assumed this was so.

Out of curiosity one day, I looked up the word "traditional." In my life, this meaningful word was totally different from the dictionary's meaning. In actuality, my previous lifestyle didn't even come close to traditional. For example, one meaning of this word is, "conforming to earlier styles and customs, according to tradition." Now . . . the lifestyle I was leading on the streets of Regina sure wasn't anything close to the early styles and customs of my Salteaux ancestors. Far from it! The drugs and the alcohol that I was consuming on a day-to-day basis wouldn't allow any room for this.

It is so plain to see now that being a substance abuser and trying to pass myself off as traditional just didn't make sense. Number one, in the traditional customs of my ancestry, there was no place for alcohol and drugs. Two, it can't be done. A person can't live two lifestyles. If they did, eventually one would win over the other. Most times, it is the booze.

All in all, the point I am trying to make in this writing is that if a person is Native they have every reason to be proud of who they are and where they come from and live a full and satisfied life according to their beliefs. Everyone has that chance. But, if they taint the traditional styles and customs of the Native lifestyle with alcohol and drugs, they have not only lost their own pride and self-worth but they have also lost their traditions. We, as incarcerated Native women, tend to try and mix these two lifestyles. It is not right . . . not now . . . not ever.

I remember when I was a little girl about four or five years old and waking up, hearing mom screaming because our dad was beating her up again. I would be scared, too, and would crawl into bed with my older sisters, and they would calm me down. I would wonder why they would always start fighting every time they drank that stuff in the green and brown bottles. I used to go and steal those bottles and empty them down the toilet, so my mom and dad would not start fighting. But, it would not help and soon it was too late. My two older sisters, young sister, and I got taken away from our mom and dad. Was I ever sad and mad at my mom and dad for not leaving those green and brown bottles alone when they knew they would only start fighting again.

I grew up thinking that my mom and dad didn't love us anymore, and, by the time I was sixteen, I was hanging around with the wrong crowd and even started drinking and getting into trouble with the law. I didn't care about anything, because Social Services would not tell me where my family was here in Saskatchewan. To make things worse, they would not tell me until I was eighteen. By that time, I was shacked up with a guy for two years and having a baby. I was terrified, because he was beating me up all the time and drinking was all he cared about, it seemed. But, I still stayed with him, because I did not know where my family lived yet. When I turned eighteen, my mom and new stepfather came down from Alberta to get my younger sister and me. That was one of the happiest days of my life. I knew they still loved us to come all that way to pick us up.

To tell you the truth, I just about gave up on my family. I tried to kill myself a few times because of what alcohol was doing to my life. I learned one important lesson from this all: never give up hope, and once you put your mind to it and say you are going to quit drinking stick with it no matter how hard it is for you. Do not learn the hard way by getting into trouble with the law and having to be separated from your children and the rest of your loved ones. Think twice about taking that first drink. Who am I going to hurt more? I am just going to hurt myself even more. I am not saying that I will never end up in here again, because when I get out there will always be those temptations to drink. I have got to work on my drinking problem and quit it for good before I can be happy with myself again. All I can do is take things one day at a time.

First published in "From Where We Stand: Women's Views on Alcohol." Prince Albert, Saskatchewan: Pine Times Productions, n.d.

Christina Rain

I am twenty-eight and married with four children, two boys and two girls. I began to write so that I could express my feelings to my husband, who was an alcoholic. I started seeing an Adult Children of Alcoholics counsellor, Bill McVey, last year, who encouraged me to publish my work.

Volcanic

One
     mountain
               of
                 emotions.
Ready
     for
        eruption.
Hot,
    burning,
           searing
                  with
anger,
      hurt,
           and
              pain.
Clouded
       and
          confused.
Too
    many
        held
           in.
Forming
       one
          VOLCANIC
                  MOUNTAIN.

Poetry or Insanity

Sometimes, I feel so lost,
not knowing what to do.
I'd like to run and hide
but that seems so hopeless too.

I try my best to rationalize
and reason with my thought.
When nothing seems to work
I feel so horribly distraught.

I tell myself that one day
everything will work out.
But at the present moment,
I just want to pout.

I know I can be sensible,
if I just take the time.
But my head is spinning 'round,
and my thoughts are out of rhyme.

I feel I have to stop,
and take a little break.
If I'm unable to do this,
I know my sanity is at stake.

I just wanted to erase
the bad things from my past.
But, I realize now that
these are the shadows I have cast.

I also know and understand,
that if I cannot cope,
then life on earth for me
. . . there is no hope.

Loneliness

Peering out from my protective skull
　gazing quietly out through my eyes
　　looking out at the dangers around
　　　hearing the harshness of one's own voice
　　　　Triggers my jump into silence
　　　　Despair
Here in a puddle, dirty, dark, slimy
　rippling my effects around
　　movement in any direction
　　　causes waves
　　　　Unbearable waves, murky with much feeling
Yet, somehow unseen
　at the same time very visible
　　Thump, thump, thump.
　　　Numbing vibrations
　　　Aching in my head
Why do I dwell
　　　　　where no man wants?
I don't know . . . maybe to be alone
　yet not really alone
　　just bobbing in and out
　　　when safe to do so
But one day it will come
　When I can see myself
　　　　　　Outside,
　　　　　　　　Move,
　　　　　　　　　　Feel,
　　　　　　　　　　　Rejoice!

For I will honestly be
　Just and only
　　ME.

No, Not Dying

Numbness, fuzziness, dumbness.
  Who's to say
    Exactly what death is
      Total unfeelingness, helplessness
As I go through the day
  But how can I be like this
    Fearful, tearful, never cheerful
      Lonely, only me
What is Death?
  The end of one phase
    Left in a daze
Groping, moping, a little hoping
  Seeking a spark
    To light up the dark
Running, falling, slipping,
  S-l-i-d-i-n-g
    Out of control
      Yah!
        That's it, no control
Floating inside some large bowl
  For everyone to look down on
    Watching, waiting, wondering,
      Feeling scared, ever so terrified
Yet feelings go denied
  Who wants to deal with it
    Lock it up deep in a pit
Then bursting in flame
  As if it were a game
    Who's in control
      Your feeling soul
        Yes, no one but your inner being
Crying, hurting, bleeding but
No, not dying
  Only living and feeling
    Your fears, yours alone are you freeing
      Scary, yes
But offering a fresh new outlook
  A porthole growing in size

That's what makes you wise
Your shadows to look upon
Your failures, your wins
They guide you as your new life begins

Elizabeth Robinson

In 1935, I was born in the General Hospital in Calgary, the first child in our family of thirteen to be born in a hospital. My childhood was spent in and around Calgary. However, Midnapore was my home town. Being of Native and French ancestry, a Métis, I was educated in the Catholic tradition. Schooling in Calgary during the early and late 1940s was difficult for a Métis child. However, because of my athletic abilities, I was able to cope with racism.

I am the mother of six children, the grandmother of six, and the great-grandmother of one. My family come first in my life. They are inspirational to my writing.

During my mid-years I went back to school to upgrade my education. One of my instructors, an English teacher, encouraged me to write. Others have also encouraged me to write. Upon leaving vocational school, I worked as a Native counsellor for alcohol and drug abusers. I decided to go to college and spent two years at Mount Royal College, in the justice administration program. Upgrading, counselling, and college were the most enlightening experiences of my life.

Writing has given me the opportunity to express myself in many ways and the opportunity to meet people. My writing is an extension of me. I like to think of myself as an elder, spiritualist, and healer.

Suppressed

Our ancestors of long ago
Their spirits are restless
Wandering about
No longer the beat of the drums
Appeases their souls
They are silent
Or is it the mighty war cry
Which ceases to exist
Le Blanc man came
In the name of the Great White Father
They took our land
Killed all our wild food
In return they gave us
Le Blanc man's food, which bloated our bellies
Le Blanc man's drink, which fogged our minds
Le Blanc man's spirit, confusing our concept of our
    Great Spirit
They gave us Le Blanc man's diseases
Smallpox, that killed us by the thousands
Suppression and threats took our freedom
A dignified Nation
In the name of civilization
They pummelled, raped, stole, and killed
They changed our ways
Spoiled our lives
Greed and power they fight amongst themselves for
We are not the only people who cry out
From the depth of our souls
Everywhere they go
Le Blanc man causes heartache and destruction
I am only one
My tears flow in sorrow
And I cry
The sound echoes across the vast universe
Never to rest in peace

Rodeo Men

They come from all over
Dressed in jeans, fancy boots, ten-gallon hats, and leather chaps
Paying a fee to try and be the world's greatest
There were even a few from down under
These mighty men of the rodeo circuit
Joined together to win
Some make it, others don't
Excitement builds when they take their spills
The roar of the crowd
Makes their hearts pound
Raw courage and guts abound
When its their turn
Working hard to be best
All is quiet when one is thrown to the ground
As the mean snorting bull turns around
Before he can do any damage
The rodeo clowns step in
Agile and quick, they do the trick
Of chasing the bull through the gate
Tears run down their faces
As they pound the ground
In frustration on seeing their score
Eight seconds in time
When the Klaxon sounds
The danger is there when they race
To flip a steer in so many seconds
A squealing, bucking bronc
Took the life of Pete Knight
Then along came one of our own
Marty Wood from Bowness
To give himself fame
All the ladies' hearts fluttered
At the evening performance
Joe Carbury's raspy voice announces
The biggest attraction of all
No where else on earth is it seen
With such fascination
"Now they're off and running."

Before it was called the chuck-wagon races
Now it is called range-land derby
They may change the name
But not the fame
Generations of men
Nerves of steel
As they get on their mark
To wait for the start
That will make or break them
The hand goes down
Drivers are taut
Four lean horses all aquiver
Chomping their bits
Around the barrels they go
Stoves all in the back
As they hit the track
Kelly Sutherland makes it to the inside rail
That half mile of hell
Looks mighty far
On the first turn
He is still ahead
Feeling the hot breath
On his neck
Of the closest team
Gives him the extra go that he needs
Thundering hooves pound the ground
Rushing wind grabs his hat
Flinging it to the track
Crushed by the other teams
On the last turn
Feet braced, Kelly turns
He catches a glimpse of four white shirts
There at his side
His faithful outriders
Sweat runs in his eyes
He shuts them
No time to wipe them
There's a roar in his ears
As the crowd rises to its feet
He opens his eyes

Knowing he has done it again
Kelly made first place in this race
Only this year it made no difference
Problems he had that told the tale
It was a big disappointment
Five times he has known what it's like
To be king of the rodeo
They accept their money
Late at night they pack their equipment
Ready to go
To the next rodeo
There are handshakes and pats on the back
Muscles are sore, some limp about
Proud they stand
Sad they are for friends who lose
They know the feeling
As they win or lose
They're mighty men
Regardless they will all be back
As they make a vow, that next time
"It will all be mine."
At the Calgary Stampede
The greatest rodeo of all

A Wink for Cecelia

The young girl stopped her bike by the side of the highway. She took a long look at the huge, red brick building with the cross on the roof. She started down the gravel road, passing under an arch, gaining speed, rocks flew. Intent on her appointment, she paid no attention to the garden before her. It was bordered with high caragana trees. The road came to a fork, the young girl took the road to the right. After a time, she came to the front doors. Getting off her bike, she leaned it against the steps. At the front door, she knocked loudly, not looking to the side of the door for the doorbell. Silently, the door swung open on well-oiled hinges. There stood a black-clad figure. The nun indicated to the girl to enter. It would be the first and last time she would use that door. She followed the nun down the long hall, and they stopped before a door. The nun opened the door and stood back, waiting for the girl to enter the room. No words had been spoken as the door was quietly closed, leaving Betty alone.

Betty stood just inside the parlor, her five-foot-six-and-a-half frame clad in faded blue jeans, sloppy grey sweat-shirt, and scruffy, once white, sneakers. One grimy stockinged toe poked out of the ragged shoe. Nail-bitten hands were tucked into back pockets. Popping noises escaped from her mouth, as her jaws worked hard on the stale smoke-tasting gum. She looked around the fancy parlor. A large (massive was more the word) desk took command of the room. It sat directly in the middle of the highly polished hardwood floor. The large high windows were covered with flimsy white lace curtains. Two high-backed stuffed chairs with starched white antimacassars sat to the side of the desk.

Her long pony-tail swung against her face as she turned when the door opened. Another nun entered the room. She stood just inside the room for a moment, looking down her long nose, over the steel rims of her silver glasses, with distaste at the scruffy creature before her. The nun's white wimple was so tight it pulled her face. It looked like it hurt her. A long black habit graced her sinister matronly figure. Her hands were tucked inside the habit's sleeves.

"Lord, what have they sent me this time?" she thought before introducing herself.

Although no words had been spoken, the feeling was mutual.

"God, what has mama gotten me into? Certainly, an education can't be this important to send me to this hell hole," her tough twelve-year-old mind thought. "Damn, I hope this doesn't take long."

The nun glided across the floor, seeming not to touch it as she made her way to sit in the chair behind the desk. She sat so straight and looked so imposing that Betty felt scared for a moment. The moment passed.

"Dispose of the gum immediately, hands out of your pockets, and stand straight. Now walk over here and pull that chair closer to the desk and sit down," she commanded in a deep voice.

Betty hastily removed her hands from her pockets and spat the gum in the waste-paper basket. "Not bad," she thought, as it landed with a wet plop.

Walking to the big chair, she struggled to pull it closer to the desk. It hurt her bony butt when she sat. She rested her arms on the arm rests, hands clasped tight in front of her as she tried hard not to fidget. The nun's head was bobbing as she looked first at the paper before her and the dirty little half-breed across from her.

"It says here your given name is Cecelia Gaudry, good French name, must be your father who is French. It also says you're Patricia Blackstock's aunt, is that so?"

"Yes, ma'am."

"You will call me Mother Superior, understood?"

"Yes, Mother Superior."

"If your given name is Cecelia, why do they call you Betty?"

"My family likes Betty better than Cecelia, and so they call me Betty, Mother Superior."

Mother Superior picked up an eraser-topped pencil and began tapping on the desk. Flipping a sheet, she scanned through the papers: "Twelve years old, grade seven, tomboy, rough language, smokes, discipline problems, and has no regard for other people's property."

She looked over the rims of her glasses at the child sitting across from her. The child sat, a smudge of dirt on her nose, nibbling on a dirty finger.

"Remove your hands from your mouth and sit on them until we are finished here."

Betty's first lesson began as she sat on her hands.

Once again, Mother Superior began to read. "Now, here is a challenge. We'll have her tamed before she leaves here." She continued to read and make notations on the paper. "Let her sit there for awhile yet. No time like the present to start her proper upbringing. It has been left unchecked too long."

Ten minutes of sitting on her hands made them numb, and, finally, when she thought her back would break, Mother Superior dismissed her with instructions to report to Sister Mary, the seventh grade teacher.

After leaving the room, Betty found a set of stairs. At the bottom, she followed the long silent hallway until she found the side door leading to the courtyard. She passed various nuns scurrying along the hall. They reminded her of penguins she had seen in science books. She laughed silently as she skipped across the courtyard. A large telephone pole stood in the centre of the yard. A single bulb hung suspended from the white shield at the top of the pole. A black and white magpie sat on this, chattering at the top of its lungs. Betty turned and hucked a large gob of spit on the dry ground. The dust was disturbed before it settled back. Whistling shrilly, she continued on her way. She was glad to be released from the stuffy parlor and the convent proper.

The classroom where she was headed was housed in the building across the courtyard from the convent. She walked up the stairs to the upper floor. Arriving at the classroom, she entered with no ceremony. Sister Mary stopped in mid-sentence and turned to see what had created the noise. All heads turned as Sister Mary spoke.

"We knock on closed doors around here, miss," said a soft voice. "Cecelia, isn't it?"

"No, it's Betty. I like Betty."

"My dear, you will be called Cecelia around here."

"Yes, ma'am."

"My name is Sister Mary, young lady, and you will address me so."

"Yes, Sister Mary."

"Now come and sit over here," she indicated a desk near the front of the room.

Eighteen pairs of solemn eyes followed her journey across the silent room. Neat rows of boys and girls dressed in white shirts and blouses, black ties, dark trousers for the boys and dark tunics for the girls.White knee socks for the girls and seventeen pair of highly polished black shoes, the school uniform. She sat a thistle in a bed of roses.

"Children, I would like you all to meet Cecelia Gaundry. She will be in our class from now on."

"Hello, Cecelia," seventeen voices choired in unison.

Betty nodded in acknowledgement and mumbled, "Hi."

Someone snickered and held their nose. Betty turned and glared aggressively.

"Children, that will be enough, back to work." She clapped the little clappers she held in her hand. The lessons began. Betty had joined the class in the middle of it and so wasn't informed of the rules and procedure of the class. That would come later. For now, she would join in the lessons. The morning went well and at precisely four minutes to twelve Sister Mary clapped her little clappers. In unison, seventeen young children rose to their feet. Betty stumbled to her feet as she scrambled to stand like the rest. Nineteen pairs of hands crossed themselves and turned on a dime to make their way to the door. Sister

Mary reached the door first and stood there, hands tucked into her habit sleeves. The first child to reach the door held it open, while seventeen children left the room single file. Then the last child left, and Sister Mary brought up the rear. Down the stairs and across the courtyard they marched, like Hitler Youth. Click, click went the clappers when they reached the door to the main hall.

They stopped abruptly to wait for Sister Mary to open the door. Betty left the group and ran across the courtyard in a different direction. She grabbed her old bike, hopped aboard, and, with rocks flying, she peddled away like crazy. With a yell, "See you later, Sister Mary," she sped off down the gravel road.

At the bottom of the hill and out of sight of the convent, she stopped. Digging deep into her pocket she withdrew a crumpled cigarette and a book of matches. She lit the cigarette and took a deep drag. As she stood, the bike between her legs, she took time to look back at the imposing building. It was then that she noticed the beautiful white statue of Jesus, holding a lamb. She choked on the smoke and said, "Forgive me, Father, but I need this. How am I ever going to get along with all those sisters and sissy kids?" she asked the silent figure.

She didn't know it at the time, but that figure of Jesus would become her refuge in the days to come. A crow cawed and Betty continued on her way home.

Lacombe Home was the building that held so many people within its bound.There were orphans, old people, retarded, and handicapped living there. The poor souls depended on the sisters for their care and keep. In some cases, whole families lived there, brothers and sisters who had lost their parents. Children were there because the government had removed them from broken homes. Times were tough. The Second World War was over, and the people hadn't gotten over the havoc in their lives. Poor people had nowhere else to go — refugees of the times. The red brick building looked huge and imposing. Inside, it was home to many. There were rules and regulations, which had better be obeyed or else. Women ruled the roost, dedicated to helping others in their care. A few to heap more misery on the lost and lonely souls. Betty would join the well-oiled machinery as a crooked little cog.

Wild and untamed, she would always be, but to keep things running smoothly she let them think her trained. It was easier for her to give in, instead of being punished for being a kid. At first, Betty entered the convent as a day student, going to classes and returning home at noon hour and after school. Later, she had to stay full-time as sickness and unforeseen circumstances left her without a mother for a time. She honestly made an effort to please the nuns, but when you're over-exuberant and full of life it's hard.

The training had begun. Girls did not wear pants. However, because of lack of money, Betty was allowed to wear her standard dress: blue jeans, sweat-shirts and scruffy old sneakers. They made concessions for the ruffian tomboy. Do this, do that, walk straight, don't slouch, don't talk, don't laugh, yes Sister, no Sister, prayers before classes, on your knees on hard wooden floors, prayers at lunch time, prayers when you returned to classes, prayers when you left for the day, prayers before meals, and prayers before bed. On every page of lessons, it was written, J.M.J. — Jesus, Mary, Joseph.

One lesson added to the school curriculum was bone-breaking hard work. Laundry day, the students left the classroom in single file, down two flights of stairs to the basement where huge machines did mountains of wash. Steam billowed everywhere. Chug, chug, chug went the giant washing machines. Hiss, hiss, hiss, the powerful mangle irons went. Every piece of laundry had to be pressed. Tons and tons of folding had to be done, filling huge baskets on wheels, stacked high with white sheets, pillowcases, towels, napkins, underwear, blouses, and shirts. The bigger boys pushed the loaded carts through the long dark tunnel from the laundry rooms to the convent proper. Everyone worked, sleeves rolled up, faces soaked with sweat, hair limp and hanging down. No time to rest, to fall behind in your job, making everyone late. Sitting on a platform high above the rest of the room was the black and white figure of a nun, watching like a hawk, every little detail, with eyes darting here and there. Click, click went the wooden clappers if you missed the beat. Novices did the nuns' wash on different days.

Click, click, "Time for lunch." All over the room, the big machines shut down, everyone scurried to their places, rolling down their sleeves, pushing damp hair from their faces. Click, click, up the stairs they went, out the door, across the yard. Head erect, back straight, feet in time to an unheard drill. Click, click, halt at the door, never a whisper or a word. Betty stumbled, bump, bump, down the line. Bodies touched, they stood so close together. Down the line she came, hands folded in her sleeves, to stand by Betty's side, unsaid words told her never to do that again, as the nun continued down the line. Click, click, open the door, walk single file down the long hall. The chimes of the noon hour peeled as the last child disappeared around the corner and down the stairs. Along another long hall. Click, click, halt at the dining-room door. No one hurried as they entered the dining-room. Rows and rows of wooden tables and chairs stood. White napkins dotted the tables before each chair. At the head of each table stood a nun dressed all in white, silver crosses hung from their necks, arms folded in the sleeves of their white habits. The children entered, to stand with folded hands behind each chair. At the north end of the immense hall stood a black and white nun on a podium. Heads bowed.

"Dear Lord, thank you for this food."

"Aye men," said a hundred voices.

Everyone was in motion, chairs scraped quietly as everyone seated themselves. The nun at the head of each table went along the long rows, dishing out the soup. Stacks of butter cut into neat little squares. Big glass tumblers of ice-cold milk sat waiting to be poured. Sitting across the table from Betty were two girls of her own age. They indicated they would like to meet her. She smiled back and said, "OK."

Click, click, her head swung around to see a nun pointing a finger at her. She bowed her head and started to eat. Everyone ate hurriedly, as time was important. Betty went back for seconds, as she never seemed to get enough to eat.

"One thing about this joint, there is enough to eat."

Plain wholesome food. Lunch was over, and it was time to return to work.

On Fridays, after afternoon classes were over, the children were allowed to play before the late meal. It was during this time that Betty was able to meet Nancy and Shirley. They questioned each other as children will do. Although Nancy was the oldest, she depended on Shirley for moral support. They were not related but looked like two peas in a pod. Nancy a little taller than Shirley, Betty was taller than them both. The three girls became fast friends. Little time was spent in play. The girls took this time to get to know each other.

Time was far too precious to be left doing nothing, as it was little enough that the children had as free time. When the girls did manage to spend time together, they left their problems behind and had carefree moments together. Time was a great factor in the sprawling building. Every moment was accounted for, to be late put a strain on everyone.

Late that fall in 1947, Betty's mother took sick and was unable to look after the child. Arrangements were made for her to stay within the confines of the convent. It wasn't the ideal thing for Betty, as she saw it, but she could handle it. All the rules and regulations would be the real killer for her. Never before had she been made to follow any signs of authority, and, now, her freedom would be taken away from her. However, it would not be that long. Somehow, she would endure the confinement. Betty was to report to the head nun who looked after the girls. The first thing Sister Mary Demon did was hand her a neat stack of blouses with ties, stockings, underwear, full slips, two heavy blue gaberdine tunics, and a pair of cumbersome shiny serviceable shoes. The convent's garb was assigned to her. Her arms were full, and to keep from spilling them on the floor she held her chin tight on the stack. She stood before Sister Mary Demon peering over the load of clothes. Sister Mary Demon, how aptly she was named, was a recruit of Hitler's regime. Tall and skinny, she looked about with silver-framed glasses perched on her beak-like nose, mouth puckered, wrinkling her lower face, her hands folded into her sleeves.

"Follow me," she commanded, as she turned briskly on her heels.

She walked with strides up three flights of steep steps. Betty scurried behind, panting with exertion when they reached the girl's dormitory. They entered the dormitory, rows and rows of perfectly made beds with tiny bedside tables beside them. Betty stood looking.

"Come, come child, time is awasting."

The child hurried to follow. Sister Mary Demon stopped before a large cupboard. Opening the door, she briskly removed two white sheets, one white pillowcase, and a grey, rough scratchy blanket. She piled them on top of everything else Betty carried, who leaned back to balance the load. She could barely see over the top.

"Come," she followed the nun like a lost sheep.

The nun halted before a bed in the middle of the large room.

"Put your things on this bed."

Betty tried to lay the load down neatly, but by this time her arms felt like lead and everything tumbled all over.

"Here, here, we will have none of that," the puckered mouth said.

Betty was sure the nun had a lemon in her mouth she was so sour. The grey striped mattress was rolled to the end of the steel bed. The nun gave it a push, and it flipped out flat on the bed springs. Betty saw someone else's urine stains upon the mattress. She wrinkled her nose with distaste.

"Make the bed, not a wrinkle, mind you," the nun stood with folded arms at the end of the bed. "Wait, I will show you how beds are made around here. I'll show you once and only once. This is the proper way."

Sister Mary Demon took one white sheet, flipped it with a snap, and folded and tucked each corner with swift movements. The sheet was perfect. Then came the top sheet, the grey blanket next, the top sheet pulled over the blanket just so. Snap went the pillowcase as she shook it out. Inside went the grey striped pillow. She smoothed out the creases and laid it on the bed. Betty stood there, watching every movement, her eyes big as she tried to grasp every detail.

"God, let me do it right," she thought. "At least the old witch made it for me this time." Not so, her good luck.

Before she could move, the nun whipped the bed bare and said, "You do it now. Hurry, I don't have all day."

Betty set about trying to make it look right. After numerous tries, it met with approval.

"Now, young lady, you will take one set of underwear, one slip, one blouse with tie, and one tunic. Don't forget your socks and shoes. You will take a bath, making sure to scrub behind your ears, and don't forget to scrub those filthy hands."

Betty shoved her hands deep in her pockets self-consciously. Withdrawing her hands, she reached for her things and took what she would need.

"Put the rest neatly in those drawers. I'll be right back."

The nun whirled on her heels and left quickly, to return just as quickly with a white bag in her hand.

"These are your toilet articles. Look after them, they are all you will get. Quickly, go bathe, and mind you had better be clean when you're finished. You have exactly seven minutes to finish."

Betty heard the threat and was to find out later that Sister Mary Demon never made idle threats, as she saw one little girl make the mistake of not washing properly. The little girl was grabbed roughly by the hair and scrubbed with a white rough face-cloth until her face was bright red and the child was sobbing silently. Betty had looked on with dismay and pity, shuddering to think it could happen to her. Betty hastily left to find the bathrooms, down the long hallway, to enter a room filled with baths, showers, sinks, and toilets.

There were no doors for privacy. It looked sterile and bare in the long room.

Hesitantly, she went about having her bath, the water barely warm. Worst of all, the yellow lye soap stank. It was impossible to wash her hair. She felt the slime from the soap and knew what it would be like mixed with cold water in her hair. However, she did wet her hair. She took the little scrub-brush and worked hard to remove every little dirt particle on her hands and feet. Finished, she climbed out of the tub and hurried to dry off. Precious moments slipped by as she dressed, half wet. Everying felt weird — cotton panties, cotton undershirt that rubbed her budding nipples roughly, the full slip. Her fingers fumbled as she did the buttons on the blouse. Over her head went the heavy tunic; the belt fit tightly around her waist. Sitting on the floor, she put on the thick white knee-high socks. She fumbled to put the black shoes on, and tying the laces she jumped to her feet. Grabbing the soap, face-cloth, and wet towel, she shoved them all into the white bag. She ran the black comb roughly through her tangled curly hair. She patted her damp hair and left the bathroom. In one hand, she carried the bag and, in the other, she carried dirty clothes and stinky sneakers. Clomp, clomp went the stiff black shoes. She skidded to a stop before Sister Mary Demon, who stood waiting, arms folded and foot tapping.

"You are four minutes late. Next time, be on time when I tell you. Umph!" She snorted, "You'll do as I say," as she surveyed the gangly child before her. "Give me those filthy clothes. They will have to be scalded and washed."

She took them between her fingers like they were deadly snakes. Nose wrinkled, she turned to leave the room. Betty stuck out her tongue at the rigid retreating back. At the head of the stairs Sister Mary Demon told Betty to go to class. Betty went down the three flights of stairs, trying to be quiet in the cumbersome shoes. Her skirt swished back and forth as she grabbed it to pull it lower. The air felt cold on her thighs and she raced across the courtyard, just in time to join the long line of children returning to class. Prayers over, class began. Deep in her tummy the rumbling told her she had missed lunch.

Betty looked up to see Nancy and Shirley looking at her. They gave her the OK sign, circled forefinger and thumb. She gave her hair a flick of her hand and put her nose in the air. Looking past the girls, she noticed Bobby Brown, that cute blond, giving her the OK sign, too. She looked him right in the eye, blushed to the roots of her hair, and lowered her eyes. Sister Mary watched the children from lowered eyes and smiled her sweet smile. Click, click, the wooden clappers sounded softly.

There were stairs all over the convent: upstairs, downstairs, front stairs, and back stairs; north stairs, south stairs, west stairs, and east stairs; stairs to the top of the convent, and stairs to the very bottom of the convent. Some were carpeted, some were bare hardwood stairs that gleamed, and some were concrete. There were short staircases and long, long staircases. In the convent, there was a very old, ornate elevator in very good repair. It had a grill sliding door and sliding doors on each floor. Within the elevator, on the wall, was a large half-circular brass gauge with numbers, Sub B, B, 1, 2, 3, and a big brass handle that slid noiselessly back and forth where you wanted it to go. If your imagination was good, you could almost see a person sitting on a high wooden chair, handle in hand, asking in a nasal voice, "Which floor, please?"

The elevator was off limits to everyone except Father Newman, the live-in priest, Sister Superior, and the very old nuns, those unable to walk from the second floor.

Betty loved elevators and hated stairs. Within two weeks, Betty knew every nook and cranny within the confines of the convent. She could be in any part of the convent with seconds to spare, removing her cumbersome shoes and racing about in stockinged feet. She would carry her shoes in her hand, or, if it was convenient, she hid them. If the need be, she would race to wherever she felt Mother Superior would be detained, race to the elevator, and ride up or down, wherever her shoes were hid. She left the elevator nonchalantly and proceeded on her way. Betty was forever trying to entice Nancy and Shirley to join her for a ride. No amount of coaxing could get them to come with her. One morning, they were late leaving the dormitory, as Nancy had a serious personal problem that embarrassed her a great deal. Those sleeping nearest her knew about her problem. They couldn't help it. Both Betty and Shirley knew and felt sorry for their friend. They were her true friends. They hurried to strip her bed, turn over the mattress, and put a clean snitched sheet on her bed, making it to perfection. Where Sister Mary Demon was, no one knew. At least the girls didn't know where she was, and, finishing the bed, they hurried from the dormitory for morning mass. Betty told the other girls it would be quicker to use the elevator. She knew that Mother

Superior would be standing by the chapel door, with hands folded and tucked into her habit sleeves, until the last person stepped through the door. Betty walked backward. As they neared the elevator door, she stood pressing the call button. On her last plea, the elevator door slid open, and without thought they all stepped through the open door. Betty slid the handle to the first floor, and they went silently down on well-oiled cables. The door slid open and the girls stepped out. They were immediately confronted by the imposing figure of Sister Mary Demon.

"The old witch must have flown down the stairs on her broom," Betty thought.

"Well, well, and what do we have here. You know you are not supposed to use the elevator?"

"Well, we were just trying it out. It's my fault. I made the others do it," Betty said in a small voice.

"Humph, a likely story. However, that is not the issue right now, Nancy," she said in a sugary sweet voice. "Do you have a problem? It seems there are sheets missing repeatedly from the cupboards and dirty wet ones in the clothes hamper. Do you know anything about them?"

Before Nancy could utter an acceptance or deny the question, Sister Mary Demon's hand snaked out of her sleeve and struck Nancy a powerful blow alongside the head. Nancy's head rocked, and she uttered a low moan, grabbing her stinging face. Betty stepped forward defensively with clenched hands, only to be stopped by a hand grabbing her and a warning look from Shirley. Helping Nancy would only make matters worse for all of them, but worst of all for Nancy.

"The three of you will be working in the scullery for the next month. Do you understand? Nancy, you will wash your sheets in cold water, in the bathtub, every time you wet them, and then you will hang them over the end of your bedside table for everyone to see, understand?" She poked Nancy square in the middle of her chest, "Now leave. You are late for mass and mind, you all, we still have the business of the elevator to discuss."

The three girls turned and walked away. Betty and Shirley walked on either side of their friend, wanting desperately to grab her and comfort her, yet knowing the puckered face watched them. They entered the silent chapel under the disapproving gaze of Mother Superior and the rest of the congregation.

After mass and before breakfast, Betty waited her chance and left the ranks of the children, racing around the front of the building to the front of the convent, down the gravel road to stand before the white statue of Jesus holding the lamb. Panting, she fell to her knees, crossed herself and breathlessly she asked, "Jesus, forgive me for getting my friends in trouble and please help Nancy."

She jumped to her feet, crossing herself again she raced to wait until it was safe to join the line of children going to class. When the chance came, she scurried, a Pippi Longstocking figure, to slip into her place in line.

Work in the scullery began next morning, hard work. Pots and pans, lots of pots and pans, by the dozens. Big ones, small ones, round ones, and square ones. Soupy water to the elbows, scrapping, washing, drying, stacking, and putting them away. Everything in its place. Loony Bill, with his large apron tied at the back with a big bow, wheeled the loaded carts one after another, unloading them for the girls and then loading them again when they were clean. Filling the cupboards. The girls were left unattended and so made the time and work go faster by talking and laughing good humorously.

One evening their good humour turned to violence. Loony Bill stood unloading a cart of soiled pots and pans. Nancy danced across the room, to lift Bill's big bow up and swing a large spatula across his backside. It was all done in good fun. Before anyone of them knew what was happening, Bill turned and threw Nancy to the floor — murder in his eye, rape in his heart. Her two friends ran to help her, but Loony Bill was a madman in strength. She was rescued only after their screams were heard by Sister Agnes, who came running with a broom to beat Bill off. Poor Bill ran down the hall like the hunchback of Notre Dame. The three scared girls were severely reprimanded and banished from the scullery to polishing furniture in the upper parlors.

This was more their style. All the really good things were up there. Parlors with beautiful furniture throughout, especially the music room, with its upright grand piano with the melodious tune. The metronome sat on top, swinging back and forth to the snappy music. Father Newman's suite was on that floor, too. The girls hated to enter his domain. They always felt he would grab one of them and cop a feel. His rooms were always left till he was not about. At times, this was impossible, and he would sit watching them like a fat black spider, ready to pounce. They learned to do his polishing in no time flat. One of the rooms they did held the preserved heart of Father Lacombe. A large apothecary jar was filled with formaldehyde, and

Betty held a finger tentatively to the jar, making the heart move about.

They always left the best for the last, the music room. Nancy would play, and the other two girls would harmonize numerous songs while dancing around the polished floors. Rugs were pulled back and their shoes were removed. They had a lovely time. Their best time came to an abrupt end one day when, in the midst of the boogie-woogie song and dance, the beautiful Sister Delphine entered the room unobserved and stood watching the three girls. They did do a good version of "In the Mood," with their sleeves rolled up and their knee socks rolled down like bobby socks, but this must stop. Click, click went the wooden clappers. The music stopped and three pairs of eyes turned to the sound. They looked round-eyed at the nun standing at the door with hands tucked into her habit sleeves. She did suggest the girls think about putting their talents to use for the Christmas concert coming up within the next few months.

Needless to say, it was time to separate these three. If ever a person could look like an angel, Sister Delphine did. You could almost see the halo above her head as she told the girls what their next jobs would be. Nancy to peel vegetables, Shirley to chapel duty, where she drank wine and got drunk, and Betty was sent to the nuns' floor to wash and starch wimples. Washing wimples was a job of forced misery, under the instructions of Sister Minerva, the tiny nun who barely reached Betty's belly button. Betty was shown the way to starch wimples. First, the water was boiled. Then, the starch was added, just the right amount to hold the wimple firm and pliable, capable of bending. Then, it was partly dried and ironed, so it fit firm but not wrinkled. Betty detested the job. It wasn't bad when she stirred the starch in the water, just the right amount, mind you. Round and round the spoon went. The mixture became thick and thicker. The minute it felt just right, Betty removed the long wooden spoon. It came out with a glop. Into the mixture went the wet, white wimples. At this point, instead of a wooden spoon you used your bare hands, plunging them into the hot mixture, turning and swirling the wimple around. First this way and then that way, the guck slid through her fingers, making squishy noises. It felt horrible. Betty stood there as the matter snaked and squirmed like a wet slug over her hand. It ran through her fingers as she hastily pulled the dripping wimple out of the guck. Her hands were red as lobsters.

"Mind you, don't drip any on the floor," the tiny nun scolded as Betty lifted the soggy mess to the hand wringer and turned the handle to watch the sticky slug squashed and land with a plop into the empty tub on the other side.

"There went Sister Mary Demon," she thought as she watched it land.

Silently, she laughed with glee. As they worked, tiny Sister Minerva talked about her family, especially her father, whom she claimed was a giant. She thought this because she said that when she would run toward him he would spread his long legs and she could run right between them. She would turn quickly and run back to be picked up in his strong arms and thrown high in the air. Sister Minerva was a delightful little person, and Betty loved her dearly, but love and work are two very different things.

Work meant less time to be idle, and Betty loved to be idle. To daydream of far-off places or hunt lions or dig for diamonds at Kilimanjaro or pilot planes or even pull a sword and kill a dragon, which, by the way, she really did with the yardstick, to stand in triumph with her foot on the dead reptile. She screamed in silent victory. One bright fall day, she could not stand the slimy work any longer, so she added more starch to the water, creating a terrible dilemma. The wet things dried to a hardness like many little boards, and, needless to say, by doing that a few times she was released from her duties. Outside the door, she removed her shoes and danced on graceful stocking feet, twisting and turning, dipping and bowing to the end of the hall, where she turned and did a deep curtsy to the unseen audience. Lightly, she ran down the stairs and through the hall, to halt abruptly before another door. Putting her shoes back on, she patted her wild hair and knocked softly on the door. Into the dark room she went. There sat the Head Sister of work details.

"Cecelia, Cecelia, what are we going to do with you? We have tried you on just about every job there is, and you just can't seem to fit in anywhere. I'll give you one more chance."

Betty wondered mischievously what her next job would be. It was into the deep bowels of the convent, but it was welcome. Fruit and desserts were more her style. Food was in her every thought as she was ordered to the kitchens. Take heart, dear reader, this child's life in the convent was not always hard work and no play.

Early morning, up before everyone else in the dormitory. All fresh from a good night's sleep and a cold-water wash made the silent walk through the halls brisker. There was the soft peel of the chimes in the big grandfather clock as it tolled the quarter hour, half hour, and the full hour. It, too, was quiet as it kept time in the massive building. Quiet, we must be quiet. No talking, no laughing, no shuffling, no coughing. It must be done quietly. God forbid if you should make a noisy fart. Mind you, proper little ladies didn't do those things. The work in the kitchen began before everything else, early in the morning so everything was ready when morning mass was over.

Betty would leave the kitchen to go to mass. The massive decorated door, done by master craftsmen, stood open to receive the many bodies that passed through the threshold each and every day. Betty walked down the middle aisle, between the rows and rows of silent pews, to reach her spot between her classmates. Dipping her hand into the holy water, she crossed herself. Bowing, she entered the pew sideways. She was first these mornings, and so it wasn't as hard to move in the confined space. Kneeling was really tough, but what really hurt was to kneel for five minutes on the hard wooden rail, with bowed head and clasped hands in prayer. She had quiet moments before the chapel filled with all the rest of the people in the convent. Betty loved the chapel. The sweet smell of incense, whiffing from the golden ball the altar boy held. White smoke curled, snaking out to reach the high ornate ceiling. Cherubs and angels graced the pale blue star-studded ceiling, laying upon cotton soft clouds. Beautiful statues stood on either side of the altar, high in their nooks. Jesus was on one side, looking down on his own with out-stretched arms. On the other side was the Blessed Mother, holding the Babe. She smiled in sweet serenity. A thousand lit candles cast a soft glow upon the figures. A draft from the airy chapel made the flames shift ever so slightly along the wall between the high stained-glass windows where special nooks held holy pictures depicting the stations of the Cross. Early morning sun shone on the coloured glass windows, creating multi-coloured sunbeams across the shiny bowed heads and adding to the celestial silence. Communion over, mass droned to a halt as the huge pipe organ began its sweet heavenly music. The chorus of many voices joined to sing in holy exultation. The last high note stopped in sweet agony as Betty listened with awesome delight. She could have sat there forever, listening in rapture as the soft click, click brought her back to reality. She had been so in tune with her surroundings that it was hard to rouse herself into motion.

Winter arrived with lots of snow and cold winds. The older boys went into the cold to clean the snow from the sidewalks and lane way. The children who had to cross the courtyard now went through the deep, dark underground tunnel to go to school. Extra time was now spent getting ready for the Christmas festivities. There would be a Christmas concert. Sister Delphine spoke to the three girls. She suggested that the girls prepare a song-and-dance routine to add variety to the Christmas concert. It was decided that they would do their best dance number. It would be an Al Jolson number, "Mammy." The girls worked hard in their spare time getting the number ready. Nancy would play the piano, and Shirley and Betty would sing and dance. Finally, the concert arrived. All day the girls practised. They never took time to eat that day. The excitement was building to a peak. They dressed early and stood backstage, watching the other children perform. As they waited for their cue, each girl had to use the bathroom. After what seemed like hours, Sister Delphine gave the girls their sign. Nancy walked to the piano and sat down. She looked different in her costume, as they all did. Borrowed boys' clothes and black shoe polish made up their costumes. Nancy turned from the piano and looked at her friends. With a resounding thrust of her nimble fingers the music started, and out came Shirley and Betty. Shirley knew how to tap-dance and so had no problems. However, Betty didn't, but, ever being the copy-cat, she did an excellent cover-up. They put their every effort into the number. At the end of the number, they stood centre stage with sweat-streaked faces and bowed time after time to the standing ovation. They had been a hit. Sister Delphine's face showed how proud she was of the three girls. The night had been a success, and it didn't matter that it would be days before the girls would be rid of the black shoe polish on their happy faces. It was late when the concert broke up. All the children had had a good time, forgetting, for a time, their problems. Time for bed, as there was work to do next morning.

As the New Year progressed, time was taken for all the children who would be making their first communion to prepare for the coming event. Betty's own first communion was her own special experience, something personal to cherish the rest of her life. She worked extra hard to learn her lessons, so that when the time came to receive her first wafer of communion she would be ready. Years later, she was to remember how awkward she felt in the white borrowed satin mid-calf gown with mutton sleeves of lace. A tiny vale of snowy white lace circled her ebony head, with spring violets. The contrast was stark. It didn't matter that she stood a head above everyone else. The thing was that she would feel equal to the rest of the children, more refined and not just the dirty little half-breed tomboy. It never changed a thing. She was still Cecelia (Betty) Gaudry, but to a child it made all the difference in the world.

After the chapel ceremony, all the children from the first communion class received their first white Bible and a white rosary, each white glass bead representing the prayers to be said. They marched in single file throughout the convent, receiving holy pictures, bookmarks, and sweet treats from the many other occupants of the convent. It was their special day.

Tiny Tim gave each child a sweet treat and a pat on the head. The sweet little man who evoked so much emotion from people they wanted to pat his head. Even Crazy Annie, who dribbled from her slack mouth, gave the children an absent-minded smile and cracked with laughter when they thanked her for the holy picture she gave them with dirt-caked claws. Old spinster, Miss Ross, sat rocking and smiled at the children who crowded around her. She handed the gifts to the children and looked off into space. Her mind was on bygone days, thinking, no doubt, about her own first communion as the children left her. Mr. Bruce sat on the long wooden bench, limp, rocking on the hard seat, holding holy pictures in his palsied hand, staring blankly as the children took a picture, unaided by the old man. The highlight of the day was an unscheduled stop at the dining-room where they were treated to ice cream and cake. Ice-cold milk slid down the gullet. Their treasures were piled in neat little stacks beside their plates. Before they removed the borrowed clothes, the children were led outside to the front of the convent, where pictures were taken. Old Father Newman stood in their midst, his white head bobbing in the bright sunlight. He patted a small head here and there. The silent statue of Jesus holding the little lamb looked on in silent approval as the camera clicked.

Betty removed the borrowed clothes and put them in their cloth bag covers. Slowly, she dressed and left to go to the kitchen. She had work to do. Sister Alphonse waited for Betty. It didn't take long to get back into the swing of things. Vegetables to be peeled, potatoes to be pared, cans and cans of fruit to be opened and emptied into large bowls. Fruit syrup sprayed and slid down the sides. It was all wiped up with a finger. It tasted good before the bowl was wiped clean with a cloth. It was the longest job she had ever stayed at in the convent. She liked it there, and Sister Alphonse was easy to get along with, a gentle, understanding woman. She knew how to laugh and she knew how to scold, at all the appropriate times.

One spring morning, a light spring rain was falling. Just before lunch, Betty left her classroom to race to her job. Every day she was let out of class early to help prepare lunch. Down the stairs she went. The cumbersome shoes now quiet and well worn. As she ran across the courtyard, there were puddles all over the yard. She hopped and skipped here and there so as not to get her feet wet. One of the older girls, Laura, the beautiful leader of the older girls, deliberately stuck her foot out and tripped Betty. She landed face first into a puddle. Dripping wet, she got to her feet. Betty turned her dirty face, purple with rage. Laura stood there. Hands on her hips, she uttered in a low voice, "Come on you dirty little squaw, there's nobody around to help you. Let's see how well you fare with me now."

All of Betty's good intentions flew to the winds, as Betty charged the older girl with head down. She roared like a wounded animal as she knocked the older girl to the ground. Laura landed with a thud on the damp ground.

"Humph," she went in a shocked voice.

In a flash, Betty grabbed the long hair in one hand, and with the other she pummelled the girl. Her element of surprise worked. The older girl was finally able to wrap her arm around the younger girl's neck, and she shoved a sharp pointed finger into the child's mouth. She hoped to rip the young girl's mouth at the corner. Instinct made Betty's strong young teeth clamp down on the foreign object in her mouth. Flesh broke, and the horrible sound of enamel on bone could be heard, as Betty tasted the salty blood running in her mouth. She spat in the older girl's face. Before she could jump to her feet, four pairs of hands held her captive. They lifted her off their friend and dragged the screaming spitting child to the centre telephone pole. With a rope, which they so conveniently held, they tied her to the pole. Securely, she was held, and one of the other girls stepped forward and said, "This is what we do to wild spitting Indians." Betty was held at the stake all noon hour. She missed her work, and she missed her lunch. When, finally, the group of older girls returned to let her go, she swore with vengeance to get even.

"I'll get even, you bitch. You just wait."

They turned their backs and left her laughing as they entered the convent.

Later that day, Betty slipped a note to her brother Elvin, who was a day student. It read, "Get me some itching powder."

After classes, she limped to her job in the kitchen. Sister Alphonse stood waiting. She had a twinkle in her eyes and a small smile, which she tried to hide from the scruffy child. A swat on the butt told Betty she understood. A few days later, Elvin slipped Betty an envelope, written on it was "Itching Powder, Guaranteed to Work."

She waited for the appropriate time and slipped unobserved into the dormitory. Rubbing her hands together like the mad professor, she ran to each of the offending girls' drawers and very deliberately sprinkled adequate amounts of powder into the crotch of their cotton panties.

Next morning after baths, the real fun began, and Betty and her friends stood back to watch. They slipped out of line and hid behind a large pillar. The line passed silently, until Laura and her friends walked by. Five big girls walked like they had itching powder in their pants, as well they did. Five girls squirmed and rubbed, as one after another their hands crept to scratch the offending area. In the chapel, they twisted and turned, rubbing their butts on the hard wooden seats. Mass masturbation it looked like from afar, as one after another they excused themselves to rush to the toilets. No amount of water removed the hellish stuff. In fact, the water made them burn. Betty's revenge was just.

Betty went to her job happy and content. Sister Alphonse wanted some things from the big cooler where all the perishable foods were kept. She asked her helper to go get them. Betty, in her hour of glory, forgot to put a block in the big door. It clicked behind her and locked her in.

"Oh! well, I might as well make the best of it," she thought, as she began to laugh.

Peels of laughter doubled her over with a stitch in her side. Tears ran down her face as she recalled the girls with itching powder in their pants. She wiped her eyes and turned to survey the massive locker. It was kind of cold in there, but "What the heck," she thought, as she saw rows and rows of dew-dipped fresh strawberries staring back at her from the counter, beckoning to be eaten. Not to worry, someone would find her when she was missed. She popped a plump strawberry into her mouth, then another and another, until she had to sit down. She felt green and sick as she held her hand over her mouth. She took deep breaths. Hours later, Sister Alphonse found her missing helper locked in the locker, rolling on the floor, gripping her swollen belly. The nun helped the poor child to her feet. Betty stumbled out the door and ran to the nearest toilet, upchucking at both ends. The place stank as she washed her flushed face with cold water. Needless to say, her cushy job was finished when Sister Alphonse discovered the missing strawberries.

Late spring was here, green grass pushed its green blades skyward. Purple velvet crocuses danced in the breeze. Pussy willows crept up the budding trees. Meadowlarks sang for a spring shower. The chickadee dee-deed in the distance. Cows bawled for food, and little lambs bleated for their mothers, like lost sheep. A colt ran and bucked on new-found legs, as he raced around the corral. He stopped by his mother and nudged at her underbelly. Oh!, how good it felt to run outside without a winter coat. To throw her arms wide and let go her silent primal scream, to greet the blue sky and soft fluffy spring clouds. The air smelt sweet with fresh earth, new grass, and even pig shit to her reborn nostrils. The dark blanket had lifted and Oh!, spring was here.

June arrived. Betty's thirteenth birthday came and went. School would soon be over. Finally, the day arrived. She had passed into grade eight. Good-byes were said on this last day. Betty raced to get her old clothes. Sister Delphine handed over a stack of clothes to the excited breathless child, all washed and pressed. Betty ran up the three flights of stairs, barely touching them. In the bathroom she stripped the convent clothes off and left them in a pile on the floor. She pulled on her panties and slid into her well-worn jeans. They felt a little tight. The old grey sweat-shirt didn't fit so loose.

"I didn't think there were this many holes in it," she thought, as she poked a finger through.

She sat on the floor as she changed socks and shoes for sneakers. Dressed, she rolled up her jeans mid-calf and took an elastic, putting her hair in a pony-tail. Picking up her report card she literally flew down the stairs, to skid to a halt before Mother Superior. Before the nun could utter a sound, Betty said, "Bye, Mother Superior, see you sometime," and was gone in a blur.

As she ran, she reached into her back pocket and, much to her delight, withdrew a wad of bubble gum. Saliva filled her mouth, and she swallowed quickly as she popped the wad in her mouth. She grabbed her old bike and with a yell she jumped aboard. Peddling like crazy, she came to a screeching halt before the silent statue of Jesus. Gravel flew. She crossed herself quickly and spoke to the silent figure, "Lord, forgive me, but this really isn't my kind of place. I know there have been times when I could have done better, and I promise to repent, truly I will. It's time for me to leave. I love you, and I will be back to see you, really I will."

She looked up at Him, crossed herself, and left. At the bottom of the hill, she stopped and looked back. She had left a piece of herself there as she noticed faces pressed against the upper windows. She waved and blew a kiss. She looked at the silent figure, and as she turned she was sure she saw Him wink.

Bernice Sanderson

Drugs and Alcohol

Drugs and alcohol have become our number one killer among our Native people. We realize this, it is spoken so often. Yet we continue to ignore the warning. It has done so much to destroy us as Native people. Our culture is dying. What must happen before we come to realize it is destroying us in many ways? We have no value of life, no understanding or compassion for our fellow human beings, no respect for our elders. Even worse, no respect for our children, our parents, and ourselves.

Is this what life is all about? Putting ourselves through bitterness, shame, and guilt? And using violence to control our daily lives, or letting others control us? We do so many things in the world we shouldn't be doing. And that is wrong. Waking up one morning, we realize we have no one to wake up to anymore but our ugly selves and thoughts. We try to take our own lives, that were given to us. It's wrong to take even that away from ourselves. Yet, it happens. We let drugs control our ways. And each dying day we become weaker, with no sense of values. We are always searching for our next high or next drunk. And trying to figure out ways to support ourselves. There are so many ways. Many of our ways will lead us to jail. We waste our lives doing sweet nothing. The circle just keeps on going the same way. When will this stop, I often wonder?

Only when we are willing to do something about it. First, we must accept things as the way they are and just go on for the best. Once we start working with our problems, many wonders will begin. We must be very careful with ourselves, and grow. It will take time.

Remember, we spent many years being sick. It will take a long, slow healing to be the people we want to be. In the end, it will be worth it all, as we work to better ourselves. Whatever it may be, always listen to those who have been there. Get closer to our Great Spirit. It's so important, look for guidance. May it be with an elder or someone very close to you that you can trust. We must learn to share our feelings and thoughts. In return, we will gain back respect, and slowly everything will fall into place. Yes, there is hope for us who care for a brighter future.

This way, as Native people, we can no longer be called drunks or losers. There are people around us who care and are willing to listen and help. We have a choice, if we only let it happen.

First published in "From Where We Stand: Women's Views on Alcohol." Prince Albert, Saskatchewan: Pine Times Productions, n.d.

Constance Stevenson

I am thirty-one years of age, living in the town of Kamsack, Saskatchewan.

I have two children, both boys, aged nine and five.

My hobbies are reading horror novels and, on occasion, writing poetry.

Prejudice (Or, In-Laws)

I am of a different race,
And I know it bothers you
But I didn't ask to be put in this place.
Are you also against the Jew?

Is it because I'm an Indian
Or, in your term, a savage?
I never asked to be Indian,
Nor am I a savage.

I see the hatred in your face
I know just what you're thinking.
Indian! You wish there wasn't such a race!
So, tell me straight and quit the hinting.

It doesn't do you good to cry,
It doesn't help me, either.
Maybe, if I left, or died,
I'd be one less bother.
(But, I'll never give you that satisfaction.)

Thanks Anyway

So tired of wearing this phoney smile,
the one that I've worn for this last while.
And, in my mind, I feel like dying,
forget about those I may leave crying.

They'll forget me in times to come,
with every day's rising sun.
In time, I won't even be a memory.
This so-called life of mine just isn't to be.

But, I'll go to my grave,
and to those who tried to save
a life that wasn't worth a damned thing,
one that's just not worth remembering,

Thanks anyway.

Mary Mae Strawberry
Translated by Ella Paul

Mary Mae Strawberry is a Cree/Stoney, originally from the Paul Band west of Edmonton. She married into the Saulteaux Reserve west of Rocky Mountain House. She is a widow and has five children.

Ella Paul translates Mary Mae Strawberry's traditional teachings.

Editors' note — The following presentation was made by Mary Mae Strawberry at a conference of Alberta Aboriginal women's groups on 16 March 1990:

I Feel in My Heart

I really don't like the way of human behaviour in the world, and that is why I stand to talk to you today. I have been in this world for a long time. I enjoyed this morning and heard good things. When I come to sessions, I bring my grandchildren. I brought, this time, a young woman because she is in this world to have children and because it is miraculous to have a baby and watch it grow.

Men step on women today because of lack of respect, and they fail to realize where they came from. Women, their minds, their hearts, are full of gentleness and love. They are like the earth — they reproduce, they are givers of life. They have a baby, they nurse that baby, they cuddle that baby, and they bring it up with love. Because of this nurturing, breast-fed babies are smarter.

I will talk about myself. I was brought up traditionally, in the times. I have no education from a school. My education came from my parents. I was widowed a long time ago, with five small children. I completed my task of raising my children. I raised my children with my hands. I worked for a living. I didn't get any public assistance or pension. I attended to my children's needs through trapping, hunting, tanning moose hides, and swapping these items for what we needed. Because of my upbringing, I never took for nothing. I always paid back.

I feel in my heart that I have almost completed my journey as a woman. To this day, I have never taken pills or any kind of white-man medicine. I am very close to Mother Earth. She takes care of me and I take care of Her, and that is why I can stand and tell you these things today. I know my role as a woman is not to sit in the house and turn buttons. My role is to work and use my hands.

This year has been difficult for me, because of grief. I lost a grandson through alcohol. That is why I decided to speak to people, because of my sorrow. Also, my year has been difficult because, this year, I only killed nine martins, fifty squirrels, and one coyote. My most precious moment is when I take my gun and go hunting. I don't take this money for myself, for the animals I sell. I take it for my grandchildren's needs. Moose hides I give to my children and granchildren for their needs.

I know I work hard, but that is what a woman should be doing. Today, I feel very sorry for young people, because they don't know how to work. They don't want to work. I want to show the youth my hands and the grip in my hands, so that maybe they will want to work and have hands like me.

Today's youth are always sitting. They are too tired sometimes to get up to get that welfare cheque. Today, their hands are only extended for free stuff. Their spare time is spent watching television and listening to the radio to tell them how to drink.

Young people, I hope, will listen to the teachings and, also, what work is. My kids have a lot of trouble. They live in Red Deer. Lots of smoking and drinking goes on in Red Deer. And parents — lots of bingo, bingo, bingo, and the bars and hotels. All parts of the family are separate. There is no family structure. My grandchildren are there. That is my worry. Then, I can't sleep. Then, I get up and do my hides.

Karen M. Watcheston

I am a Cree woman. I was born in the spring of 1958. I was raised on the lands near the Ochapowace Reserve, in the Crooked Lake area in the south-eastern part of Saskatchewan. I am proudly the great, great, granddaughter of Chief Red Dog Star, who was the hereditary chief of the Star Blanket Nation. His mother was a Cree and Sioux woman. His daughter, my kohkom (grandmother) Hortence, is my mentor, who calls me Kaye (Crow). I also have a twin, Sharon.

My passion for literature and poetry stems from my mentor's great wisdom and strength, and the devoted love and respect she had for the new written language, in spite of its heavily male-dominated roots. This vestige of pride within our culture is our vehicle through which our people will be able to survive and live through the harsh transition on this wheel of life and process.

Through our journey of language, we, as women, must illustrate the great power of the quill and the strength it has woven within the quill's feathers, and within our own quilting of living. We, the mothers of life and the holders of the "seed within," must unite and carry for all this gift of flight and breath into the nostrils of the winds. We must make our own stand on this path of the living and take the right to be the "keepers of our own gardens." Within each of us, we have the right to gaze upon a star and make a wish upon that star. Then, to be able to dream a dream — then, have the right to live it.

I am presently raising my own two beautiful daughters against the landscape of the hues of taupe. I am proudly somebody's mother. My children and I reside in the foothills of the Rocky Mountain area, in the majestic city of Calgary. I will be writing the rest of my life for the sheer love I feel for it and myself.

Beyond the Wheat Field

She was alone in her kitchen while the lives of her children went on around her in the other rooms of their house. She stood for a moment and looked out the open window where the late summer day was gathered in the pale streaks of the cloudy sky. It had become clear to her that she was growing and enjoying this habit of solitude, being a woman alone with herself and her children. That moment at that window, she very much enjoyed the peacefulness and the sense of independence it brought to herself and her young family.

In her reflection, she could see her faint pleasant smile, crooked at one corner and shyly sincere. Her face glowed with warmth under her hair that was as black as a raven's coat. Her cheek-bones, she knew, were those of her Musum's. His face, and hers, were as proud and stern as that of their Cree heritage, of the people generations before them.

As a young girl, she remembered her Musum. He had said that her eyes told of many stories, of immense feelings, and of honesty. If she would look into the beholder's face wanting nothing save the truth, a face could never lie. She could remember his voice saying, "A face will not lie to you, the mouth will. And if you look long and hard at a person's eyes, they cannot." He said of her eyes, "When you are a happy and honest child they dazzle and dance, but when you are sad and distant from your heart they will be cold and dull, for they seek the truth from some fierce edge of awareness. Look long and hard. They will not lie to you, my girl, for the truth you can see and only in a lie will you not be able to see your own reflection."

The body she held stood proudly in her reflection. She was proud as she recalled the care she had taken at the time her children were born. Many an evening she had spent exhausted from the painstaking workouts she would do. As she worked out, she thought of why she was doing this to herself: to be part of that young, vibrant girl in the fields again, which she would now be able to share with her own daughters.

She wanted to be part of and share their youth and her memories of her Musum's home, of a grand, free childhood, and that's what brought her these treasures. One could not be fat and unhurried when the early days of the land and the fields required so much energy and prolific zest. There had been a time when being quick and sinewy meant running in the field, being alone with only the morning breakfast milk and the dawn behind her. That was a time remembered as a time when she was at repose with her thoughts and a time when time was truly her own.

It was to be a possession, cherished forever. She would never take for granted her solitude and its precious memories, which she would share with her own daughers, whose innocence was as hers had been, treasured, and for all the children to come.

Looking again into the window, she could see her face was as healthy as the wheat in the fields beyond the reflection. The stalks of wheat stood there, touched by nothing but the wind. In this moment, she found contentment, for she knew that it was here that she had found peace.

The late evening breeze that had whistled in her ears as though she were a young fawn was not whistling of the years rolled in these fields of wheat. The breeze whispered to a world within itself and beyond it. It had become a sound she could hum whenever she needed a pleasant, safe space to think and be alone, a place where she could be comfortable with herself and her solitude. It was also a sound she would remember with passion.

This wheat field beyond this wind, that had brought her family its life and its abundance, had also brought with it death and somber, morose idleness. The wheat with its restoring powers was not bringing her as she stood at this window anything but pain and sudden resentment, for she knew that it had been the wheat and not the fields that had taken her Musum from her childhood.

She would not soon forget the wheat's power to change from being a truth and life-giver to being a noxious enemy. She knew this field with its wheat was capable of feeding a hungry Indian, and, as easily, it could kill one with its fermented liquid. She knew well of its poetry and power over men and its capacity to control.

She would not remember the wheat as the taker of lives, as the taker of her Musum's last breath. Life was to be found in this wheat field. In the wind's whistle was the answer to her own happiness. And it would be here in this field and in this reflection that she could find her own truth and its worth, for in these she was able to find solitude.

As she stepped closer to the open window, she took a long hard look into the reflection of herself before going to her children in the other rooms. Perhaps it was a kind of certainty and a call from honesty that had brought her here this evening. There was a fierce fire about the reflection she now saw before her that she would recall in her thoughts in the evenings to come.

Standing alone, she did not mind the thought of not having anyone to share these moments of reflection with. Save for the voices of her children, the moment was restful, and she relished the place she had made for herself alone and for her children.

She heard her Musum's voice calling her from her youth, "Come my girl. We have work to do and seeds to tend, for we want this field good and ready for the Sun-dance, and the time, she will not wait for anyone. We will sing as we talk and work. Then we will dance in the field. Come my girl."

His eyes seemed to dazzle and dance in the reflection now, as she smiled at the vision. It had for a moment brought her to a time and a field in which her own youth would be forever embossed on the window pane. It brought her to a moment when her old Musum's voice could remind her that this was our field forever, to reflect upon whenever we needed to be with ourselves and our solitude.

Each year, it was to bring all our children closer to a day when we all could sing and dance with the life the seed had brought for us, the seed from which we all came, and in which our children could find comfort, freedom, and a home. It was a field that would always bring our children good memories and lessons about life that we could all now carry into this field of life's processes. It was a field to be shared throughout our lives, as learners and lovers of life, a field to be wandered as a peaceful honest solitude.

There was no longer any time to ponder precious solitary thoughts. Her children in the other rooms were ready for their story and their own solitudes. She knew that they would sleep peacefully tonight with only a wheat field as their blanket. Life had brought her here tonight to enjoy and live and not to wonder at the cost of the seeds her Musum had paid so harshly for so many nights before.

Gayle Weenie

I am Cree, originally from the Sweetgrass Reserve, and I now live in Saskatoon. I started writing mainly out of frustration when a close friend suggested that I do something positive with some of my pent-up negative energy.

Sun-dance

You can hear the drums
You can hear the chants
You can hear the rattles
You can hear the flutes

You can see children playing
You can see people laughing
You can see tents in a circle
You can see the sacred lodge in the centre

You can hear the crier
You can see the colourful offerings up around the lodge
You can smell the sweetgrass burning
You can feel the warmth of the sacred fire burning

You can see the dancers in rhythm with the drum beat
You can see the servers inside the lodge
You can see families with their giveaways enter the sacred lodge
You can hear their thanksgivings and prayers

You can hear the singers on horseback
As they sing in unison around the lodge
You can see young and old, sit and watch
You can feel the spirit of our forefathers

Ah! The Sun-dance — the most sacred of our ceremonies
It has been practised for years
It must be carried on for more
Because it is so

Nohkom

Grandmother   – I miss you
               – I can see your smile
               – I can hear your laughter
               – I can feel your comfort
               – I can taste your bannock
               – I can hear your stories
               – I can hear your jokes
               – I can see you standing tall, proud, and happy
               – I wish we'd had more time

Grandmother   – I miss you

Grandmother   – Watch over me and all my family

The Eyes of an Indian

Grandmother used to say, "Never look anybody in the eye"
It is a sign of respect
It is a sign of politeness
Never look at the eyes of an Indian

Oh Grandmother, we did not always listen
We peeked
We looked when you weren't looking
To see the eyes of an Indian

Oh Grandmother, it was not to be disrespectful
When we looked
We saw kindness, joy, and love
In the eyes of an Indian — yours

Oh Grandmother, it is difficult now
White man say, "Look at me"
So we look awkwardly
With the eyes of an Indian

Oh Grandmother, if only you can see what I see
Sometimes there is scorn, anger, and ridicule
Often there is unkindness and hurt
Even in the eyes of many an Indian

Oh Grandmother, maybe it was your way
Of protecting us from seeing a broken spirit
If only we had been mindful of our ways
And never looked at the eyes of an Indian

Jessie Winnipeg-Buller

I am the second youngest of eleven children, six of whom are deceased. I was born on the Blackfoot Reserve, located near Gleichen, Alberta, on 27 March 1940.

I remembered this story and others being told to me by my late parents, Jack and Ellen Winnipeg. My father was part Scots, although he spoke good Blackfoot and hardly spoke English. My parent's Indian names were Dark Daughter and Eagle Bear Medicine. My Indian name is Singing Away Woman, which my late aunt gave and blessed me with when I was an infant. I am thankful to my aunt and blessed by this name.

I am happily married to my non-Native husband. I have eight beautiful children and fourteen grandchildren. I enjoy painting and drawing and am presently taking art classes.

I am planning to do another bedtime story. I thank my Heavenly Father for everything, especially for saving my soul. I really enjoyed writing this story. I hope you will enjoy it.

An Indian Maiden and the Stars
(An Old Blackfoot Bedtime Story)

Before the white man came, long ago, on a clear starry night, two young maidens were out for a stroll around the camp. One of the maidens said, "I am going to wish on the brightest and most beautiful flashing star to be my husband."

The two maidens parted company. The wishful maiden started back to her tepee when, all of a sudden, a tall, handsome brave stood in front of her. The brave was dressed in buckskin and feathers. The brave told her, "Your wish has been granted. I am the star that you wished upon for a husband, and I have come for you." The brave said, "You cannot come back to your people when you leave them, because your wish is a curse upon you."

The maiden and the brave went at once to the sky where he had come from. Although the maiden was happy that her wish came true, she did not realize the consequences of her wish.

The maiden and her husband lived happily in the sky with their baby, who was a fragile star. One day, the husband told his wife not to dig out a huge pumpkin that was growing in their garden. As the days went by, the maiden's curiosity got the best of her. She slowly started to uproot the pumpkin, which she wasn't suppose to dig, but she succeeded in digging out the plant. To the maiden's surprise, the plant left a big hole in the ground. As she looked down through the hole she noticed something moving around down below. The maiden was surprised and overjoyed because she recognized the place as her people's camp.

However, seeing her people, the maiden felt homesick and was very sad and cried aloud for her home. When her husband realized what his wife had done by digging the pumpkin out, he felt disappointed by his wife's disobedience toward him. He had told her how he had warned her about digging or removing the pumpkin.

"Now, because of your disobedience, you and our baby will have to be roped down from this home," the brave said.

He gathered enough vines and strips of hide to use to rope his wife and baby back down to her people. The maiden and her husband said their goodbyes.

"As painfully as I feel about you leaving, I must warn you," said her husband. "Our baby is fragile and must be kept safe and protected at all times until he grows up to be a man."

As the maiden made her way down toward her people's camp, there was a boy whose eyes were badly infected. But he could still see, and he looked up and started shouting, "I see something coming down from the sky and it is coming toward us."

But the people just laughed at him and did not believe him because they thought that he was just seeing things. When the maiden reached the ground, she was welcomed by her relatives and the rest of her people.

The maiden was so happy to return to her people's camp that the warning of her husband about their baby's care was not taken seriously by the maiden. The baby was mostly with her, as she secretly cared for her child. The excitement of home, family, and friends were her busy activities of the day. The maiden had been gone a long time, and her people wanted to visit with her. The days went by, and the maiden was happy. Although she did miss her husband, she had their son for comfort. The baby was hidden near her bed, but children were near the baby, and, without realizing, one of the children took the star baby and ripped it apart. Then it was thrown to the floor.

When the maiden realized that her baby was missing, she looked around and saw on the floor her torn baby, who was turning into stardust. The maiden was shocked and cried till she could no longer cry.

Debbie Wiper

I was born at the Royal Alexandra Hospital in Edmonton, on 21 January 1970. I am twenty years old and reside in Calgary. I composed these stories in treatment for physical and emotional abuse. During the summers of 1986, 1987, and 1988, I was involved in the Wood's Summer Stock Theatre. Last year, it was well publicized throughout the city. That is how I began writing and acting out my experiences. Thanks to Clem Martini, Barry Mickelson, and Laura Bachynski for their support and time and to all the audiences who came to our productions.

H.E.R.

I woke up in a moisturizing kind of space. I wondered what had happened to cause this painful thought. Many times, I had wondered what could have made it eerie and uncaring, and all that came to my mind was H.E.R. People had thought I was crazy. One day, I had found myself in a position where I was going to say where is everything going and everything fading and getting foggy with peace forever and not having to think of what's H.E.R. name. Unfortunately, I found myself woken up by someone saying, "Let's go open the Christmas presents." Wanting to reply with #@*!!, I walked slowly out into the living-room. There stood a tree beautifully decorated, lights shining and glowing off the wrapping paper. I found myself for a minute thinking of happy thoughts and not all the sad moments. There was one present under the tree for me. I sat on the couch and wondered what was inside. The boy was gone and the tree had no glitter anymore. Slowly, tearing off the paper to finally get to the box itself, I held my breath for a minute before lifting the lid. I thought I heard someone saying something without paying attention and with a quick flash of lights, darkness, eeriness, I found myself dead. She had torn me apart. H.E.R.

Thinking Back, Summer 1988

I was too old to play with dolls and too young to be out after midnight, but I knew the difference when something was wrong with someone. This person, "The Enemy," was acting different.

"The Enemy," that was my name for her. As a young person, sometimes we label people, and then they have to hold up their reputation. Maybe that's what she was doing.

It was really weird to see her like that. She didn't notice me as I looked in through the bedroom door. I saw only a few minutes of it, but it was pretty scary. I saw things that were done. Her, pulling her hair, making faces in the mirror, crying very softly. It all looked very abnormal.

I know at the time I wanted to yell at her, tell her she was crazy. Look I wanted to say, look at what you're doing to yourself. Is this what I'll do when I grow up?

She was supposed to be a role model for me. I didn't say anything, of course. She would have told me, mind your own business, said, it's your own fault, get out of this room before you regret it. So I slipped back and let the door fall . . . shut.

There was a time when I would have put that person down in every way.

Now, when I think about "The Enemy," I feel sorry for her.

Broken Heart

To say you know someone
is a statement unknown.
To risk your sensitivity
is a challenge
that should be taken if you
don't want to be alone.
To feel some kind of friendship
for someone
is very special.
I take this on,
knowing that a day will come
when we'll part in good or bad,

a time where we'll cherish
together
in laughter and in tears.
To save a space in my heart,
which is now empty
filled with pain and fear,
knowing that special
someone for parts of life
which were quite difficult
but her being there stopped
the pain.
Now I realize the risk
was not worth taking
and so I stand alone,
with a piece of my heart
cutting my hand.
Do I try again?

Mary Young

Born in Bloodvein, Manitoba. Attended high school in Winnipeg and graduated with a bachelor of arts from the University of Winnipeg. Currently working as a Native Student Advisor at the University of Winnipeg.

Heart in Two Hands

Apparently, she came into this world hopping out of her mother's womb and from birth she almost always knew what was in store for her. Other times, things around her were discouraging but they somehow pushed her, moved her, and she would look forward to the future. She often thought, "What could I do to make this world a better place? How can a little girl find peace, love, and harmony, not only for her family but for all Native people?" It didn't seem so difficult; people were the same. We had things in common.

As she grew older, she continued to ponder, she became strong, strong enough to leave home. Her feet could carry her for miles. Her feet didn't ache, but her heart ached for a better world, more understanding, and more communication. The city seemed so big, so cold, and the people were different. She would walk home from school thinking about home and friends, and she often thought, "I wonder if they know this feeling I'm carrying around?" All she knew was when she wrote home she would never consider mentioning it. I'm not weak. I can do it. She dug deeper to try and figure out her feelings. She took her heart with both hands and she saw there were different compartments. There was loneliness, for sure, there was depression, not much though, there was definitely doubt, and she could see doubt had touched all the compartments at one time or another. But then she smiled. There was that special place in her heart for her family she left so long ago. She missed their laughter, their stories, and their smiles. She often went through the reasons why she left, and this would remind her of the goals she had set for herself. She wondered if she could accomplish these goals. Would anybody understand what she was trying to do? Besides, who would pay attention? Did anybody else see things like she did? Not all Indians were drunks, or are they?

Robin Young

I was born and raised in Cold Lake, Alberta. I am of French and Chipeywan Indian descent. I am in my late twenties.

Though I am college educated, most of what I write comes from experience and what I learn through the teachings of life.

Reflections

1

"I remember feeling helpless when I was growing up. Especially when Mother was getting beaten up. I can't count how many times that I wished I was grown up, just so I could break the arm that struck my mother. At the same time I would be mad at her for going out with men who just used her."

2

"I grew up in a 'don't' world. It was always 'don't' do this or 'don't' touch that. Sometimes, when I reflect back today, I wonder what would've happened had I said, 'Why not?'"

3

"I never realized that there was two of me when I was abusing alcohol. Or I knew that I possessed two very separate personalities, and it wasn't until my decision to abstain from over-drinking that I'd stopped denying that there was in fact a bad side to me. When I was drinking heavily, the negative personality always won over the positive side, like inside myself there was a great battle going on between the two sides of me.

I can say that the real Robin had a few close friends who really cared about me and the other Robin had a hell of a lot of drinking buddies, but no close friends.

When it seemed that the negative Robin was going to win the battle and she'd pulled all the stops, that's when I realized that I was breaking down and I was going to just lie down and stop fighting. But Robin's true friends came along and pushed me, like grab hold of your senses and really just have it out with this terrible Robin and I was given the encouragement and a touch of strength through the grace of God.

I can look back at some of the really stupid things I'd done while I was drunk and tell myself that the person doing those things wasn't the real me, and that line of thinking has helped my sobriety. At the same time, I don't deny that the things I'd done weren't done by me, because I do need to take responsibility for my actions and that part of me has to pay the consequences of those actions."

The Final Cry

He closed his eyes — did he like the darkness?
He let his heart beat — did he feel the pain?
He let his mind wonder — could he turn off the thoughts?
He thought about his childhood days — was he really a happy child?

He let his arm slowly rise — could feel a pulling sensation.
Did he really want to do this — maybe there was another way.
Suddenly he could feel himself floating — hey was that "me" down there?

. . . .

"I had a friend who took his own life, and it was very difficult for me to deal with. When I first heard about what he'd done, I just blocked all feeling, like I thought it couldn't have happened because I'd seen him a couple of days before.

I don't recall crying, even at the funeral. It wasn't because I didn't care, but I refused to accept it.

I blamed myself for the longest time, because I'd seen the signs and I had this feeling that he'd do something to himself and I saw the vacant stare in his eyes, but I realize now that I'm not at fault. When a person chooses to end their life, it's really their decision, and no one is at fault.

Today, I'm grateful that I knew this young man and I think about him sometimes, especially when I'm walking close to a river, because he and I use to walk close to water, and it's a nice serene place to remember him."

Don't

Don't be silly,
   of course the sky is blue.
Don't be dumb,
   you know the grass is green.

Don't run,
   I can't stand to see you fall.
Don't laugh,
   can't you see I'm talking.

Don't go anywhere,
   I'll be back soon.
Don't let anyone into the house,
   you don't know who might come by.

Don't be silly,
   of course I'm not drunk.
Don't be stupid,
   of course beer bottles break.

Mind Game

"Dad, could we play ball?"
"I'm busy right now, ask me later."

Later

"Dad, could we play ball now?"
"I have things to do, ask your mother."

"Mom, could we play ball?"
"I'm busy, go ask your father."

And so

"Come on, ball."

· · · · · · · · · ·

"I didn't play when I was a child. What I did do though was re-enact what I saw the adults around me do. Most of the time, I observed them drunk, so I had a lot of fights and arguments in my plays. One time, I beat the crap out of my imaginary friend. Why? Because he didn't use my imaginary door."

Afterword

The circle has neither beginning nor ending. It has always been. The circle represents the journey of human existence. It connects us to our past and to our future. Within the periphery of the circle lies the key to all Native philosophy, values, and traditions. All things living depend upon its equilibrium. If it is unbalanced, the effects on our physical, mental, and emotional health can be devastating. Native peoples have experienced continuous change in the last two hundred and fifty years, and the circle has suffered stresses beyond imagination. Yet, it remains intact like the original people of this land. The women are the keepers of the circle. They have the power to nurture and to replenish the life forces. Through our writing, we are maintaining our Nativeness in this fast-paced, often foreign contemporary society. The written word has given us our voice, and we have begun the healing process. We are writing the circle.

Robin Melting Tallow